The Economics of Overtime Working

Numerous individuals throughout international labour markets work hours in excess of their standard contractual hours. Overtime working is a vital consideration in the employment and wage decisions of many households and firms. From a policy perspective, overtime is at the centre of interest in the work sharing/ unemployment trade off. Robert Hart presents the first comprehensive economic evaluation of this phenomenon, examining theoretical, empirical and policy aspects of overtime hours and pay. In a comparative assessment of labour supply, labour demand and compensating differential models of overtime behaviour, he utilises detailed international evidence drawn from the United States, Western Europe and Japan. Policy initiatives linked to job creation, work sharing, absenteeism and payroll taxation are critically assessed and presented in an intuitive manner. Displaying analytical rigour and empirical expertise, Robert Hart's work extends far beyond a mere summary of existing research to enliven and inform debate.

ROBERT A. HART is Professor of Economics at the University of Stirling. He is a labour market economist and acknowledged authority on the economics of working time. He is the author of *The Economics of Non-Wage Labour Costs* (1984), *Working Time and Employment* (1987), *Human Capital, Employment and Bargaining* (with Thomas Moutos, 1995) and *Work and Pay in Japan* (with Seiichi Kawasaki, 1999).

The Economics of
Overtime Working

Robert A. Hart

CAMBRIDGE
UNIVERSITY PRESS

PUBLISHED BY THE PRESS SYNDICATE OF THE UNIVERSITY OF CAMBRIDGE
The Pitt Building, Trumpington Street, Cambridge, United Kingdom

CAMBRIDGE UNIVERSITY PRESS
The Edinburgh Building, Cambridge, CB2 2RU, UK
40 West 20th Street, New York, NY 10011–4211, USA
477 Williamstown Road, Port Melbourne, VIC 3207, Australia
Ruiz de Alarcón 13, 28014 Madrid, Spain
Dock House, The Waterfront, Cape Town 8001, South Africa

http://www.cambridge.org

First published 2004

Printed in the United Kingdom at the University Press, Cambridge

Typeface Times 10/13 pt.   *System* LaTeX 2_ε [TB]

A catalogue record for this book is available from the British Library

Library of Congress Cataloguing in Publication data

Hart, Robert A.
The economics of overtime working / Robert A. Hart.
     p.   cm.
Includes bibliographical references and index.
ISBN 0-521-80142-7
1. Overtime. I. Title.
HD5111.A3H37   2004
331.25′72 – dc22   2004043567

ISBN 0 521 80142 7 hardback

For Shirley, with apologies for all the overtime I have caused.

Contents

Figures

Tables

Preface

Three economists – Frank Brechling, Sherwin Rosen and Ronald Ehrenberg – stimulated my original interest and approach to the study of working time. Their seminal 1960s/early 1970s contributions are highlighted in chapter 1. More recently, Stephen Trejo has provided researchers with fresh insights into the evaluation of working time policy initiatives in relation to overtime working. The direction of Trejo's work has made me realise that the important ideas on working time of H. Gregg Lewis should have also played a part in the early formulation of ideas. I can only plead 'better late than never' and hope that this present contribution makes some amends.

I will not attempt at this stage to persuade potential readers of the value of devoting a complete monograph to overtime working. Chapters 1 and 2 attempt to motivate the entire topic. The overview in chapter 1 presents in an accessible manner most of the core labour market issues that are explored in more depth at later stages. The international facts and figures in chapter 2 also cover many of the key areas of later concern. Chapters 3 and 4 deal with the theory of overtime working from the perspectives of labour supply, labour demand and models that attempt to combine the two sides of the market. Chapter 3 deals with the overtime decision in general while Chapter 4 concentrates specifically on the role and interpretation of the overtime premium. Two empirical chapters follow. Chapter 5 is concerned with studies of the determination and effects of overtime hours while chapter 6 deals with overtime pay. Labour market policy issues form the subject of chapter 7. Finally, chapter 8 contains some brief speculation on the future of overtime work.

Stephen Trejo made a number of very helpful suggestions on a key part of the text. Martyn Andrews, Sarah Brown, Ronald Ehrenberg, Thorsten Schank and Hui Wang also offered useful comments. Recent ideas in this area have benefited from research collaborations with David Bell, Yue Ma, Jim Malley, Robin Ruffell and Ulrich Woitek. Elizabeth Roberts helped me greatly in assembling the graphs and figures. Of course, none of these individuals is implicated in any remaining errors and misconceptions.

Finally, I should like to acknowledge the encouragement and support of Ashwin Rattan who was the Economics Editor at Cambridge University Press when this monograph was commissioned.

1 Overview

Overtime working implies that actual hours of work per period are in excess of standard contractual hours.[1] An example of standard time is a 35-hour workweek consisting of five 7-hour weekdays. If an individual works a 50-hour week then this would entail 15 weekly hours of overtime. This may be spread over weekdays, or confined to specific weekdays or it may involve, additionally or solely, weekend work.

For the vast majority of workers, overtime hours are remunerated at a different rate of pay from standard hours. Typically they command a premium that consists of a fixed multiple of standard hourly pay. A premium of time and a half applies to most overtime workers in the United States. This means that a worker receives 50 per cent more for working an overtime hour than a standard hour equivalent. Double time, time and a quarter, time and a third are other common multiples found elsewhere. Over the week, overtime hours may not be paid at a constant premium. It is not uncommon, for example, for workers to receive a higher premium for weekend compared to weekday overtime activity. Overtime is not necessarily paid at higher rates than standard time, however. For a minority of workers, overtime hours are remunerated at the same rate or even at a reduced rate. Further, some workers are rewarded indirectly for undertaking overtime. The most common practice in this latter respect is for the firm to offer days off in lieu.

In some countries, the rules governing pay and hours of overtime working – i.e. the level of the premium and the maximum number of per-period standard hours after which overtime pay applies – are imposed through government legislation. At one end of the spectrum, the government sets the overtime premium at such a high level that few firms exceed it. At the other end, all aspects of pay and hours are set at firm level within a much more *laissez faire* labour market climate. In between these extremes, less severe constraints apply with respect to coverage and/or the level of the premium. The outside regulator need not be the government. It is not uncommon for a national-level union or a federation of employers to formulate overtime rules that are then adopted by member firms.

---

[1] Alternative expressions for standard hours include 'normal hours', 'straight time hours' and 'regular hours'. This book adopts standard hours throughout. Despite its (Oxford) dictionary status, 'regular hours' is especially misleading. As we will see at several later stages, many workers and employers view overtime working itself as a regular work activity.

Whether or not overtime rules are imposed by outside legislation, there is still the question of whether employees within a given firm can opt voluntarily to work overtime if such work is available. While many employees can exercise such a choice, there are also many cases in which the overtime decision is taken unilaterally by the employer and that it is a condition of employment that reasonable amounts of overtime be undertaken when requested. Given that varying degrees of freedom do exist across firms then we might expect that employees who face relatively significant within-firm mandated overtime hours may be compensated for the related disutility (Ehrenberg and Schumann, 1984).

It has recently emerged that many individuals claim to work unpaid overtime. This is especially true of managerial and professional workers. This may well represent a short-run state of affairs, with payment taking the form of deferred compensation. For example, individuals may choose to work longer hours than stipulated in their contracts in order to achieve recognition from their peers that they hope will lead to future accelerated promotion and/or pecuniary reward. There are several other possible explanations for the unusual claim of offering labour services in the workplace for no pay, and this topic will be visited at several stages in the text. To simplify matters, the following convention will be followed. When referring to 'overtime' or 'overtime working', it is always implicit that it is *paid overtime* that is under consideration. Otherwise, the term 'unpaid overtime' will be used.

Overtime working might be regarded as a peripheral activity, representing at best a small fraction of a firm's labour input and payroll. In fact, although there is a wide international variation in incidence, overtime is a quantitatively important labour market phenomenon in respect both of its contributions to total labour input and to take-home pay. It is a particularly significant component of work time in several major economies. As examples, average weekly overtime in all industries in Japan and the United Kingdom is roughly 3 hours per week and between 3 and 4 hours among non-supervisory production workers in the United States. Moreover, the proportions of males working overtime reached as high as 0.4 in UK and US manufacturing in the late-1990s cyclical peak. An individual working average overtime hours in these countries would receive in excess of 20 per cent of total direct remuneration in the form of overtime pay.

But, of course, high incidence alone is insufficient reason to devote a monograph to the topic. Until relatively recently, the main interest has derived from economic analysis that has treated overtime as an important element of active labour market policy at national, industrial and firm levels. On the demand side, overtime has been viewed as representing a relative speedy form of short-term factor adjustment on the firm's intensive margin that involves costs and returns that distinguish it from alternative factors, such as stocks of employment and capital. A substantial policy oriented literature has grown around the idea of exogenously manipulating these costs, usually through government legislative intervention, in order to achieve employment policy goals. Work sharing in the form of more employees working fewer hours has been the central interest. On the supply side, it is common to treat an individual worker as supplying hours that maximise utility subject to a budget constraint. If optimal hours are higher than (by assumption) a standard workday constraint the individual would wish to work overtime hours. Suppose, however, that an individual wants to work no more than maximum standard hours while the firm – perhaps due to technical or organisational constraints – requires longer hours. The firm may attempt to 'encourage' a supply of overtime by paying a premium for additional hours. In other words, overtime pay may be seen as a means by which the firm establishes patterns of working time that would otherwise not have been forthcoming. As we will see later, one application of this possibility is the use of overtime pay to discourage absenteeism.

Since the early 1990s, there has been a serious challenge to the notion that there is significant scope for policy intervention in respect of overtime pay and hours. This has arisen from an alternative approach to modelling hours' determination. Both firms and workers have preferences over wage-hours combinations. *Ceteris paribus*, job attributes are viewed in terms of their associated per-period lengths of scheduled working hours. The wage acts as a compensating differential for jobs of different lengths.[2] Contrary to traditional demand and supply analyses of working time, hours are treated as indivisible blocks of time, such as the required length of the working day. Suppose that the parties reach agreement over an average hourly wage and the number of daily hours. Assume that maximum daily standard hours and the overtime premium are set by legislation. The terms of the wage-hours agreement can be maintained in the face of a mandatory change in the overtime regulations. For example, an increase in the mandated premium can be exactly offset by a reduction in standard hourly rate so as to leave the average hourly wage and daily hours unaltered.

It is worth spelling out in a little more detail the ideas behind the two most dominant approaches, the workers-hours demand model and the wage-hours compensating differential model.

1.1 The two core models

The two leading workers-hours models that motivate the core debates on overtime working were introduced in the 1960s.

Brechling (1965) was the first to develop in detail the workers-hours demand model. Output, capital, technology and factor prices are treated as exogenous to the cost minimising firm. The firm produces output at the lowest cost combination of workers and average hours per worker. The study contains many of the results that, perhaps, are more immediately associated with later work. Among several long-lasting features, it distinguishes between equilibrium outcomes that represent short-time working or maximum standard time working or overtime working. It shows how changes in factor prices and in standard hours move us away from these equilibria. Substitution between workers and hours is central to its analysis. It explores what were later to become the most important working time topics in United States and European policy debates. For the United States, an economy with mandatory overtime rules, this concerned the employment effects of a rise in the overtime premium.

---

[2] Interestingly, the logic of this approach is most easily seen against the background of a labour demand set-up in its strictest form. Suppose we lived in a world where all employment contracts imposed purely employer-determined fixed hours and fixed hourly pay. Supply-side considerations cannot be suppressed under these conditions. Thus, 'we can think of individuals as shifting amongst employers until, in equilibrium, each individual is working in a job which offers him the [fixed] hours he would have liked to work, given the pay and tax parameters' (Ashworth, McGlone and Ulph, 1977).

Suppose we fix the capital stock and the level of technology. If the firm employs overtime hours in equilibrium, a rise in the premium produces a workers-hours substitution – i.e. substitution away from the margin that experiences the price rise. As for Europe, governments and unions have long been fixated on policies designed to induce work sharing through cuts in the standard workweek. Brechling shows that, for cost minimising firms working overtime in equilibrium, a reduction in standard hours produces a *fall* in employment and a rise in average overtime hours. This perverse result has stubbornly recurred over a large number of model variants on Brechling's original theme. It has been a dominant argument among economists who have advised against such policy interventions.

Might it be more realistic to concentrate on fixed work schedules consisting of indivisible daily hours rather than on the optimal fine-tuning of average hours in the face of relative factor price effects? Technological, organisational and customer considerations may lead firms to select the most cost effective daily lengths of production and business trading hours. Different attitudes to work and leisure – prompted by such factors as personal characteristics, family circumstances and peer group influences – may induce individual suppliers of labour to search for the job length/wage earnings combination that optimises their utility.[3] Market equilibrium may then be thought of as reflecting the satisfaction of joint preferences across employers and individual workers with labour demand equal to labour supply at all job lengths. In effect, the wage acts as a compensating differential for jobs of different length. In essence, this is the core motivation behind the influential work of Lewis (1969a) into the determination of daily hours. It brings together the hours preferences of firms and workers by determining the mutually agreed daily hours and wage earnings combinations.

Why does the Lewis approach carry radical implications for the standard demand model? Let the firm and its employees agree, via the above process, to an average hourly wage of w_0 for a 10-hour working day. Suppose that maximum standard hours and the overtime premium are set by legislation. Trejo (1991) nailed down the critical point. At the time that wages and hours are set, the parties will encompass these exogenously imposed hours and pay rules, adjusting the standard hourly rate in order to achieve w_0. For example, suppose that the mandated overtime premium is 1.5 times the standard hourly rate and that daily standard hours cannot exceed 8 hours per day. Then, w_0 would be the average of 8 hours of standard pay plus 2 hours of overtime 'weighted' at 1.5 times the standard rate. Now, suppose that the government increases the overtime premium to 2 times the standard rate. The average hourly wage would rise above w_0 because the 2 hours of overtime would now receive an increased weight. But the parties would wish to stick to their original wage agreement because this jointly satisfies their preferences with regard to a job length of 10 hours per day. To maintain a given equilibrium, they could simply agree to retain w_0 by a suitable reduction in the standard hourly rate.[4] Alternatively, if the government reduced

---

[3] There is evidence that workers match with their preferred lengths of jobs. For example, based on the Canadian Survey of Work Reduction, Kahn and Lang (1995) show that, in general, workers who state that they prefer to work fewer (longer) hours do in fact work short (long) hours. Increased job tenure appears to lead to more satisfaction with length of hours suggesting that hours matching improves with seniority.

[4] Actually, Ehrenberg and Schumann (1982a, p.135), without reference to Lewis' paper, realised this point: 'One plausible response to a legislated increase in the premium is for . . . [firms and employees] . . . to voluntarily

maximum standard daily hours, the average hourly wage – for given daily hours – would again rise because fewer hours would be weighted by the lower standard rate and more by the higher overtime rate. Again, the parties would be happy with a downward adjustment of the standard rate that served exactly to offset the increase. Contrary to the Brechling model, the initial hours equilibrium is unaffected by these interventions. This implies that there is no incentive to alter the workforce size, or other input factors, given such a government intervention.

An interesting issue surrounds the question of why the Lewis model, and not standard neoclassical supply-side analysis, has offered the main challenge to the workers-hours demand model. There is a well-established supply-side literature that deals with the time allocations of individuals facing differing wage schedules. Unfortunately, it has little or nothing to say about the demand side of the problem. But overtime working is essentially a firm-level activity and there is an undeniably important element of employer input into most overtime decisions.[5] However, in most instances overtime is a voluntary activity and so the employer cannot unilaterally impose overtime work on individual workers. Herein lies a major problem. The supply-side reactions of employees to changes in overtime rules are predicted to differ radically from those emanating from demand considerations. For example, a rise in the overtime premium is likely to induce the supply response of a greater willingness to work overtime – or to offer more overtime hours per period – while the demand reaction would be to substitute out of overtime and to employ more workers. Models that have attempted to integrate traditional demand and supply analyses of pay and hours have proved to be intractable and largely unhelpful. Yet, standing alone, labour supply models cannot offer a serious alternative to workers-hours demand because cutting out employer-based decision making is simply too far removed from reality. The Lewis approach side steps these problems by regarding the length of per-period working hours as defining a job attribute over which employers and employees register preferences (Trejo, 2003).

1.2   Key developments and issues

Why did the workers-hours labour demand model dominate the study of overtime working during the 1970s and 1980s? Arguably, and especially in a European context, job creation policy was a dominant labour market theme of this era and so economists wanted to work within a framework that offered the possibilities of influencing employment outcomes through working time policy interventions. Workers-hours substitution by optimising firms in the face of factor price changes provided a simple means of arguing the pros and cons

agree to a reduction in the level of straight-time wages, or fringes, or both, leaving total compensation for the initial number of hours unchanged.' Owen (1989) also raises this issue but emphasises that legislation introduced to change the premium may well also attempt to prevent employers from offsetting downward adjustments of standard rates. Owen also points out that there are potential difficulties of reducing standard rates under actual union contracts.

[5] Lewis (1969b) emphasises that a motivation of his approach to working time is to overcome the inadequacy of received theory that stems from 'its exclusive reliance on the supply side to explain hours data. The theory assumes that hours of work per employee per period of time is a matter of no consequence to employers.'

of such policy initiatives. The subsequent rise of the Lewis model might then be seen as an *ex post* rationalisation of the general failure of government and union policy to influence work sharing outcomes. A simpler, but not necessarily unconnected, explanation of early demand-side dominance lies in the fact that two distinguished labour market economists produced seminal pieces of work along the lines pursued by Brechling. The first emphasised the role of fixed, or hours-independent, labour costs in the demand model and contained an empirical application related to US railroads (Rosen, 1968). A PhD student of Brechling undertook the second, and arguably most important study of all. Thus, Ehrenberg (1971a) rigorously developed static and dynamic versions of the cost minimising model and provided detailed empirical work. Economists went down the labour demand route because this work stimulated a broad range of theoretical, empirical and policy issues that were not only confined to the working time domain.[6]

In common with a number of contemporary studies, Brechling's 1965 paper is also concerned with the analysis of time-wise adjustment between actual and desired employment within the context of the labour demand model.[7] Nadiri and Rosen (1969) extended this area of demand analysis to embrace both labour and capital dimensions. Suppose the firm envisages a long-term expansion of production. It may undertake this by a combination of (a) a larger workforce, (b) a greater utilisation of the existing workforce, (c) an expansion of its stock of capital, (d) a greater utilisation of its capital equipment.[8] The extent to which it will have recourse to one or other action is likely to embrace considerations of relative prices. As already intimated, the overtime wage premium is likely to be a key consideration in (b). *Ceteris paribus,* a rise in the overtime premium, in relation to other marginal input costs, is now far more difficult to evaluate. Outcomes depend on degrees of complementarity and substitutability among factor inputs.

In the short term, the adjustment potential of each input factor is conditioned by its own adjustment speed and the relative adjustment speeds of the other factors. If we were to concentrate on this time frame – and rule out adjustment of capital – then the workers-hours adjustment problem may still be extended to include the stock of inventories. As investigated by Topel (1982), the firm may face the choice – involving an evaluation of relative prices – of increasing overtime hours or reducing inventories below planned levels as its response to an unanticipated short-run increase in sales. Nakamura (1993) brings overtime hours directly into dynamic factor demand analysis of the Japanese labour market. It is found that an output shock stimulates an overshooting of overtime to compensate for a slow adjustment of employment to a new long-run level.

---

[6] While cost minimisation dominated the early workers-hours studies, it was later expanded to embrace profit maximisation. The best contribution is that of Calmfors and Hoel (1988). In several notable instances, this served to complicate predicted outcomes. For example, a rise in the premium produced workers-hours substitution (the substitution effect) but the rise in total labour costs for given output caused a reduction in sales that impacted negatively on the workforce size (the scale effect). Net outcomes were rendered ambiguous.

[7] Perhaps developments of the workers-hours model in this direction is most associated with the work of Fair (1969; see also Fair, 1985).

[8] Of course, there are other ways of increasing production. For example, on the intensive margin, the firm might try to encourage more effort per unit of time rather than change the length of the time unit itself.

Overtime is treated as one of the firm's most important intensive margin responses in the interrelated factor demand literature. This margin has also featured prominently in the analysis of the relationship between marginal cost and price over the business cycle, with the work of Bils (1985) providing the leading example. Overtime hours have been found to respond more quickly than employment stock to fluctuations in business activity. One reason for this is that overtime decisions are more easily reversible than employment hiring decisions. This helps to avoid the risk of writing off sunk human capital investments if market predictions turn out to be inaccurate. So, changes in overtime can be used as a short-term employment reaction to cyclical change in the face of uncertainty over the length and potential extent of the perturbation. Even when relative factor responses have been fully assessed, overtime may temporarily diverge from planned levels due to adjustment impediments in capital and labour inputs. Overtime's relationship to marginal cost and wage earnings over the cycle stems from similar considerations. Some firms will respond to an upturn in the cycle by extending both the average overtime hours of existing overtime workers and the proportions of their total workforces working overtime. If overtime hours are paid at a higher marginal rate than standard hours then marginal labour costs to the firm will rise. These rises will be greater if longer weekly hours themselves involve a higher marginal overtime premium (e.g. weekend working).

Most of the best known time-related overtime-adjustment investigations derive from factor demand models. But how do studies of employment and hours adjustments relate to the Lewis compensating differential model? We have already noted that this model has provided a radical alternative to demand-side developments in the comparative static evaluation of workers-hours reactions to mandatory changes in pay and hours. At the heart of this challenge is the idea that firms and workers jointly express preferences over jobs of given lengths. This suggests that hours, including overtime hours, contain important job-match effects. One of the latest developments in the study of overtime working is to uncouple pure dynamic adjustment speeds of hours from the influences of fixed effects. In fact, if job matching is a quantitatively important phenomenon then a failure to account for it in dynamic time-series analysis of overtime would tend to produce underestimates of the true speed of hours adjustments.

Most theoretical developments relating to overtime working in the workplace describe a homogeneous workforce, with all workers either participating or not participating in overtime. While this convenient assumption has helped considerably with problems of modelling tractability, it clearly is not representative of the experience of many overtime firms. Overtime working is largely a voluntary activity and not all eligible workers elect to work extra hours. Moreover, the firm itself may not experience sufficient demand to justify extending all workers' hours and so may attempt to select what it believes to be those individuals most suited to working longer hours. For whatever reasons, partial overtime coverage is commonly observed. This raises several extensions and questions concerning existing models. We need to find explanations of how changes in factor prices and standard hours affect *both* average overtime hours *and* the decision over whether or not to participate in overtime. We might even need to query the premises on which the various modelling approaches are based. Take the Lewis model as an example. Suppose that employees in a typical firm either do or do not engage in overtime and, if they do, that they work different numbers of weekly overtime hours. Does this mean that the firm specifies a number of jobs of different lengths and finds workers with different preferences by paying a range of compensating differential wage rates? This may cause industrial relations problems if workers with the same ability and hourly productivity are paid different average hourly rates.

Overtime hours changes entail production, labour cost and wage effects. With respect to the last of these, overtime plays a key role in the study of the cyclical behaviour of real hourly earnings. At the aggregate level of the firm or industry, hourly earnings decompose into average standard wages, the average overtime premium and the proportion of the workforce working overtime. At the micro (individual-based) level, researchers are increasing keen to distinguish between standard hourly pay and hourly earnings (i.e. including the effects of overtime pay). In fact, the use of hourly earnings in studies of wage cyclicality and cross-section/time-series wage curves involves an important issue concerning overtime. Even if the wage rate and the premium were to remain constant, earnings can still fluctuate if the length of weekly hours is itself changing over the cycle. In particular, if weekly hours vary procyclically then so can the earnings of overtime workers even if standard hourly rates and the premium were to remain unchanged. This is because the proportion of premium to total pay would vary procyclically. This raises a critical issue in relation to Phillips curve and wage curve studies. Hours effects may serve to obfuscate pure wage effects with estimated earnings/unemployment elasticities representing composites of wage curves and hours curves.

Suppose each of the main components of daily earnings – i.e. standard pay, overtime pay and the proportion of overtime to total hours – display cyclical time-series behaviour. A critical question is whether the components are responding primarily to the same cyclical indicator. For example, fluctuations in standard pay may vary positively with all phases of the business cycle. Economists typically proxy the business cycle by an output- or employment-based indicator. By contrast, overtime pay and hours may respond to shorter-term fluctuations in demand towards the peaks in economic activity. For example, if firms find it difficult to adjust employment and capital inputs in tight labour markets towards the peaks of cycles, they may opt to employ longer overtime hours or to rundown inventories at a faster than planned rate. For this type of reasoning, overtime fluctuations have been argued to link closely with inventory cycles. Gaining an understanding of the influences of various cyclical indicators on wage earnings is usefully aided by the adoption of frequency domain methods of decomposing (stationary) time series into harmonic waves of varying phases and amplitudes. Recent work on the behaviour of wage earnings over the cycle has moved in this direction.

As already indicated, in some countries pay and hours conditions applying to overtime working are largely worked out at the level of the firm while, in others, firms are subject to high degrees of exogenous constraints. However, even in the latter cases, overtime decisions are undertaken that lie outside the domain of regulation. For example, large numbers of firms in the United States pay overtime rates for hours that occur *before* maximum permitted weekly standard hours have been reached.[9] The question then arises as to why, given wages and hours are determined within the workplace, firms opt to pay overtime premia for marginal hours. One simple, but potent, explanation involves custom and practice. Long-term efficient contracts necessitate agreements over both wages and working hours. Suppose the firm takes standard weekly hours as given, perhaps following an industry or local labour market norm. Also, suppose that the firm requires working hours to be in excess of standard hours. How is premium pay determined in these circumstances? There is an indeterminacy problem if the parties attempt to set the optimal length of overtime hours and two optimal wage rates, i.e. the standard and overtime rates. It is far simpler for the firm and its workforce to allow the premium to be based on an historic norm, subject to custom and practice, and then to concentrate bargaining on the standard wage. In this event, firms facing the custom of a relatively high premium can achieve a competitive average hourly wage by setting relatively low standard rates. Firms experiencing low premiums would set relatively high rates. This argument is very much in the spirit of the Lewis model and applies, especially, to unregulated labour markets.

Premium pay for overtime may also be adopted by the employer as a simple means of attempting to offset potential difficulties among workers with diverse preferences over per-period lengths of working hours. Overtime schedules may be designed with the aim of curbing dissatisfaction, and associated poor work performance, with respect to pure standard time arrangements. The use of overtime in this way may help to improve matters when all employees in the firm are required to work the same length of daily or weekly hours. Greater potential difficulties arise when equally productive employees in the same occupation and/or involved in interactive job tasks within the firm undertake different lengths of per-period hours. It is not easy in these instances to pay different average hourly wage rates for different hours provision while also avoiding adverse industrial relations repercussions.

In recent times, European statistical sources have reported on the phenomenon of unpaid overtime. Managers and professional workers, in particular, report working significant numbers of weekly hours beyond those stipulated in their contracts and for which they receive no additional payments. This is in contrast to paid overtime which is especially prevalent among blue-collar and lower-paid workers. Aggregated across all individuals, unpaid hours are roughly comparable in number to paid overtime hours. Of course, for most individuals, there is no such thing as working for nothing in a long-run context. Early work concentrated on studying the longer-term consequences of offering such hours. These include accelerated promotion, above-average pay rises for given work characteristics and the link of unpaid work to remuneration systems linked to company performance.

Unpaid work also has implications for the study of wage earnings. Unpaid hours serve to drive a wedge between paid-for and effective hourly wages. If, at any given time, company managers work more than contracted weekly hours while non-managers work only paid hours then their effective hourly wage differential will be less than the wage differential if only paid-for hours are measured. This may impact, for example, on the analysis of returns

---

[9] Trejo (1993) provides evidence that suggests that over 20 per cent of overtime receives a premium for marginal hours worked before the 40 weekly standard hour limit set under the US Fair Labor Standard Act (FLSA) regulations.

to education. Suppose that in their early careers, managers and professionals work more unpaid hours than other workers. More highly educated individuals are likely to work as managers and professionals. In the early work years at least, returns to education will be exaggerated if paid hours rather than effective hours are used to deflate gross wages. Of course, working unpaid hours may help managers and professionals to enjoy steeper wage profiles at later stages in their careers but this does not detract from the strong possibility that wage-tenure and wage-experience profiles will differ with and without the accommodation of unpaid overtime.

The remainder of the text attempts to explore in greater depth these broad areas of interest.

2   Facts and figures

At the level of the firm, the quantitative significance of overtime working is best described in terms of its contributions to physical labour input and to labour cost. On the input side, suppose for simplicity that all workers in the firm are full-time employees and that they all work, at least, the maximum number of standard hours. Then, answers to four key questions are required in order to assess the quantitative importance of overtime:

(1) What is the size of the firm's workforce?
(2) What is the maximum number of daily or weekly standard hours?
(3) What proportion of the firm's workforce works overtime in any given period?
(4) How many per-period hours of overtime do overtime workers work?

Through time, information on (1)–(4) allows us to establish changes in the firm's total overtime requirement. In the next period, and for given output, the total would rise if, *ceteris paribus*, there were rises in the workforce size, the proportion of workers working overtime, the number of overtime hours worked by overtime workers and if maximum standard hours were reduced.

In evaluating the cost side, the following four questions with respect to overtime workers are of key importance:

(1) Are overtime hours paid or unpaid?
(2) For paid overtime, what is the marginal hourly rate of pay?
(3) Does the rate in (2) vary with the number of per-period overtime hours?
(4) Are the standard hourly wage rate and the overtime premium functionally related?

At first glance, we might query the relevance of question (1). If workers provide overtime hours free of charge, then why be concerned about cost implications? One important reason is that overtime working refers to a sub-set of total weekly hours and the price of each hour worked affects average hourly cost. If workers 1 and 2 undertake the same weekly standard hours at the same hourly rate and worker 1 works five hours of paid overtime and worker 2 five hours of unpaid overtime then clearly the average hourly earnings of worker 2 is less than those of worker 1.

This chapter is designed to give a number of initial descriptive insights into the aspects of the overtime breakdowns suggested by the foregoing questions.

2.1   Overtime hours per employee

To set the scene, we begin by examining a popular macro descriptive measure of the incidence of overtime – weekly overtime averaged over all employees (i.e. overtime and non-overtime). Figure 2.1 provides national-level all-industry time series of this variable for a selection of OECD countries. Figure 2.2 shows the equivalent manufacturing data for the same countries plus the United States.

Three observations stand out. First, the time series reveal large international differences in the amount of weekly overtime working per person. At one end of the spectrum, Australia and Canada average less than 1 hour throughout industry while, at the other, Japan and the United Kingdom average between 3 and 4 hours. As we discuss in section 2.4, these differences are likely to derive, in part, from variations in the degree of legislative control governing the practice of overtime working. Second, in all countries, weekly overtime in manufacturing is higher than for all industries taken together. Third, overtime appears to be highly cyclical.

In fact, overtime hours are procyclical. Using the British New Earnings (NES) Survey Panel from 1975 to 1999, and measuring the cycle by fluctuations in GDP around trend, Kalwij and Gregory (2000) find that a 1 per cent movement above trend is associated with a 1.2 per cent rise in overtime. Using the German Socio Economic Panel (GSOEP) for the period 1984–97, Bauer and Zimmermann (1999) find that, during boom periods, changes in overtime feature importantly in firms' reactions to demand fluctuations. They find that a 1 per cent increase in output growth in a boom period leads to a 2.4 per cent increase in overtime hours. Of this overall overtime reaction, 71 per cent consists of an increase in overtime hours of those workers already working overtime with the remainder due to an increased incidence of overtime working. In Japan, overtime has been found to be especially cyclically volatile, especially during the 1970s where its rate of change was found to exceed that of output (Tachibanaki, 1987; Nakamura, 1993).

A more detailed description derives from US experience. Figure 2.3 shows weekly overtime per manufacturing employee in the United States, based on Bureau of Labor Statistics (BLS) monthly data from 1956 to 2001. Superimposed are the National Bureau of Economic Research (NBER) estimated business cycle peaks and troughs.[1] Several features stand out:

(1) Overtime provides an extremely sensitive indicator of the *timing of the 'bottoming-out' of major recessionary periods.* Included here are the two OPEC supply shocks of the middle and late 1970s. In general, major NBER troughs appear either to coincide precisely with overtime troughs or overtime leads them by a month or two. There are several strong labour market reasons for overtime providing such an accurate indicator of trough periods. For example, where labour turnover costs are high or where there are high sunk investments in labour, firms may tend to use variations in labour utilisation as a buffer to demand downturns. At these times, overtime hours are reduced or eliminated.

---

[1] NBER, US Business Cycles Expansions and Contractions, http://www.nber.org/cycles.html.

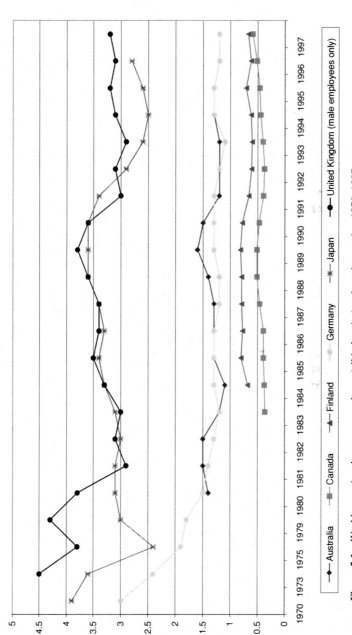

Figure 2.1 Weekly overtime hours per employee (all industries): selected countries, 1970–1997
Source: OECD, *Employment Outlook* (1998).

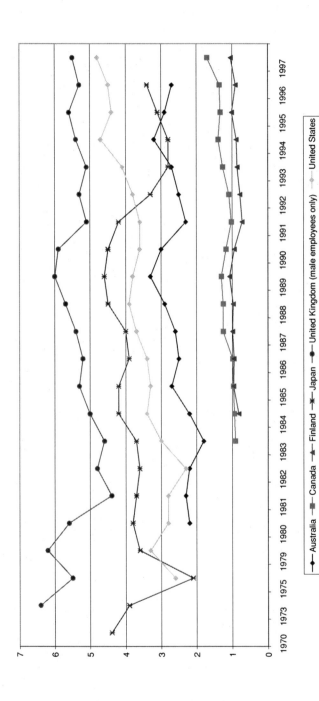

Figure 2.2 Weekly overtime hours per employee (manufacturing): selected countries, 1970–1997
Source: OECD, *Employment Outlook* (1998).

Australia — Canada — Finland — Japan — United Kingdom (male employees only) — United States

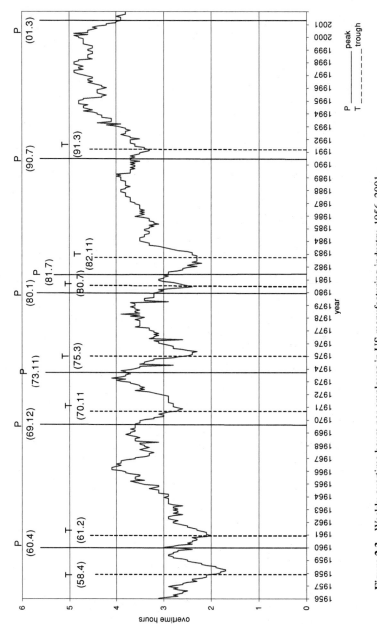

Figure 2.3 Weekly overtime hours per employee in US manufacturing industry, 1956–2001
Source: Bureau of Labor Statistics, Establishments Survey. NBER Business Cycle Reference Dates.

An upturn will involve an initial move towards normal rates of labour utilisation before more employment is undertaken.[2]

(2) Interestingly, *peaks in weekly overtime and NBER-identified peaks* coincide less precisely than their respective troughs. It is hard to account for this asymmetry except in so far as the major recessions may well have unequivocally affected the large bulk of industrial activity whereas peak activity tended to hit different industries at different times. In fact, typically, overtime peaks tend to pre-date NBER peaks by several months.[3] This might occur for two main reasons. First, high-overtime industries may peak earlier than the overall industrial average. For example, demand downturns may well hit manufacturing plants, such as auto makers, more speedily than service industries, such as utility supply. Secondly, overtime is a leading cyclical indicator and might pinpoint cyclical turning points more speedily than more broadly based measures of cyclical economic performance used to calculate the NBER reference dates.

(3) Several overtime peaks and troughs, such as in the second half of the 1960s and the middle 1990s, occur *independently of 'official' NBER peaks and troughs*. In important respects, this may reflect a short-term attribute of overtime behaviour. When the economy is buoyant and a fall in demand occurs, there will clearly be considerable uncertainty over the length and depth of the subsequent downturn. Many firms will be highly risk averse about undertaking relatively costly worker layoff decisions. Reductions in overtime offer the potential to reverse labour input decisions relatively costlessly if forecasts of deep recessions prove to be incorrect. This 'first line of defence' aspect of overtime working will result in overtime cycles that do not coincide with cycles in which, *ex post*, major peaks and troughs are identified.

(4) The 1990s witnessed one of the longest periods of sustained growth in US history. From early 1991 to early 1997, average weekly overtime in manufacturing increased by 1.6 hours and reached 4.9 hours, the highest since the BLS published these data in 1956. Given ever-tightening labour markets as the decade of growth progressed, it is not surprising that firms gave ever-greater recourse to more intensive use of existing employees. In fact, overtime growth in US manufacturing during the 1990s was far more impressive than employment growth.[4] Hetrick (2000) notes that a common factor among those industries exhibiting the strongest growth in overtime was a highly skilled

---

[2] Despite incurring marginal premium payments, increasing overtime in the initial phases of an economic recovery may constitute an optimal strategy for some firms. In the first place, increasing labour utilisation among existing employees allows better job matching by giving firms time to search for and to hire new recruits while meeting increasing output demands. Secondly, employing new workers involves once-over costs of hiring and training. If firms are unsure over whether a given demand increase signals a long-term upward trend or whether it merely represents a temporary blip in economic activity, they may seek to avoid incurring sunk costs during the initial phases of an economic recovery. An increase in marginal labour cost through increasing overtime might be deemed to be smaller than the potential costs associated with inaccurate cycle forecasts.

[3] In fact, in the latest period, the overtime peak occurred in April 2000, preceding the official NBER peak by 11 months.

[4] Hetrick (2000) provides interesting details that lie behind the data in figure 2.3. More than half of the 20 industries within US manufacturing had overtime increases of at least 1 hour between 1991 and 1997. There were exceptional increases in motor vehicle manufacture (4.4 hours), iron and steel foundries (3.7 hours) and in industrial machinery and equipment, refrigeration and service machinery (2.9 hours). A particular influence on the increase in overtime was that manufacturing employment was shifting towards component industries in which overtime increases were among the strongest.

workforce. Skill shortages, combined with reluctance by employers to invest heavily in training new recruits given uncertainty about the length of the cyclical upturn, were probably large factors in determining this unprecedented growth in overtime. Hetrick notes that the 10 industries with the largest overtime growth had more than 17 per cent of their employment in high-skilled jobs and compared to a figure of 8 per cent in the 10 industries with the least growth in overtime.

These overtime observations are particular interesting when set against the comparable patterns of manufacturing employment. The US trends in employment and overtime are shown together in figure 2.4. First, especially in more recent times, overtime changes have been more sensitive to changes in the cycle than employment. While overtime turned round exactly in phase with the cycle in March 1991, manufacturing jobs continued to decline until July 1993. During the downturn, 683,000 jobs were lost and a further 400,000 after the recession officially ended. Second, while overtime grew strongly to reach record levels between 1991 and 1997, growth in employment was less impressive and, in 1997, ended at a level nearly 700,000 lower than in the pre-recession peak of March 1989. From March 1991 to January 1998, the number of production workers in manufacturing increased by 601,000. Hedrick calculates that if overtime increases during the same period were translated into full-time equivalent jobs then this would account for a further 571,000 jobs.

2.2   Proportion of overtime to total workers

As discussed by Leslie (1991), changes in the amount of overtime working occur along two main channels. First, average overtime per overtime worker fluctuates through time. Second, the proportion overtime to total workers also varies. Therefore, the total change in overtime working would be expected to result mainly, though not only, from changes in these two components. Before examining this relative contribution, we begin by concentrating on the proportion of workers working overtime.

Let us start with a few simple aggregate observations, provided by Pannenberg and Wagner (2001), that concentrate on workers who overwhelmingly work paid overtime. Data are taken from the GSOEP and the British Household Panel Survey (BHPS). For the period 1991–8, the proportion of blue-collar West German employees working overtime varied between 37.2 per cent (1993) and 46.8 per cent (1997). Their comparable average weekly overtime hours varied between 5.8 hours (1995) and 4.8 hours (1992). For British non-managerial workers, between 58.8 (1997) and 52.7 (1991) worked overtime and averaged between 10.1 (1995) and 8.8 (1992) hours. Note that, although both countries display relatively high proportions of overtime workers, when overtime hours are translated into overtime hours *given overtime is worked*, weekly overtime is considerably greater than the all-employees numbers presented in figures 2.1 and 2.2. There is a fair degree of fluctuation in these variables – especially if we were to translate the statistics into total weekly hours of overtime provided in the two economies. However, Pannenberg and Wagner also note a large degree of *persistence* in the incidence of overtime in both countries. Taken over

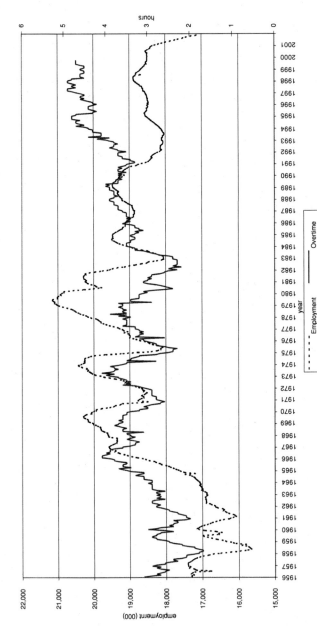

Figure 2.4 Employment and average weekly overtime hours in US manufacturing, 1956–2001
Source: Bureau of Labor Statistics, Establishments Suvey.

all full-time employees, 35 per cent of West Germans and 50 per cent of Britains worked overtime over the entire period.

The incidence of paid overtime working varies greatly by occupation. As we will see in section 2.7, there is a relatively high incidence among plant and machine operatives and a very low incidence in managerial and professional occupations. Table 2.1 shows the British male and female occupations with the highest incidence of overtime in 2001. Apart from non-managerial manufacturing occupations, overtime is commonly undertaken, for example, among workers involved in road and rail transport.

Figures 2.5 and 2.6 present manufacturing industry data on the proportions of workers working overtime for three of the countries shown in figure 2.2. Figure 2.5 shows the proportion of US manufacturing employees working more than 40 hours per week.[5] A comparison with the fluctuation of average overtime per employee in the United States, illustrated in figure 2.3, reveals a very similar procyclical pattern. Note also that the prolonged growth in the economy in the 1990s is matched by a very significant growth in the proportion, from 22 per cent in 1982 to almost 40 per cent by 1997. In the case of Australia in figure 2.6, high proportions of overtime workers in manufacturing – varying between 25 per cent and 40 per cent of the workforce – contrast with Finland where the proportions deviate little from 11 per cent. Note from figures 2.2 and 2.6 that both the incidence and average hours of overtime are low in Finland. As we will see, this economy has particularly stringent legislative constraints on overtime working, an important consideration when making these sorts of comparisons.

As stated at the outset of this section, it is important to link the notions of overtime hours per worker and the proportion of overtime workers. As a preliminary insight, this is undertaken with reference to the British New Earnings Survey Panel Data (NESPD). Since the incidence of paid overtime is very low among managers and professionals (see section 2.7), we exclude occupations in these categories. The overtime graphs in figure 2.7 refer to full-time male and female workers as well as part-time female workers for the period 1975–2001. For each category of worker, they depict weekly overtime averaged over all workers and average weekly overtime per overtime worker. For example, male overtime per worker averaged between 2 and 4 overtime hours while overtime workers averaged between 8 and 10 overtime hours. Of course, the difference is due to the fact that – as shown in the equivalent proportions' graphs in figure 2.8 – between 21 and 45 per cent of male workers worked overtime during this period. An interesting feature of these latter data is that significant proportions of both full-time and part-time females work overtime. In fact, part-time female overtime workers average slightly more weekly overtime hours than their full-time equivalents and, by the end of the period, the incidence of overtime working among part-timers was on a par with full-time females.[6]

---

[5] The graph is constructed from unpublished data from the BLS Current Population Survey (Employment and Earnings). Following FLSA rules (see section 2.4), an overtime worker is regarded as someone working in excess of 40 standard hours. In fact, this is not strictly accurate because some workers are paid overtime for hours less than the 40 legal maximum.

[6] Two main possibilities may account for high average overtime among part-time females. First, their work may be concentrated into several long working days, of which part is eligible for overtime compensation. Second, they may work more unsociable hours – such as evening and weekend work – and receive a higher proportion of overtime hours as a compensating differential.

Table 2.1 *British male and female occupations with a high incidence of overtime working (NES), 2001*

Males	%
Ambulance staff	76.9
Crane drivers	75.5
Bookmakers	73.9
Agricultural machinery drivers and operatives	72.2
Railway station staff	70.6
Telephone fitters	70.6
Milling machine setters and setter-operators	69.6
Cable jointers, lines repairers	69.1
Rail signal operatives and crossing keepers	67.7
Grinding machine setters and setter-operators	66.7
Metal plate workers, shipwrights, rivetors	65.1
Furnace operatives (metal)	64.3
Mechanical plant drivers and operatives (earth moving and civil engineering)	64.3
Bus and coach drivers	64.1
Steel erectors	63.6
Coach and vehicle body builders	63.4
Auto electricians	63.3
Labourers in foundries	61.9
Welding trades	60.0

Females	%
Bookmakers	75.0
Ambulance staff	62.5
Hospital ward assistants	53.8
Postal workers, mail sorters	49.3
Police officers (sergeant and below)	47.9
Other food, drink and tobacco process operatives n.e.c.	44.1
Glass product and ceramics makers	43.5
Bus and coach drivers	42.4
Drivers of road goods vehicles	41.5
Radio and telegraph operators, other office communication system operators	40.4
Bakery and confectionery process operatives	38.6
Inspectors, viewers and testers (metal and electrical goods)	38.5
Counter clerks and cashiers	38.3
Printing machine minders and assistants	37.9
Caretakers	37.8
Plastics process operatives, moulders and extruders	37.8
Bakers, flour confectioners	37.5
Other health associate professionals n.e.c.	37.5
Launderers, dry cleaners, pressers	36.4
Machine tool operatives (inc. CNC machine tool operatives)	36.1
Counterhands, catering assistants	35.2
Assemblers/lineworkers (electrical/electronic goods)	34.2
Medical radiographers	33.9
Debt, rent and other cash collectors	33.3
Other assemblers/lineworkers n.e.c.	32.7
Other personal and protective service occupations n.e.c.	32.6
Metal working production and maintenance fitters	31.9
Packers, bottlers, canners, fillers	31.4
Storekeepers and warehousewomen	31.4

Notes: Full-time employees. Occupation included if sample size is 20 or more workers.

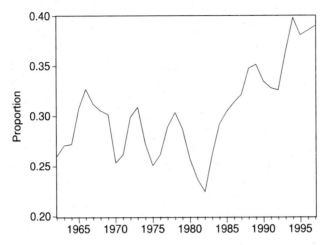

Figure 2.5   Proportion of workers working overtime in US manufacturing, 1962–1997
Source: BLS, Unpublished data.

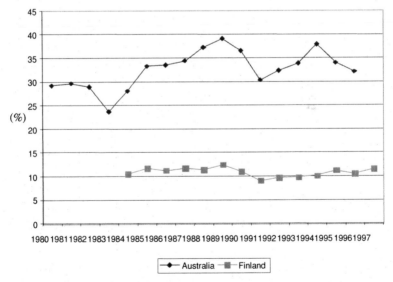

Figure 2.6   Percentage of employees working overtime in Australia and Finland (manufacturing), 1980–1997
Source: OECD, *Employment Outlook* (1998).

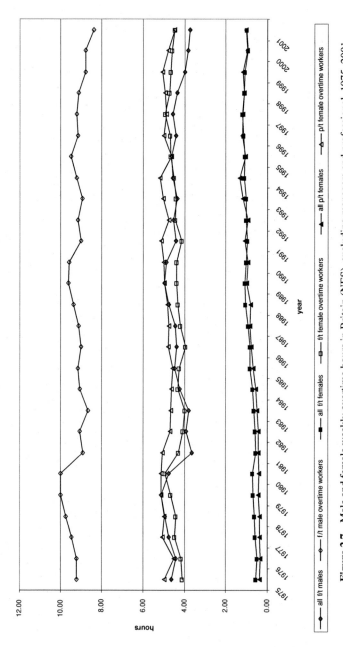

Figure 2.7 Male and female weekly overtime hours in Britain (NES), excluding managers and professional, 1975–2001
Note: f/t = Full-time.
p/t = Part-time.

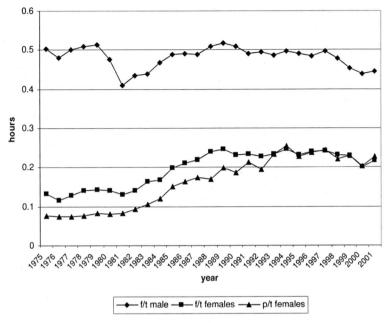

Figure 2.8 Proportion working overtime in Britain (NES), excluding managers and professionals, 1975–2001
Note: f/t = Full-time.
p/t = Part-time.

For the ith category of worker ($i = 1, 2, 3$) in figures 2.7 and 2.8, total overtime (V_i) is the product of the number of workers (N_i), the proportion working overtime (λ_i) and the average overtime hours of workers working overtime (o_i). As a simple indication of the relative volatility of each component to a change in total overtime, we have $\dot{V}_i = \dot{N}_i + \dot{\lambda}_i + \dot{o}_i$ where $\dot{V} = d[\ln(V)]/dt$, $\dot{N} = d[\ln(N)]/dt$ etc. The standard deviations of the rates of change of each component measure its relative contribution to the total overtime variability (see, for example, Gordon, 1982). Results are summarised in table 2.2. For each category of worker, all three components of total overtime contribute significantly to overall change. Of the two components of particular interest here, o and λ, changes in the proportions of workers working overtime account for more of the total variability than changes in overtime per overtime worker. Of course, these relative contributions will change for different sub-periods of time and for different industrial and occupational disaggregation of the data. This simple exercise merely underlines the fact that changes in overtime working are inadequately described by changes in overtime hours undertaken by existing overtime workers.

Much of the foregoing material is highly aggregative and yet most analysis of overtime-related labour market problems has taken a far more micro approach. A critical issue from an analytical viewpoint is how overtime incidence is distributed across firms or plants in a given industry. So what proportion of employees work overtime in the workplace? This is a very important issue. As we will see in chapter 3 and elsewhere, while a large

Table 2.2 *Standard deviations of rates of change of the components of total overtime hours (NES), 1975–2001*

	Full-time males	Full-time females	Part-time females
Mean overtime hours of overtime workers (o)	0.032	0.041	0.052
Proportion working overtime (λ)	0.044	0.076	0.099
Number of workers (N)	0.044	0.062	0.079
Total overtime hours (V)	0.069	0.085	0.124

Table 2.3 *British proportions of employees who regularly work overtime or hours in excess of the normal working week, by largest occupational group within the establishment (paid or unpaid hours)*

	Weighted % (based on 2,191 establishments)
1 All (100%)	14
2 Almost all (80–99%)	9
3 Most (60–79%)	10
4 Around half (40–59%)	12
5 Some (20–39%)	13
6 Just a few (1–19%)	23
7 None (0%)	19

Source: 1998 WERS – main management interview.

part of the theory of overtime proceeds as if *all* workers in a given establishment either work or do not work overtime in any given period, recent work has acknowledged a more realistic assumption. In many overtime firms fewer than 100 per cent of workers in given occupations regularly undertake overtime. British evidence in table 2.3 is presented from the 1998 Workplace Employee Relations Survey (WERS) based on a management survey in 2,191 establishments. Overtime incidence is reported in respect of the largest occupational group in each establishment and covers both paid and unpaid hours. Only 14 per cent of establishments report that all employees work overtime, while 19 per cent indicate that none works overtime. The remaining 67 per cent report varying proportions of overtime participation, ranging from most workers to just a few. Andrews, Schank and Simmons (2002) present evidence on overtime working in German plants from 1996 onwards based on the Establishment Level Panel Data Set of the Institute of Employment and Research (IAB). It is found in their sample[7] that all operatives work *only* standard hours in 55 per cent of plants. Of the 45 per cent of plants that work overtime, only 10 per cent of these employ

---

[7] The sampling frame in this study is biased towards large plants, with 50 per cent of plants employing more than 5,000 workers and only 0.25 per cent employing fewer than 100 workers. In the case of Britain there is a slight bias towards higher proportions of workers working overtime in large-sized firms.

overtime over their entire workforce. The average proportion of workers working overtime in overtime plants is 41 per cent.

2.3 Overtime hours and standard hours

As we explore in chapter 4 and elsewhere, a central interest in the study of overtime working is the relationship between overtime hours and standard hours. In important instances, maximum lengths of standard hours are set outside of the firm's control, at national, regional or industrial level. Interest has focused on how decisions to reduce these hours impact on the firm's utilisation of existing labour relative to its extensive margin hiring policy. A critical issue concerns whether firms, faced by such hours reductions, are working overtime schedules or not.

Trends in total hours and standard hours for British males and females from 1975 to 2001 are shown in figure 2.9. For males, a very shallow downward trend in the standard component of total hours contrasts with somewhat more cyclical behaviour on the overtime margin of total hours. Total hours also display cyclicality among females while standard hours are somewhat more steeply downward in the early 1980s. Female standard hours exhibit an unfamiliar feature, however. Thus, there is a marked *upward* movement in standard hours after 1993, a year that marked the start of exceptionally strong real growth. Bell and Hart (1998) examine this phenomenon for one-digit NES industries. In general they find that in male-dominated industries – such as metal goods, engineering, vehicles and 'other manufacturing' – female and male standard hours exhibited similar downward trends. By contrast, in industries with high proportions of female workers – such as banking and 'other services' – there were procyclical movement of standard hours in both the mid-1980s and the mid-1990s.

Elsewhere in Europe, against the background of relatively high and long-term unemployment, work sharing policies have been pursued more vigorously than in Britain. Germany has been at the forefront of these developments. Figure 2.10 shows that effective yearly working time in (West) Germany fell, in a more or less unbroken trend, from 2,081 hours in 1960 to 1,503 hours in 1997. In important respects, German metal work and printing unions have been at the forefront of effecting hours reductions (see Hunt, 1998). The path of overtime follows a more tortuous route, however. It rose steeply in the 1960s, reaching a peak of 157 annual hours per worker in 1970. Against the background of the two OPEC supply shocks it had decreased to less than half this total (66 hours per year) by 1982. Since then it has remained stable, representing about 4 per cent of effective working time. In a shorter time perspective, figure 2.11 shows that mean weekly contractual hours of full-time German males fell from 41 to 38 hours between 1984 and 1997 while weekly overtime remained stable at around 2.5 hours.

Based on the 2001 British NES, figures 2.12–2.14 explore additional associations between overtime and standard working. First, as shown in figure 2.12, the standard hourly wage declines in overtime hours. Lower-paid workers work more overtime. Second, weekly wage earnings in figure 2.13 rise monotonically in overtime hours. As the week lengthens, and assuming no change in the rate premium pay for overtime (see section 2.6), the downward

Figure 2.9 Total hours and standard hours: United Kingdom, males and females (NES), excluding managerial and professional workers, 1975–2001

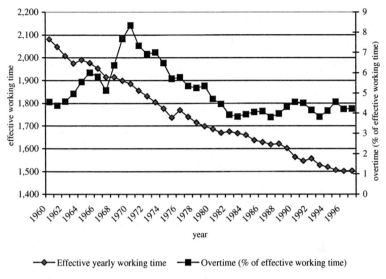

Figure 2.10 Working time and overtime in Germany, 1960–1997
Source: Kohler and Spitznagel (1996).

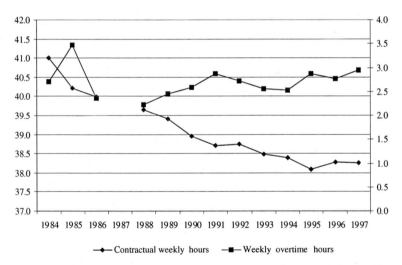

Figure 2.11 Weekly contractual hours and overtime hours in Germany (GSOEP), 1984–1997
Source: Bauer and Zimmermann (1999),based on data from the GSOEP. The numbers refer to full-time working male West Germans who are not employed as civil servants.

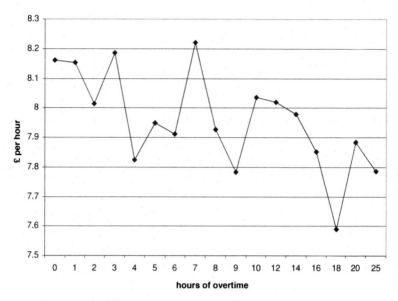

Figure 2.12   Average standard hourly wage rate, by hours of overtime (NES), 2001

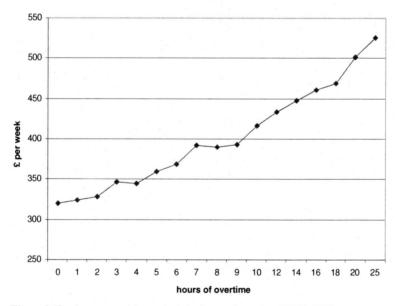

Figure 2.13   Average weekly earnings, by hours of overtime (NES), 2001

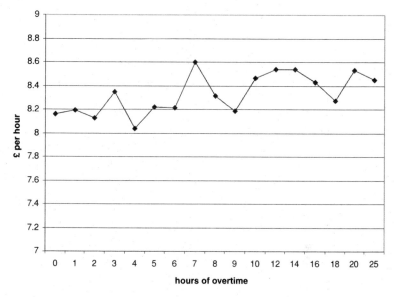

Figure 2.14   Average hourly rate of earnings, by hours of overtime (NES), 2001

influence of the standard wage on weekly earnings is more than offset by the positive effect of rising overtime hours on wage earnings. In effect, as shown in figure 2.14, the average *hourly* rate is quite flat in relation to weekly hours of overtime.

We will return to this evidence in chapter 4 in a discussion of the role of the overtime premium.

2.4   Legislative limits

A very significant part of the literature on hours of work has been devoted to analysing the effects of legislative limits imposed by governments in order to control the conditions under which overtime is worked. As will be reviewed later, much of this work concerns the work sharing implications of altering one or more of the limits.

Four types of intervention are most commonly observed internationally,[8] these are:

(1) a maximum number of daily or weekly standard hours after which hourly overtime premium pay comes into effect
(2) minimum levels of overtime premia
(3) overtime hours subject to a maximum daily or weekly limit
(4) (highly related to (i) and (iii)), a maximum weekly total hours limit.

---

[8] Other regulations may also impinge on the practice of overtime working. Examples would include the prescription of minimum rest periods and the length of night shifts.

The most frequently quoted example of an attempt to control dimensions (1) and (2) of hours of work is the US Fair Labor Standards Act (FLSA) that sets a standard weekly hours limit of 40 and a minimum premium of time and a half times the standard hourly rate. As for (iv), the most significant recent example has been the 1998 European Working Time Directive, enacted by EU member countries in the late 1990s, which limits the length of working time for each 7-day period to 48 hours.

The degree of legislative control ranges from countries like New Zealand and the United Kingdom, where there are virtually no regulations outside those agreed through individual collective bargains, to the United States, where very significant proportions of workers are covered by the FLSA rules (Hunt, 1998). But the FLSA does not cover all employees (see Trejo, 1993) and the 48-hour EU limit can be exceeded through agreement between employers and workers. In fact, legislation throughout the industrialised world is complex and subject to varying degrees of partial coverage.

The OECD (1998) provided a useful summary of (i)–(iv) for a large number of member countries in 1996. These are reproduced in table 2.4 and should be read 'as typically applied' and by no means indicative of the experience of all workers in each country. The information conveys two important points. First, intervention is common and *laissez faire* economies like the United Kingdom represent the exception, not the rule. Second, there exists a rich variety of rules and regulations concerning the timing, length and payment of overtime hours.

2.5   The overtime premium

There is relatively little published work, especially at the micro level, that deals specifically with the measurement of the overtime premium. This almost certainly reflects a general lack of suitable data. Fortunately, the British NESPD allow us to gain important insights. The UK labour market is of special interest in the study of the premium, because, as indicated in section 2.4, it is largely free from legislative interference. Here, we examine a number of general characteristics of the premium, leaving theoretical and econometric developments to later chapters.

Following Bell and Hart (2003a), let hourly earnings (i.e. the hourly wage rate inclusive of overtime), e, be given by

$$e = \frac{h_s w + pwv}{h} \qquad (2.1)$$

where h is total weekly hours worked, h_s is standard weekly hours and w is the standard hourly wage (i.e. the hourly wage exclusive of overtime), p is the average overtime premium, and $v = (h - h_s)$ is overtime hours. Re-arranging we obtain

$$p = \frac{(e/w)h - h_s}{v}. \qquad (2.2)$$

The NESPD allow us to derive individually based estimates of p since they provide data on each of the variables on the right-hand side of (2.2).

Table 2.4 *Legislative limits to standard and overtime working, 1996*

Country	Standard weekly hours	Premium for overtime hours (in excess of standard hours)	Maximum overtime hours	Maximum weekly hours
Australia	38–40	50% for first 4 hours, then 100%	None	None
Austria	40	50%	5 (10 during 12 weeks per year)	50
Belgium	40	50% for hours week-day hours 100% for weekend hours	10	50
Canada	4–48	50%	None	None
Czech Republic	40.5	25%	8	51
Denmark	37	50% for first hour then rising to 100%	None	48
Finland	40	50% for 2 hours then 100%	5	45
France	39	25% for first 8 hours then 50%	9	48
Germany	48	25%	12	60
Greece	40	25% for first 60 hours per year 50% for second 60 hours per year	8	48
Hungary	40	50%	12	52
Ireland	48	25%	12	60
Italy	48	25%	12	60
Japan	40	25%	None	None
Korea	44	50%	12	56
Luxembourg	40	25% blue-collar, 50% white-collar	8	48
Mexico	48	100%	9	57
Netherlands	40	None	15	60
New Zealand	40	None	None	None
Norway	40	40%	10	50
Portugal	40	50% for first hour then 75%	12	54
Spain	40	–	2 (average 80 hours per year)	47
Sweden	40	None	12 (maximum 200 hours per year)	48 or 52
Switzerland	45 or 50	25%	16	61 or 66
Turkey	45	50%	3 hours per day 90 days per year (i.e. 270 hours per year)	– .
United Kingdom	None	Collective agreement	None	None
United States	40	50%	None	None

Source: OECD, *Employment Outlook* (1998).
Note: – No data given in the original sources.

Concentrating on male overtime workers, the average premium in (2.2) is shown between 1975 and 2001 in figure 2.15, together with average weekly overtime hours. Apart from the second half of the 1970s and early 1980s (a period that embraces the aftermath of two great OPEC supply shocks), both variables display relatively modest fluctuations. Overtime hours peak quite markedly in the late 1970s, coinciding with a trough in the average premium. This may represent a compositional effect: the high overtime hours may have included many workers that did not normally work overtime and who received relatively low premium rates. Thereafter, the premium averaged 1.3 times the standard rate and overtime workers average about 9 hours per week. Clearly, after the extremely volatile late 1970s/early 1980s, the average overtime premium displays virtually no cyclical tendency.

In chapter 4, we explore cross-sectional regularities in the average overtime premium. These are used to motivate arguments as to why custom and practice may play important roles in determining the overtime premium in economies where there is little or no legislation governing the timing and payment of overtime hours.

What about international evidence on the shape of the overtime premium schedule? In order to explore this question, data availability dictates that we use more aggregate data than shown so far. Following Hart and Ruffell (1993), Hart, Malley and Ruffell (1996) and Hart and Malley (2000), we may express the mean marginal overtime premium, p, as follows

$$p(v) = k + \sum_{i=1}^{n} m_i(v)^i + \eta \qquad (2.3)$$

where k and ms parameters and p and v are defined in relation to (2.1). Suppose that (2.3) refers to a given industry and so the function depicts, for a given standard wage, the rise in the industry's wage costs as average overtime increases. For example, we may be interested in investigating (2.3) for a homogeneous occupation in a single industry. If the ms are zero, then overtime is compensated at a constant premium for all overtime hours (e.g. $k = 1.25$).

However, it is not difficult to imagine that the mean premium *rises* as average overtime in the industry increases so that the ms are found to be greater than zero. Imagine that an industry-level agreement established three different constant premiums, with the payment of each depending on the time of the workweek that overtime is undertaken. For example, work on weekday evenings is compensated at the lowest constant rate, work on Saturdays at a higher constant rate and Sunday working at the highest constant rate. Normally, we would expect overtime to vary across the workforce. Imagine that we start in a recession, at the trough of the cycle, with most employees working no overtime. As the cycle picks up, with higher output demand in the industry, the distribution of overtime working will be weighted more and more towards higher premium rates. Depending on the precise step-intervals and the specific premium rates, various shapes of rising mean premium functions can be generated (Hart and Ruffell, 1993). The polynomial in (2.3) is designed to accommodate a range of possibilities (see also Shapiro, 1986; Bils, 1987).

A priori, we might expect significant differences in the estimates of (2.3) from country to country. The United States sets $k = 1.5$ for hours in excess of $h_s = 40$ (see table 2.4). This

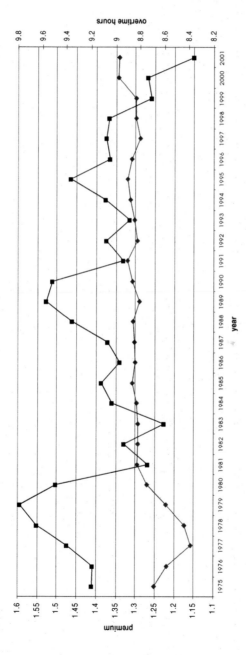

Figure 2.15 Average overtime premium and average overtime hours for male non-managerial workers working overtime, United Kingdom (NESPD), 1975–2001

Table 2.5 *Estimated average premium schedule for three countries*

Japan		United Kingdom		United States	
Period	1958–90	Period	1981–8	Period	1960–90
No. of observations per industry	33	No. of observations per industry	3	No. of observations per industry	31
No. of industries	16	No. of industries	23	No. of industries	16
FIML estimates		OLS: Pooled 1981, 1984, 1988		FIML estimates	
Parameter	Estimate	Parameter	Estimate	Parameter	Estimate
k	1.25 (n/a)	k	1.30 (0.11)	k	1.50 (n/a)
m_1	0.153 (0.00e-3)	m_1	−0.050 (0.10)	m_1	0.0008 (0.38e-4)
m_2	−0.082 (0.75e-4)	m_2	0.009 (0.027)	m_2	−0.0006 (0.21e-4)
m_3	0.0077 (0.81e-5)	m_3	−0.001 (0.002)	m_3	0.0001 (0.32e-5)

Source: Hart, Malley and Ruffell (1996).
Note: The figures in brackets are standard errors.

is a relatively high mandatory rate by international standards. Consequently, we would not expect a great deal of 'action' from the m-parameters in (2.3); in fact, of workers working over 40 hours, Trejo (1993) indicates that less than 5 per cent receive a premium rate other than time and a half. At the other end of the spectrum, the United Kingdom has no national rules and regulations covering the length and payment of overtime. There is more scope here for rising schedules to apply. In between these two cases, Japan sets a lower mandatory premium than the United States[9] and, again, there may be evidence of a rising schedule. In other words, while a low mandated rate might suffice to compensate relatively low weekly overtime hours, longer hours may require higher premiums in order to induce sufficient labour supply.

Industrial-based results for the three countries, using a third-degree polynomial specification, are presented in table 2.5. Details of data and estimation are given in Hart, Malley and Ruffell (1996). In line with the findings in figure 2.16, the United Kingdom exhibits no evidence of a rising schedule, with $k = 1.3$ and with insignificant ms. Less surprisingly, the United States estimates reveal no variation around $k = 1.5$. The complete dominance of

[9] The data presented in table 2.4 generally simplify much greater underlying complexity. In the case of Japan, a 25 per cent minimum overtime premium must be paid under the following circumstances: (a) daily work hours exceed 8 hours; working on a holiday which comes once every week, (b) working on any day of the four holidays which come regularly within each 4-week cycle, (c) working between 10p.m. and 5a.m. If more than 8 hours are worked on any given holiday then hours must also be remunerated at a minimum of 25 per cent. If, for example, the agreed working day is 7 hours then the employer need not pay an overtime premium for the eighth hour. The base wage that is used as the basis for computing overtime premiums is specified by law for all types of wages and benefits; some components are excluded for the base while others are included.

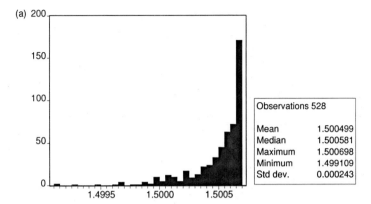

Figure 2.16a Distribution of average overtime premium, United States

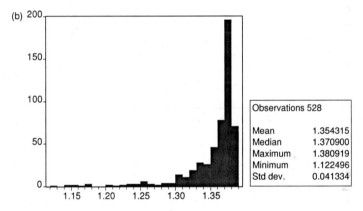

Figure 2.16b Distribution of average overtime premium, Japan
Source: Hart and Malley (2000).

the mandatory rate is illustrated in figure 2.16b(a); this shows the distribution of premium rates from the US data set. By contrast, the m estimates for Japan are more significant and reveal that as average overtime hours increase from 0 to 1, the average overtime premium rises from 1.25 (the minimum) to 1.32. As would be expected from these results, the dispersion of Japanese premium rates in figure 2.16b(b) is considerably wider than in the United States.

2.6 Wage earnings decomposition

A recurring issue throughout this text concerns the implications of decomposing average hourly wage earnings into standard wage and overtime components. It will be shown that this type of breakdown can have important implications for studies of wage determination and the behaviour of wages over the business cycle. It is useful at this stage to discuss a number of the main empirical issues. The developments concentrate on the US labour market. As shown in table 2.4, one advantage of this economy is that regulations concerning the operation and payment of overtime hours are essentially simple.

Following Hart, Malley and Woitek (2003), express average hourly earnings at time t as a geometric average, e_t^*, that is

$$e_t^* = e_t^{o^{\lambda_t}} w_t^{1-\lambda_t} \tag{2.4}$$

where e^o is average earnings of overtime workers, w is the standard hourly wage and λ is the ratio of overtime to total workers. (Estimates of λ_t are shown in figure 2.5.) Under FLSA regulations, maximum weekly standard hours are 40 and the premium is 1.5, and so we can express average earnings of overtime workers as

$$e_t^o = \frac{w_t[40 + 1.5 \times v_t^o]}{40 + v_t^o} \tag{2.5}$$

where v_t^o is the average overtime hours of overtime workers.

Substituting (2.5) into (2.4) and taking logs gives

$$\log e_t^* = \log w_t + \lambda_t \log \left[\frac{40 + 1.5 \times v_t^o}{40 + v_t^o} \right] \tag{2.6}$$

If $\lambda = 0$ in (2.6), there are no overtime workers and the standard wage is the representative compensation for all workers. If $\lambda > 0$, then $e^* > w$ due to the fact that a proportion of weekly hours for overtime workers is compensated at the hourly premium rate. The extent to which e^* diverges from w is dependent on (a) the proportion of overtime to total workers, λ_t and (b) the size of the average premium mark-up,

$$\log \left[\frac{40 + 1.5 \times v_t^o}{40 + v_t^o} \right].$$

Effectively, the mark-up is the weight (≥ 1) which attaches to w for overtime workers to achieve their average hourly earnings. Obviously, the size of the weight is determined by the number of overtime hours of overtime workers and on the level of the premium.

It turns out that the geometric average of earnings, as expressed in (2.6), provides extremely close estimates to the published average earnings data. Three aspects of the decomposition of the earnings rate over the period 1962–97 are presented in figures 2.5 and 2.17. First, figure 2.17(a) shows the share of the wage rate within the earnings rate, averaged over all workers (i.e. overtime and non-overtime). This graph is constructed with respect to the earnings rate provided by BLS (w/e) and with the geometric average (w/e^*).[10] Second, figure 2.17(b) shows the share of the wage rate within the earnings rate for overtime workers only (w/e^o). This latter graph – along with the proportions of overtime workers in figure 2.5 that uses the same data – reflects the growing importance of overtime working in the 1990s.

---

[10] The shapes of the two graphs are identical. The fact that w/e lies below w/e^* stems from the fact that $e^* < e$ under the geometric compared to the arithmetic mean (except when $\lambda = 1$ in which case $e^* = e$).

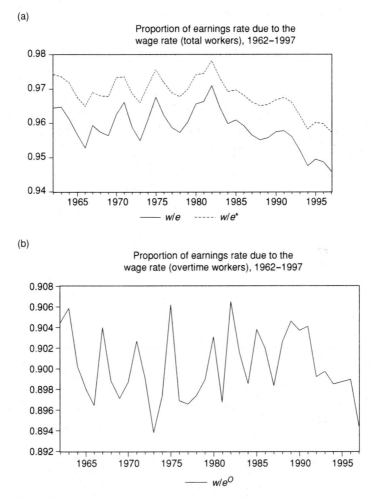

Figure 2.17 Decompositions of the earnings rate, 1962–1997

2.7 Paid and unpaid overtime

In recent years, there has been growing interest among European labour market researchers in the phenomenon of unpaid overtime. At this stage, it will suffice to present some information on the incidence of unpaid work. This topic will be returned to at a number of later stages throughout the book. While we concentrate here on British data, detailed breakdowns are also available for Germany (Bell *et al.*, 2000).

Figure 2.18 shows paid and unpaid hours of overtime averaged over all British male workers from 1987 to 2001. Three features stand out. First, paid-for overtime is quantitatively more important than unpaid overtime. Second, the downward trend in paid overtime over

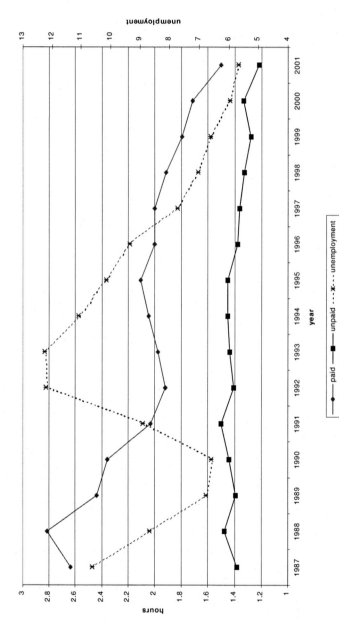

Figure 2.18 Average overtime hours (all males, United Kingdom) (LFS), 1987–2001

the period has been considerably more marked than unpaid overtime. In fact, by 2001 paid overtime averaged 1.5 hours a week compared to 1.2 hours of unpaid overtime. Third, paid overtime appears to be more procyclical than unpaid overtime. Note that the particularly large reduction in paid overtime hours in the late 1980s–early 1990s coincided with a major increase in the rate of unemployment. By contrast, the incidence of unpaid overtime was little affected by this recession.

The overtime series in figure 2.18 hide an important aspect of the incidence of paid and unpaid overtime, however. In large part different types of worker undertake these two categories of overtime work. We now explore occupational breakdowns.

Table 2.6 shows the distributions of weekly unpaid and paid overtime for British male and female workers in 2001. The occupational contrasts are stark. For males, 54.5 per cent of managers and 48.2 per cent of professionals claim to work unpaid overtime; this compares with 4.5 per cent of plant and machine operatives. However, only 7.5 per cent of managers and 13 per cent of professionals work paid overtime; this contrasts with 45.9 per cent of plant and machine operatives. The female comparisons convey a broadly similar picture. Significant percentages of both male and female managerial and higher professional workers claim to work extensive weekly unpaid overtime. As examples in this latter respect, 13 per cent of male managers and 23.8 per cent of female professionals claim to work 13 or more unpaid overtime hours per week.

What are the implications of the occupational incidence of unpaid overtime for hourly earnings? Table 2.7 shows two average hourly earnings calculations for British males and females. The first is paid-for hourly earnings. This consists simply of weekly earnings divided by the weekly number of paid-for hours. The second is actual hourly earnings. This is always equal to or smaller than its paid-for equivalent because weekly earnings are now divided by the sum of paid and unpaid weekly hours. As we might expect from the earlier information, the two average earnings measures compare closely for less-skilled occupations. For managers and professionals, however, relatively high levels of unpaid hours result in actual hourly earnings that are between 84 and 91 per cent of their paid-for equivalents.

Similar outcomes can be expected when the sample is categorised by academic qualification. More complex and less regulated jobs are likely to match with higher levels of educational attainment. This expectation is confirmed in Table 2.8. For both males and females, actual hourly earnings for those holding degrees are considerably lower than their paid-for equivalents. Actual earnings are also significantly lower than paid-for earnings for those holding other higher educational qualifications.

Pannenberg and Wagner (2001) examine the ways in which various overtime patterns influenced the evolution of monthly earning distributions in Britain and West Germany during the 1990s. Based on data from the GSOEP and BHPS, they estimate linear regressions in which the dependent variable is the individual percentile in the earnings distribution in year t. Explanatory variables cover types of overtime compensation as well as a wide range of other controls. Using the individual-based regression estimates, earnings mobility tables are predicted for different patterns of overtime incidence and compensation. These are undertaken with respect to individuals starting at a given percentile on the earnings

Table 2.6 *Unpaid and paid weekly overtime, by three occupation groups in (LFS), 2001*

Males

Occupation	Weekly unpaid overtime hours (%)						Weekly paid overtime hours (%)					
	0	1–6	7–12	13–20	21–40	No. of individuals	0	1–6	7–12	13–20	21–40	No. of individuals
1 Managers and administrators	45.5	24.7	16.9	9.7	3.3	2,011	92.5	3.8	2.5	0.9	0.3	2,011
2 Professional	51.8	25.9	11.7	7.2	3.5	1,459	87.0	7.2	3.2	2.0	0.7	1,459
8 Plant and machine operatives	95.5	3.2	0.8	0.6	0.0	1,415	54.1	16.9	16.5	8.3	4.1	1,415

Females

Occupation	Weekly unpaid overtime hours (%)						Weekly paid overtime hours (%)					
	0	1–6	7–12	13–20	21–40	No. of individuals	0	1–6	7–12	13–20	21–40	No. of individuals
1 Managers and administrators	50.4	29.3	13.3	5.6	1.5	875	91.0	5.0	2.9	0.7	0.5	875
2 Professional	38.6	20.7	16.8	15.9	7.9	897	93.2	3.9	1.5	0.9	0.6	897
8 Plant and machine operatives	96.6	1.9	0.8	0.8	0.0	268	72.4	14.6	8.6	4.5	0.0	268

Table 2.7 *Paid-for and actual hourly earnings by occupation £ per hour), 2001*

	Male earnings			Female earnings		
Occupations	(1) Paid-for	(2) Actual	(3) (2) as % (1)	(1) Paid-for	(2) Actual	(3) (2) as % (1)
Managers and	18.58	16.39	88.2	14.42	12.85	89.1
administrators	(15.4)	(13.7)		(11.5)	(9.3)	
Professional	17.29	15.68	90.7	16.12	13.48	83.6
	(11.0)	(10.3)		(12.3)	(11.3)	
Plant and	8.38	8.32	99.2	6.21	6.17	99.4
machine	(6.1)	(8.3)		(2.5)	(2.5)	
operatives						

Notes: Figures in brackets are standard deviations.

Table 2.8 *Paid-for and actual earnings, by educational qualification (£ per hour), 2001*

	Male earnings			Female earnings		
Occupations	(1) Paid-for	(2) Actual	(3) (2) as % (1)	(1) Paid-for	(2) Actual	(3) (2) as % (1)
Degree level	18.54	16.52	89.1	15.15	13.16	86.9
	(14.6)	(13.0)		(11.1)	(9.1)	
Other higher	13.80	12.82	92.9	11.42	10.51	92.0
educational	(10.2)	(9.2)		(9.7)	(9.2)	
School leaving	10.79	10.35	95.9	8.57	8.25	96.3
certificate	(8.9)	(8.5)		(6.4)	(6.1)	
Youth training	8.25	8.25	100.0	4.40	4.40	100.0
certificate, etc.	(3.9)	(3.9)		(0.9)	(0.9)	

Notes: Figures in brackets are standard deviations.

distribution – possessing an assumed set of characteristics of that group – and ending at a percentile position in time period $t + 3$. In both countries, individuals with persistent paid or unpaid overtime are predicted to end in a significantly higher earnings percentile than if no overtime is worked. For example, a German starting in the 10th percentile is predicted to reach the 14th percentile if no overtime is worked over the 3-year period and to reach the 20th percentile if either paid or unpaid overtime is persistently worked. The British paid/unpaid overtime predictions are particularly interesting. Again assuming a start in the 10th percentile, an individual who persistently works paid overtime will end up at the 17th percentile, but at the 22nd percentile if persistent unpaid overtime is undertaken. There are a few qualifications to these latter results – especially a higher than average correlation between working unpaid hours and the incidence of bonus payments – but they point to an interesting line of investigation. Working unpaid overtime today may lead to better employment returns in the future and this may underline the main reason for such overtime behaviour. We report further on this issue in section 5.6.

2.8   Summary

The main conclusions arising from this chapter are as follows.

- There are wide international variations in industrial averages of weekly overtime within OECD countries – ranging from 1 hour to 6 hours per manufacturing worker (overtime plus non-overtime).
- Overtime hours are procyclical and leading indicators of cyclical turning points.
- The proportion of employees working overtime also varies procyclically.
- In many overtime firms, only a fraction of the workforce in given occupations regularly works overtime.
- In the evaluation of changes in total overtime hours it is important to differentiate between hours of existing overtime workers and the proportion of the workforce working overtime.
- Male standard hours have exhibited monotonic downward trends in recent decades.
- There is some evidence of cyclicality in female standard hours.
- The degree of regulation of maximum weekly standard hours and minimum overtime premia ranges from strong comprehensive control with high overtime premia (e.g. the United States) to virtually no control whatsoever (e.g. the United Kingdom).
- In the unregulated UK economy, the average overtime premium is acyclical.
- There is international evidence that the overtime premium is invariant to the number of weekly overtime hours.
- At the macro level, studying the cyclical behaviour of average hourly earnings requires wage decomposition into the standard hourly wage, the overtime wage and the proportion of employees working overtime.
- Professional and managerial workers in Germany and the United Kingdom report that they work significant numbers of unpaid weekly overtime hours.
- Unpaid overtime drives a wedge between paid-for and actual hourly wages earnings.

3   The overtime decision

In this chapter, we investigate the decision to work overtime hours in the workplace. The literature has explored this issue from three different perspectives. These are (a) the overtime supply choice of the individual, (b) the firm's demand for overtime, and (c) worker-firm contractual bargaining agreements over hours of work. Within all three approaches, it is common to accommodate interventions by outside agencies – usually the government, but including industry-level agreed rules and regulations – that effectively impose exogenous constraints on the practice of overtime working. It should be emphasised, however, that supply-dominated studies almost invariably embrace aspects of demand while demand analysis is often extended to admit some degree of supply-side decision making.

Suppose we were to concentrate on an individual's decision to supply hours of work. In the case of overtime, the question arises as to the role played by the wage premium for hours worked in excess of standard hours. This typically involves considerations that lie beyond the usual supply analysis of a participating individual.[1] Leaving aside possible mandatory rules in respect of overtime compensation, payment of a premium for a sub-set of daily working hours implies action by an agent to provide an *incentive* to work longer hours than would have been the case with only a single rate. It suggests overt intervention to induce, for part of the working day, a substitution effect that overwhelmingly dominates the income effect. Implicitly, therefore, the premium reflects the presence of a demand-side action by a firm in order to 'encourage' a given supply outcome. If the premium is targeted towards a specific worker, then the firm may be acting as a discriminating monopsonist that is able to tailor its hiring rules to individual supply prices. More commonly, the worker would be working, formally or informally, as part of a work team. In this event, the firm may set a premium rate that it believes will persuade most team members – some marginal, some intra-marginal – to prolong their workday. This may serve to reduce the transaction costs of relative wage setting and to avoid intra-group disputes over differential rates.

---

[1] A 'pure' supply scenario involving overtime would best be envisaged in terms of a self-employed worker. The optimal length of working day can be written down in terms of the usual utility analysis. Decisions to work in excess of this preferred work allocation – perhaps due to rush orders, unusual contractual commitments or special family circumstances – can be undertaken according to a set of implicit rules determined by the individual and not subject to the binding constraint of a third party.

What about workplace employment and hours decisions undertaken unilaterally by the firm? In the simplest demand approaches, it is assumed that all employees work the same overtime hours. In the case of production line operations and team oriented work, this may not be a bad first approximation to reality. In many cases, however, it is an unrealistic assumption since we observe that only a part of the total workforce works overtime (see section 2.2). In this event, average overtime hours are influenced by both the length of hours of overtime workers and the proportion of the workforce participating in overtime. Questions concerning which individuals work overtime and which do not almost certainly involve the need to accommodate supply-side aspirations. Even where firms dominate in overtime decision making, they would probably allow – in fact, they may be legally obliged to permit – some degree of worker discretion over whether or not to participate in overtime activity. In fact, it may well be more cost effective for the firm to encourage self-selection rather than itself investing in time and effort to find suitable and willing overtime workers.

In the absence of dominant demand- or supply-led overtime decision making, the parties may need to agree strategies on how to deal with overtime scheduling. The obvious way of reconciling differing approaches is through collective bargaining and, not surprisingly, one focus in the literature has been on the construction of union-firm bargaining models. However, this area has proved to be the most difficult in which to make significant progress. There are serious problems to overcome. Changes in overtime working affect the firm's revenue and costs as well as union members' hourly earnings and leisure time. The good news to the parties of a rise in overtime hours is increased revenue and enhanced earnings. The bad news is a rise in unit labour costs and a fall in utility associated with forgone leisure. Finding an optimising balance is not a simple task. In fact, as we shall argue at various stages, the parties are likely to resort to 'custom and practice' in respect of overtime pay and hours in order to circumvent potential indeterminacy problems.

A more tractable, and perhaps more realistic, approach side steps the problem of integrating the apparatus of the neoclassical supply-side analysis of individual hours' preferences with workers-hours demand. An important aspect of a given job's attribute is regarded as its associated length of per-period hours. Depending on technological, business trading and organisational constraints, a range of different job lengths is required across firms. Different utility preferences and budget constraints among individuals lead them to search for a range of job lengths and associated wage earnings. The wage acts as a compensating differential for jobs of different lengths. Market equilibrium is achieved when preferences are matched, with labour demand equal to labour supply for each job length.

We begin by reviewing the basics of the individual overtime supply decision. Here, particular emphasis is given to the implications of constraining pure supply decisions through the imposition of a maximum length of daily standard hours and a minimum overtime premium. We then turn attention to pure demand and to demand-dominated decision making. It is subsequently recognised, however, that demand-led overtime decisions do not normally ignore potential supply-side constraints. In the first place, we highlight a number of modelling developments that try to capture the fact that only a fraction of the firm's workforce may actually work overtime. Second, where overtime is undertaken, we explore the possibility that the length of overtime spells may be subject to supply constraints. For example, the firm may take on board the fact that longer per-period overtime hours may require increasing marginal premium payments in order to offset a rising opportunity cost of leisure. Third, it is recognised that not only the length of working hours but also the concomitant supply of effort may feature in the firm's decision making. Demanding longer daily hours may also require a wage setting strategy that provides incentives to workers to avoid reductions in work application as the working day lengthens.

Some attention is then given to union bargaining models that embrace working time issues. The great bulk of the literature in this area ignores hours of work. Yet workers are especially interested in levels of weekly or monthly take-home-pay and not merely the hourly rate for the job. Firms are concerned with both intensive and extensive margins of production. Progress in this area has been somewhat limited, with monopoly union and right-to-manage approaches achieving the most progress. Again, this has much to do with the fact that in efficient contract models in which the parties bargain over all aspects of pay, overtime premia are indeterminate. This helps to explain the common observation that unions and employers are often content to follow a fixed set of rules concerning overtime premium rates and the schedule of overtime hours to which each rate applies.

Mandatory overtime rules are then dealt with more explicitly. It is shown that where the parties reach long-term agreements over the length of a job and its associated wage earnings – with hours in effect being treated as indivisible – they will simply act to offset changes in mandated rules through the mechanism of flexible standard hourly wage rates. Once employee/employer wage-hours preferences are jointly satisfied, working time policy effectiveness is essentially eliminated.

Overtime hours in most of these foregoing developments are remunerated at a premium rate of hourly pay. In general terms, 'paid overtime' simply refers to the practice of working per-period paid hours in excess of a contractually specified norm.

As we have seen in chapter 2, the great bulk of paid overtime is undertaken by nonmanagerial/professional workers. But many managers and professionals also have job contracts that specify their lengths of hours. We know from section 2.7 (see table 2.6), that high proportions of these workers claim to work unpaid overtime – i.e. unpaid hours worked in excess of those stipulated in their contracts. In other words, their hours exceed their contractual standard hours but their contract does not provide for additional payments. As we will discuss, one clue to the distinction between paid and unpaid overtime lies in the complexity of job tasks and the associated ability to forecast and to monitor task completion times. Other explanations, discussed in section 5.6, include treating unpaid overtime as work activity that receives deferred compensation. The latter may take the form of accelerated wage increments and/or job promotion.

3.1 Labour supply

The term 'overtime' generally refers to hours that are worked in excess of a required per-period minimum number. The most familiar examples of the latter are the standard workday and standard workweek. In many instances, agreements over the length of the standard workweek are reached through union collective bargaining agreements. It is quite common for the firm to insist – i.e. to adopt a 'take-it-or-leave-it' stance – that all employees work hours at least up to a prescribed number of standard hours. There are several reasons why firms seek to unify working time in this way. First, large and complex business organisations may require a high degree of formal work scheduling in order to minimise organisational costs. Second, adopting a common standard working day helps to maximise available trading hours across vertically and horizontally integrated industrial or commercial sectors. Third, team working – involving interactive job tasks and skills – may be most productive if all members of the team keep the same working hours. Fourth, line production necessitates the attendance of all line operatives over a given production interval. Fifth, cost considerations may dictate that heating, lighting, canteen and recreational facilities are provided to the maximum number of workers for specific parts of the working day. Sixth, a standard length of hours may be imposed on the firm by an outside agency. A common example of the latter is a public sector company that is required to adhere to workweek lengths prescribed by national or regional government. In the private sector, agreements between employers associations and national-level unions may impose hours' standards on individual member firms.

In the following discussion of an individual's supply of overtime hours in a single job,[2] it is assumed that the worker faces a standard workday constraint. This serves potentially to introduce a form of hours' rationing since the imposed hours may not correspond to the individual's preferred hours (Killingsworth, 1983).

In the neoclassical model of an individual's supply of hours, utility is maximised subject to a budget constraint. Utility is derived from combinations of consumption and leisure while the budget constraint consists of real wage income (the real wage rate times hours) and real non-wage income. Suppose, initially, that there is no standard workday and no overtime. There is a single hourly wage rate and the budget constraint is depicted by the line 0–a–b in figure 3.1, with 0–a representing the amount of consumption at zero working hours and where the slope of a–b is equal to the real wage. An indifference curve – e.g. u_0 in figure 3.1 – represents combinations of consumption and leisure that provide the individual with the same level of satisfaction. Indifference curves are assumed to be convex. A point on an indifference curve depicts the negative of the marginal rate of substitution of consumer goods for leisure. The optimal consumption/leisure combination occurs at a point of tangency between an indifference curve and the budget line. In figure 3.1, p represents such a point, with the desired weekly hours given, h^* and associated utility, u_2. Hours can be readily translated into equivalent desired daily leisure time. In effect, p represents an unconstrained interior solution where the worker is free to choose the length of the working day given the fixed wage.

Now, suppose an industry-wide agreement leads to the imposition of a standard workday, consisting of h_s standard hours. The individual is required to move from p to c and work $h_s > h^*$. The worker is likely to accept the new conditions because utility associated with c (u_1) is greater than the alternative utility (u_0) which is equivalent to non-wage income, a,

---

[2] We ignore labour supply involving dual job holding. For an extension of supply along these lines – involving overtime work and pay – see Frederiksen, Graversen and Smith (2001).

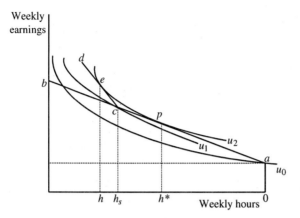

Figure 3.1   Overtime and 'overemployment'

combined with $h = 0$. In effect, acceptance of the new conditions implies that the worker becomes 'overemployed' in the sense that the required hours are in excess of the utility maximising hours.[3] Two, perhaps related, scenarios may then arise.

In the first place, the worker may attempt partially to rectify the position – by moving towards the preferred point p – through taking spells of absenteeism. In fact, the greater the gap $h_s - h^*$ the greater the tendency to be absent given diminishing marginal utility of leisure.[4] This suggests a positive association between the number of required standard hours and absenteeism. In fact, the relationship between absenteeism and overtime working has proved to be a catalyst in the development of ideas concerning the effects of overtime in the labour market, and this topic is returned to in more detail in chapter 7.

In the second place, assuming the firm can play the role of a discriminating monopsonist, it may seek to offset potential absenteeism and low morale by offering an overtime premium for hours worked in excess of h_s. The increased slope of the budget line, c–d, represents this premium pay and tangency point e depicts the return to equilibrium hours – though now consisting of $h_s + (h - h_s)$ – and a regaining of initial utility, u_2. The possibility that there is a negative trade off between payment of an overtime premium and the rate of absenteeism for some employees may provide a clue as to why the firm may offer premium pay as part of a guaranteed contract. However, we leave discussion of this kind of generalisation to chapter 4 where the role of the premium is scrutinised in more depth.

Of course, this analysis is very partial and, in particular, begs questions relating to the firm's hours and employment requirements in relation to revenue and cost. Even if the firm wishes to expand labour input, it would still need to consider the relative costs of paying

---

[3] The marginal rate of substitution between income and leisure at point c (i.e. the slope of u_1) is greater than the economic rate of substitution between income and leisure (the slope of the budget line, a–b).
[4] Brown and Sessions (1996) discuss this and many other aspects of absenteeism. A rise in the wage rate produces income and substitution effects that serve, respectively, to increase and decrease the tendency to be absent. An increase in non-wage income has a pure income effect and, providing leisure is a normal good, increases the tendency to be absent.

an overtime premium to selected overemployed existing workers (net of reduced absentee costs) compared to hiring new recruits. But, at least, introducing an overtime schedule may well offer the best intensive margin way of dealing with overemployment, *ceteris paribus*. Paying a premium for overtime hours would be expected to induce a relatively large substitution relative to income effect since it is confined to *marginal* daily hours. Increasing the standard wage as an alternative strategy would involve a much larger offsetting income effect.

An alternative supply scenario is illustrated in figure 3.2. Initially there is no overtime and, at the given wage rate, the worker is in equilibrium at the unconstrained point p and offers h^* hours of work. Suppose that the government mandates the length of the standard workday or workweek consisting of h_s hours.[5] It also stipulates a minimum overtime premium that attaches to the standard hourly wage for hours in excess of h_s. Provided the firm complies with individual preferences, the worker in figure 3.2 will benefit from such legislation since average hourly pay will rise given that $h > h_s$. In the scenario depicted, the worker will move from p to q, given a larger income than substitution effect, and offer h hours of which $h - h_s$ will be remunerated at the premium wage.[6] The firm may well be reluctant to pay this higher compensation, however. In effect, it would be receiving less labour service at a higher average hourly wage rate. If it refuses to pay overtime wages under these exogenously imposed rules, it will be obliged to offer the worker h_s hours at point c. In this event, the worker would be 'underemployed', with actual hours falling short of desired hours. The costs associated with this type of constraint may be low worker morale coupled with intensified job search for alternative employment. The government might not be completely unhappy over such repercussions. If figure 3.2 depicts a typical reaction to the imposition of h_s then labour service available to the firm is reduced. The government might believe that the internal costs of worker underemployment might be more than offset, in terms of total welfare, by the external benefits of new jobs created in order to restore the employment shortfall. In other words, its intervention might represent an overt employment policy of job creation by means of work sharing.

In figure 3.2, the worker maximises utility at the given standard wage rate at point p but is prevented from attaining this optimum by the exogenous imposition on the firm of a higher marginal price of labour input. Suppose that the firm, too, prefers to operate with a wage-hours combination compatible with point p. In other words, both parties are happy with job length $0 - h^*$ and associated wage earnings at p. Can the parties reach an agreement that effectively circumvents the sub-optimal solution resulting from the required overtime payment rule beyond h_s? The answer is that they can do so, partially, if they are willing and able to reach an agreement over the standard wage, w (see Ehrenberg and Schumann, 1984; Trejo, 1991; Filer, Hamermesh and Rees, 1996). As depicted in figure 3.3, they could agree to lower w up to h_s, the point at which the legislation takes effect. The reduction is such

---

[5] See Costa (2000) for an analysis of an initial introduction of mandatory rules pertaining to overtime working. This concerns the US Fair Labor Standard Act (FLSA) of 1938.

[6] Of course, targeting premiums at the level of the individual is unrealistic in most work situations. It is more usual for a group of workers to face a single premium and then to make a voluntary commitment on whether or not to work overtime. For an empirical investigation of this latter set-up in a US context, see Idson and Robins (1991).

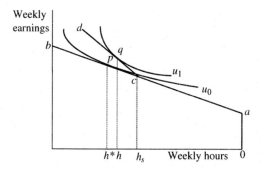

Figure 3.2 Overtime and 'underemployment'

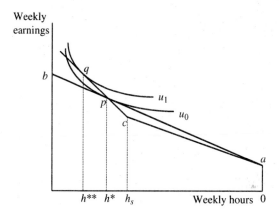

Figure 3.3 Overtime with standard wage compensating differential

that the slope of the standard budget line $a-c$ compared to $a-b$ is just sufficient to offset the steeper slope of the overtime budget line to the left of c so that h^* hours can be purchased at the same cost as in figure 3.2. The solution is only partial in the sense that at point p the worker is again underemployed by $h^{**} - h^*$ hours since q would be the preferred utility maximising point. We take a closer look at this type of wage-hour agreement in section 3.7.

Of course, this analysis is not relevant only to the case where mandatory overtime rules are imposed by government. Due to production and organisational constraints, the firm itself may require the worker to work longer overtime hours than those equivalent to utility maximisation. The firm may then compensate the worker by an appropriate increase in the standard wage. Clearly, a compensating wage differential could be paid if the worker is required to work fewer hours (overtime or standard) than desired. Ehrenberg and Schumann (1984) analyse compensating differentials for the case of the firm requiring 'too many' overtime hours.

3.2 Labour demand

From the viewpoint of an individual supplying hours to a firm, it is not realistic to ignore demand constraints in decisions concerning overtime. On the other side of the coin, it might be regarded as equally unrealistic to conceive of pure demand oriented decisions. Yet, such a demand literature exists and it has produced several useful bedrock ideas and insights – from theoretical, empirical and policy perspectives – on which to build when attempting more realistic portrayals of the labour market. This is also the motivation behind this section, with the express aim of capturing the central demand issues in the simplest possible modelling framework. Generalisations on the approaches adopted here can be found in the considerable existing literature on this subject. The seminal contribution is Ehrenberg (1971a), while Hart (1984, 1987) and Contensou and Vranceanu (2000) provide large surveys and considerable analytical details.

One simplification, in particular, should be highlighted. It is sufficient for present purposes to assume that the firm requires workers to work overtime hours in equilibrium. Brechling (1965), Calmfors and Hoel (1988), Bhattacharya, DeLeire and MaCurdy (2001) and Andrews, Schank and Simmons (2002) provide solutions to demand models where short-time working is undertaken or at corner solutions where workers work maximum standard hours with zero overtime.

Labour services

Suppose that the firm faces a given output, level of technology and flow of capital services. The production function can be inverted and expressed equivalently in terms of a labour services function. Letting N be the number of homogeneous workers and h the homogeneous per-period hours worked per worker, this is written generally as

$$L = F(N, h) \qquad (3.1)$$

where $F_N > 0$ and $F_h > 0$.

Ehrenberg (1971a) introduced a special class of labour services function belonging to (3.1) that has proved very popular in the subsequent literature. Suppose that (3.1) were to feature on the revenue side of a firm-level cost minimising or profit maximising problem. Then, Ehrenberg argued that it is intuitively plausible that equilibrium hours are invariant to scale.[7] In fact, Ehrenberg derived a class of multiplicatively separable labour services functions that satisfy the scale invariance property. These can be expressed

$$L = AN^\alpha g(h) \qquad (3.2)$$

where A and α are constants with $0 < \alpha \le 1$ and where $g(0) = 0$, $g'(h) > 0$ and $g''(h) < 0$. As h increases, L increases at a diminishing rate and L and N are positively related.

While (3.2) introduces a significant degree of simplicity in its description of the effects of N and h on labour services, it nevertheless provides a reasonable degree of 'believability'

---

[7] Such a property is highly convenient when it comes to estimating hours' demand functions, a consideration that perhaps helped to encourage Ehrenberg's intuition!

in its representation of the production process. Various authors have argued that the sign of $g''(h)$ may switch as the working day lengthens (see, especially, de Regt, 1984 as well as Barzel, 1973, Feldstein, 1976 and Booth and Schiantarelli, 1987, 1988). For example, at low values of h it might be the case that $g''(h) > 0$; marginal productivity rises after an initial period in which productive effort is affected by 'warming-up' or setting-up activity. Towards the end of the working day – that is, for large values of h – 'winding-down' activities, perhaps aided and abetted by fatigue or boredom, may produce $g''(h) < 0$.

A particularly simple way of adding economic flesh to the $g(h)$ function is suggested by FitzRoy and Hart (1985) and Hart (1987). Let τ be set-up or 'get-ready' time. If $h < \tau$ then $g(0) = 0$. If $h > \tau$ then

$$g(h) = (h - \tau)^\beta \tag{3.3}$$

with $0 < \beta < 1$ and so $g''(h) < 0$. Average productivity initially rises and then falls for $h > \tau/(1 - \beta) > \tau$.

Cost minimisation

We start with a simple and familiar core workers-hours demand model. We will refer to it at later stages as the *standard model*. It stems from the work of Brechling (1965), Rosen (1968) and Ehrenberg (1971a). Standard hours, h_s, are treated as an exogenous variable. For simplicity, homogeneous workers are employed for the same number of weekly paid-for overtime hours.

Recalling that it is assumed that the firm operates on the intensive margin in the overtime region; total costs are given by

$$C = cN = \{w[h_s + k(h - h_s)] + z\}N \quad h > h_s \tag{3.4}$$

where c is total per-worker cost, w is the standard wage, k is the overtime premium and z are hours-independent (or 'fixed') costs.[8]

Let output be predetermined which implies that labour services is fixed at $L = \overline{L}$. In general terms, the firm's cost minimising objective is expressed

$$\min_{h,N} C = cN \tag{3.5}$$

subject to $F(h, N) = \overline{L}$.

The determinant of the bordered Hessian matrix for the problem in (3.5) is given by

$$\Delta = \lambda\left[F_h^2 F_{NN} + F_N^2 F_{hh} + \left(2F_h^2 F_N\right)/N - 2F_h F_N F_{hN}\right] \tag{3.6}$$

where λ is a Lagrangian multiplier and where $\Delta < 0$ is required in order to satisfy the second-order conditions for a minimum.

---

[8] Fixed costs comprise two main elements (e.g. Ehrenberg, 1971a; Hart, 1984). First, they consist of turnover-related costs such as hiring, training and redundancy costs. Second, some elements of company fringe benefits (e.g. private health cover, vacation pay, private pensions) and statutory payroll taxes (health, pension and unemployment insurance contributions) may consist of hours-independent payments.

The problem in (3.5) is explored using the multiplicative form of labour services given by (3.2); thus, the production constraint is given by $\overline{L} = AN^\alpha g(h)$.

The Lagrangian $J = \{cN - \lambda[\overline{L} - AN^\alpha g(h)]\}$ entails the first-order conditions $J_h = J_N = J_\lambda = 0$ which give, respectively

$$wkN = \lambda AN^\alpha g'(h) \tag{3.7}$$

$$c = \lambda A\alpha N^{\alpha-1} g(h) \tag{3.8}$$

$$\overline{L} = AN^\alpha g(h). \tag{3.9}$$

Combining (3.7) and (3.8) gives

$$\frac{\alpha wk}{c} = \frac{g'(h)}{g(h)} \tag{3.10}$$

or the firm equates the ratio of marginal costs at the intensive and extensive margins to the ratio of their respective marginal products. Note that the value of h derived from (3.10) is independent of the level of output. This property stems directly from the fact that the inputs in (3.2) are multiplicatively separable.

Simplifying further, we now adopt the expression for $g(h)$ in (3.3). The production constraint then becomes

$$\overline{L} = AN^\alpha (h - \tau)^\beta. \tag{3.11}$$

Evaluating the second-order condition in (3.6) for this labour services function produces the requirement that

$$\frac{\alpha kwL^2}{N(h - \tau)}(\beta - \alpha) < 0. \tag{3.12}$$

Thus, assuming $h > \tau$, the second-order condition requires that the returns to workers exceed returns to hours, i.e. $\alpha > \beta$. This is a well-known result, and one that we will return to at several later stages, and especially in section 5.3.

We now apply function $g(h) = (h - \tau)^\beta$ to the first-order equilibrium condition in (3.10). For $h > \tau$, $g'(h) = \beta g/(h - \tau)$ and $g'(h)/g(h) = \beta/(h - \tau)$. Substituting this latter result into (3.10) and rearranging produces

$$h = \frac{\beta z + \alpha\tau wk - \beta wh_s(k - 1)}{wk(\alpha - \beta)}. \tag{3.13}$$

We can now examine two results that have featured prominently in the analysis of the overtime decision. As we will see later, each result has been challenged in empirical work as well as in alternative theoretical approaches.

First, given (3.12) holds, it follows that

$$\frac{\partial h}{\partial k} = -\frac{\beta(z + wh_s)}{wk^2(\alpha - \beta)} < 0 \tag{3.14}$$

or a rise in the premium reduces average hours. Given positive marginal products and (3.11), it follows that $\partial N / \partial k > 0$. The rise in k increases the marginal cost of an additional hour and employing a new worker (since the overtime hours of the new worker have increased in price). But the cost rises in the former are more than proportional to the latter, with the result that the firm substitutes workers for hours. These results are illustrated graphically in figure 3A.1 (p. 79).

Second, we have

$$\frac{\partial h}{\partial h_s} = -\frac{\beta(k-1)}{k(\alpha - \beta)} < 0 \tag{3.15}$$

or reduced standard hours are associated with a rise in total hours. Again, $\partial N / \partial h_s > 0$ follows automatically. A cut in standard hours has no effect on cost on the intensive margin – given a single premium applies to all overtime hours – but increases cost on the extensive margin since a lower proportion of a new worker's time is paid for at the lower standard wage rate.

It will also prove useful to note that

$$\frac{\partial h}{\partial z} = -\frac{\beta}{wk(\alpha - \beta)} > 0 \tag{3.16}$$

which implies that $\partial N / \partial z < 0$. A rise in hours-independent costs of labour induces the firm to substitute in favour of the intensive margin.[9] For strictly equivalent reasons, the same hours-worker substitution occurs for an increase in set-up time, τ.

Profit maximisation

What if the firm is a profit maximiser? The firm now chooses output and, retaining previous functional forms, this implies that L replaces $\overline{L}$ in (3.11), that is

$$L = AN^\alpha (h - \tau)^\beta. \tag{3.17}$$

Setting output price to unity, the new problem is expressed

$$\max_{h,N} \pi = L - cN. \tag{3.18}$$

where cN is defined in (3.4).

First-order conditions require $\pi_N = \pi_h = 0$, which give, respectively

$$\frac{\alpha L}{N} = c \tag{3.19}$$

and

$$\frac{\beta L}{h - \tau} = wkN. \tag{3.20}$$

---

[9] That we would expect the employment and hours effects of a change in h_s and z to be the same can be illustrated in a simple way. From (3.4), cost per worker can be re-written as $c = wkh + \hat{z}$, where $\hat{z} = z + (1-k)wh_s$. Here, $\hat{z}$ is fixed cost in the sense that it is independent of endogenous hours, h. It follows quite simply that $dN/d\hat{z} < 0$ and $dh/d\hat{z} > 0$. Note that a cut in h_s causes $\hat{z}$ to rise as does a rise in z.

From these two first-order conditions, we establish that in equilibrium the firm equates the ratio of marginal products of workers and hours, α/β to their respective marginal costs, $c/wk(h - \tau)$. This is equivalent to (3.10) under cost minimisation with, again, the choice of production function ensuring that hours of work are scale invariant.

Maximisation requires that (3.19) and (3.20) are satisfied, as are the second-order conditions given by $\pi_{NN} < 0$, $\pi_{hh} < 0$, $\pi_{NN}\pi_{hh} - \pi_{NH}^2 > 0$. This last expression is the determinant of the cross-partials of the objective function,

$$D = \begin{vmatrix} \pi_{NN} & \pi_{Nh} \\ \pi_{hN} & \pi_{hh} \end{vmatrix} = \begin{vmatrix} \alpha(\alpha - 1)L/N^2 & \alpha\beta L/(h - \tau)N \\ \alpha\beta L/(h - \tau)N & \beta(\beta - 1)L/(h - \tau)^2 \end{vmatrix} > 0. \quad (3.21)$$

Note that $\pi_{NN} < 0$ implies that $\alpha < 1$ and $\pi_{hh} < 0$ implies that $\beta < 1$.

Does profit maximising behaviour produce divergent results from those obtained under cost minimisation? It will suffice to explore two outcomes.

First, what are the effects of a change in standard hours? Using Cramer's rule, we obtain

$$\frac{\partial N}{\partial h_s} = \frac{w(1 - k)N\pi_{NN}}{D} > 0 \quad (3.22)$$

and

$$\frac{\partial h}{\partial h_s} = \frac{w(1 - k)N\pi_{Nh}}{D} < 0. \quad (3.23)$$

A fall in h_s is associated with a fall in employment and a rise in average total hours. This is in line with the cost minimisation findings – see (3.15) – but with a somewhat extended explanation. The fall in employment occurs not only through the substitution effect, as in the cost minimisation case, but also via a scale effect. The fall in h_s raises c in (3.19) since a given output is produced at a more expensive mix of standard and overtime hours. Given diminishing returns – see (3.17) and (3.3) where $g''(h) < 0$ – employment must reduce as a result of this scale impact. Thus *both* substitution and scale effects serve to reduce employment in the event of a cut in standard hours. Since the choice of a multiplicatively separable labour services function in (3.17) renders hours to be scale-independent, the hours' result in (3.23) is due to a pure substitution effect.[10]

Second, what are the consequences of a change in the overtime premium, k? In this case, we obtain

$$\frac{\partial N}{\partial k} = \frac{w(h - h_s)N\pi_{hh} - wN\pi_{Nh}}{D} \quad (?) \quad (3.24)$$

and

$$\frac{\partial h}{\partial k} = \frac{wN\pi_{NN} - w(h - h_s)N\pi_{Nh}}{D} < 0. \quad (3.25)$$

As in (3.14) under cost minimisation, a rise in the premium produces a fall in standard hours due to the substitution effect. Employment rises as a result, but this is offset by a negative scale effect. A rise in k raises per-worker cost, c and so the net impact on employment

---

[10] These conclusions with respect to h_s also apply to changes in fixed costs, z or a change in set-up time, τ.

is ambiguous, as revealed by (3.24). Again, however, the hours' result in (3.25) matches (3.14) under cost minimisation given the scale-independence of hours. The outcomes in (3.24) and (3.25) are illustrated graphically in figure 3A.2 (p. 79).

A rising overtime schedule

The foregoing cost minimisation and profit maximisation problems provide illustrative examples from a class of models that have been influential in the policy literature. They have featured in debates concerning the impacts on work sharing of changes in standard hours of work and relative workers-hour factor prices. Yet, the optimising problems they describe contain two immediately serious shortcomings that relate directly to their (typical) formulation:[11]

(1) One problem stems directly from the popular adoption by theorists and empiricists of the *multiplicatively separable labour services functions* belonging to (3.2). As we have shown above (see (3.12)), optimal solutions require higher returns to workers than to hours of work. In fact, most empirical studies find relative returns that lie in the opposite direction. This problem has led to several strands of research. From a purely empirical angle, it has produced more careful attempts at specification and testing of functional forms in order to check the degree to which estimates of relative returns are affected by model misspecification (see DeBeaumont and Singell, 1999). This issue is investigated in section 5.3.

(2) Even more problematic are the findings in (3.15) and (3.23) whereby a fall in per-worker standard hours leads to a rise in per-worker total hours, that is $\partial h / \partial h_s < 0$. The overwhelming empirical evidence supports a positive partial derivative with, typically, a fall in standard hours leading to a less than proportional fall in total hours. In other words, overtime rises as only a *partial* offset.

One theoretical approach deals simultaneously with both types of problem in (1) and (2). It relates to a possible crucial weakness inherent in the foregoing demand formulations. Santamäki (1983) suggested that the typical specification of the firm's cost function, as represented in (3.4), may be oversimplistic. A clue to the potential problem is given by considering the work sharing effects of a cut in standard hours. For example, as shown in (3.15) in the cost minimising model, a fall in h_s leads to a substitution effect whereby N falls and h rises. Why does this occur? The fundamental reason is that in the cost formulation in (3.4) all overtime hours are assumed to be remunerated at the single rate, k. Therefore, on the intensive margin, changing hours in the overtime domain has no marginal cost implications. But it does carry direct implications for extensive margin costs since, for given output, per-worker marginal costs are directly related to the mix of standard and overtime hours within total hours. If h_s falls, the cost of a new hire rises relative to the cost of an extra overtime hour and hours-worker substitution is required to maintain cost minimising equilibrium.

---

[11] Other problems relate to the scope of labour market coverage offered by these modelling approaches. These issues are raised at later stages.

Santamäki points out that this result has predominated in the demand literature because analysts have ignored the possibility that the cost of overtime might be a *rising function* of overtime hours worked.

Why, *a priori*, might we adopt the notion of a rising overtime schedule?

(a) An individual's *opportunity cost of leisure is likely to rise in marginal overtime hours.* The firm may recognise this by paying higher premiums as more weekly overtime hours are undertaken. British workers have reported that the premium varies in this way (Brown *et al.*, 1986) and there is also more limited evidence at company level (Incomes Data Services, 1997). Now, assume each worker faces rising steps in premium pay as overtime hours rise. Suppose that a firm consists of workers *who undertake different amounts of weekly overtime* as well as those who work only standard hours. Then, we would expect that the proportion of workers facing a given marginal hourly rate would increase as average hours rise thereby producing the outcome that the firm's average marginal rate will rise as hours rise.[12]

(b) As we have seen in chapter 2 (see section 2.2), an important part of the change in total overtime hours consists of changes in the proportion of workers working overtime. If a firm attempts to meet an increase in desired overtime by this means, then this implies that the average overtime premium will rise.

Following Hart and Ruffell (2000), we re-write the cost expression in (3.4) to allow for an average premium rate, a. Thus,

$$C = [w(h_s + av) + z]N, \quad h > h_s \tag{3.26}$$

where $v = (h - h_s)$. Now, let the firm's marginal overtime premium, s, increase continuously with overtime hours, that is

$$s = k + mv, \quad m \geq 0, \quad k \geq 1 \tag{3.27}$$

where both k and m are treated as exogenously determined parameters. The total payment for overtime is given by

$$awv = w \int_0^v s(v)dv = w(kv + \tfrac{1}{2}mv^2). \tag{3.28}$$

Substituting (3.28) into (3.26) gives

$$C = [w(h_s + kv + \tfrac{1}{2}mv^2) + z]. \tag{3.29}$$

---

[12] Note that the aggregation of workers facing different amounts of overtime is crucial to this argument. If all workers work the same overtime and if, in discrete intervals, overtime pay rises as the length of overtime hours rises then the results of the standard model would not essentially be altered. To see this, let cost in (3.4) of a 'typical' worker to be given by $c = k_1 w(h - h_1) + k_0 w(h_1 - h_s) + wh_s + z$, with $k_1 w > k_0 w > w$. In effect, h_1 is a second kink point in this firm's isocosts. Here, the first period of overtime is remunerated at, say, time and a half and the second period at double time. This can be re-expressed as $c = wk_1 h + \tilde{z}$, where $\tilde{z} = (k_0 - k_1)wh_1 + (1 - k_0)wh_s + z$. Then, as in n. 9, it follows that $dN/d\tilde{z} < 0$ and $dh/d\tilde{z} > 0$ under cost minimisation.

What if expression (3.29) replaces (3.4) in the profit maximisation problem developed on pp. 53–5? Full developments are given in Hart and Ruffell (2000) as well as in Santamäki (1983) for a somewhat different modelling set-up.[13] Two key findings stem from the most feasible ranges of m, k and z values:[14]

(1) first-order conditions are consistent with returns to hours exceeding returns to workers
(2) the outcome $dh/dh_s > 0$ is derived, a result contrary to the standard model; a decrease in standard hours may now be associated with a fall in total hours.

Clearly, if a fall in h_s at current output is associated with marginal cost increases in *both* workers and hours then straightforward hours-worker substitution is no longer guaranteed. An alternative theoretical underpinning of the observed $\partial h/\partial h_s > 0$ is discussed in section 3.3.

While the possibility of a rising overtime schedule allows us to obtain some theoretical underpinning to empirical findings that are at odds with the standard model, we must be cautious over the generality of this explanation. British evidence suggests that the schedule is flat in relation to numbers of hours worked (Bell and Hart, 2003a; see also table 2.5 for wider international evidence). In fact, if we include individuals who undertake overtime at a premium rate that is *lower* than the standard hourly wage rate, the schedule tapers slightly downwards in long overtime hours (see figure 4.1, p. 87). In fact, in an Italian context, it is reported that the cost of an overtime hour of work is *less* than that of a standard hour (Giannelli and Braschi, 2002).[15] Thus, while we report some evidence of a rising schedule in the case of Japan (see the discussion in relation to table 2.5), this may well turn out to be an exception rather than a rule.

Extensions

Explicit differentiation between standard and overtime hours in production
So far, we have differentiated between standard and overtime hours on the cost side of the firm's optimising problem. What about explicitly differentiating between these two types of hours in the production function? One obvious reason to undertake such a separation relates to a firm employing two distinct types of worker – those who undertake overtime and those who do not. We leave theoretical discussion of this important area to section 3.3. Suppose that, in the spirit of the foregoing, the firm employs a homogeneous workforce with

---

[13] Santamäki (1983) provides more generality than Hart and Ruffell (2000). The latter authors concentrate on a Cobb–Douglas labour services function since their main contribution is to assess empirically the parameter values that satisfy the first-order conditions.

[14] An exception is if k is high and m is low in (3.29) (e.g. $k = 1.5$ and $m = 0.01$).

[15] These two authors raise an interesting observation that may have wider implications beyond the Italian labour market. They find that, although the overtime premium is likely to be higher than the standard hourly wage rate, overtime hours are nonetheless cheaper because other direct and indirect costs associated with the standard workweek do not apply to overtime working. Thus, indirect labour costs – such as holiday pay, thirteenth-month bonus and severance pay – are negotiated within the standard wage contract. Total average hourly standard pay – i.e. incorporating the standard wage plus these other add-ons – is generally found to exceed average overtime hourly pay. This is an interesting area to pursue. Elsewhere, it may well be the case that formally agreed indirect compensation attaches to contracts covering standard working time. This would serve to reduce the cost of employing an extra hour relative to an extra worker compared to the narrower dichotomy between the standard wage rate and the overtime premium.

each individual member working the same per-period hours. If the latter were to include overtime hours, might there still be reason to separate standard and overtime hours in the description of the production process? At least one line of argument advanced by Hart and McGregor (1988) would seem to lend support to such a separation.

The daily/weekly lengths of standard hours are often fixed by collective bargaining. In fact in many instances they are set exogenously to the firm, at national or industrial levels. Such hours are sometimes referred to as 'normal' hours. They set the norms for lengths of production runs, business trading hours, delivery times, inter-company communications, canteen and other company service provisions and so on. As suggested by several of the items in this list, normal hours are often common across similar firms within national or regional boundaries. Overtime hours, by contrast, may involve unilateral decisions by firms to extend the length of hours during specified periods. In part, this may merely reflect the fact that they allow the firm to meet unforeseen and short-run changes in (i) product demand and (ii) labour inputs (e.g. sickness and absenteeism). In other words, they extend normal workday operations to permit a longer production run. But, in other important respects, the firm may view overtime working as time available to effect more efficiency during its strategically most important normal time operations. Obvious examples of such time use would include set-up time, maintenance work and stocktaking. In particular, set-up time may involve preparations that facilitate the efficient running of the next day's normal work time activity. To the extent that overtime may involve different, though interrelated, activities from normal time may also imply that it becomes important to distinguish between the productive returns of the time components of total hours.

Within the cost minimising framework encapsulated on pp. 51–3, Santamäki (1984, 1988) introduces the special case of labour services function in (3.1) expressed as

$$L = N^\alpha h_s^{\beta_1} \left(\frac{h}{h_s} \right)^{\beta_2} \tag{3.30}$$

where the sufficiency conditions require that $\alpha > \beta_2$. If $\beta_1 = \beta_2$, (3.30) reduces to $L = N^\alpha h^\beta$, or the marginal productivity of hours is independent of the length of standard working hours.

Suppose, however, that $\beta_1 > \beta_2$ in (3.30), or overtime hours are marginally less productive than normal hours. This implies that the marginal product of hours decreases in the number of overtime hours. This may have significant consequences from our earlier cost minimisation results. Consider, for example, the outcome for the standard model in (3.15). If overtime is worked in equilibrium, a fall in standard hours is predicted to produce a rise in total hours and a fall in employment. (This would be the outcome using (3.30) with $\beta_1 = \beta_2$). Santamäki shows that if $\beta_1 > \beta_2$ the total hours' effect continues to hold but the employment outcome is now ambiguous. The fall in standard hours is more than offset by a rise in overtime, such that total hours rise. But, by assumption, overtime hours are not as efficient as standard hours and so this reaction may fail to compensate sufficiently to meet the cost minimising firm's production constraint. *Both* overtime hours *and* employment could increase in this scenario.[16]

---

[16] The profit maximising outcomes incorporating the labour services function in (3.30) are discussed in Schank (2001).

A discussion of empirical studies that attempt to differentiate between standard and overtime hours in production is undertaken in section 5.3.

Additional production inputs
So far, the demand-based discussion has concentrated on models in which the problem is to determine optimal combinations of hours and workers to produce either exogenous or endogenous output. It has been assumed that other production inputs are fixed. Adding additional inputs tends generally to preclude unambiguous outcomes to changes in decision variables.

What if the model is extended to accommodate variability in hours, workers and the stock of capital? In the event of changes in *hours-related* payments, effects on employment demand are not clear-cut (Hart, 1984; Hamermesh, 1993). Suppose that the overtime premium is set exogenously by the government and that a decision is made to raise it. In the two-input cost minimisation model with equilibrium overtime, it is predicted that average hours will fall (see (3.14)) and that employment unambiguously increases. Cost minimisation in this context is conducive, therefore, to effecting work sharing outcomes. With variable capital added to the model, matters are not quite so straightforward. A rise in k increases the ratio of variable to fixed labour costs thereby improving the relative price of a marginal worker compared to a marginal (overtime) hour. But it also raises the price of total hours (i.e. workers times average hours) relative to the user cost of capital, *ceteris paribus*. Without more detailed knowledge of the degrees of complementarity or substitutionability between inputs, it is not possible to determine net employment or hours outcomes. Ehrenberg and Schumann (1982a) estimate a demand-for-overtime equation that is derived under the assumption that labour is the only variable production input. They then attempt to quantify the implication of admitting a scale dimension to the problem.[17]

Apart from changes in the stock of capital, the degree of capital utilisation is also a potentially important consideration in the assessment of hours changes. Calmfors and Hoel (1989) investigate connections between working time and the operating time of the capital stock, as represented by the number of shifts in operation. The number of shifts is treated as a choice variable. If anything, a cut in standard hours under this set-up holds even less prospects for employment creation than under a single-shift system. Suppose in terms of figure 3A.1 (p. 79), workers–hours equilibrium in a single-shift firm was at the isocosts kink point, *e*. Workers are employed for maximum standard hours but with no overtime. A cut in standard hours in this position is likely to lead to an employment increase.[18] With a

---

[17] Ehrenberg and Schumann (1982a) estimate the effect on employment of increasing the overtime premium from time and a half to double time (see section 7.1). The simple demand structure on which their regression equation is based implies that the wage elasticity of demand is completely inelastic. Based on their estimates, they discuss the impact of such a premium increase if all workers initially work a standard workweek of 40 hours and 3 hours of overtime. Although high for their estimation, they suppose that this causes a reduction of 1.2 hours of overtime per week. In turn, and based on their upper-bound employment estimates this would lead to a 3 per cent increase in full-time (40-hour) jobs, given constant total hours. But total hours are unlikely to remain constant. So, using a long-run wage elasticity of labour demand of -0.3 based on the survey of Hamermesh (1976) (see, also, Hamermesh, 1993), they estimate that total hours would decline by 0.24 per cent. Further arithmetic leads them to reduce the previous estimate of new jobs created by 0.25 percentage points.

[18] Assuming that the firm moves from the initial kink point to the new kink lying to the left, employment will increase since the working time reduction is binding.

flexible number of shifts the employment prospects are not the same. Given fixed costs of employment, a cut in standard hours decreases the marginal cost of shift work more than the marginal cost of employment. The increase in the relative factor cost of employment causes a substitution towards a greater use of capital that in turn tends to increase the number of shifts and to a decrease employment.[19]

But even with capital fixed under a single-shift system, the problem remains that working time deals only with one aspect of labour utilisation on the intensive margin. Individual workers may additionally have scope to vary their hourly work effort. As in the efficiency wage literature, suppose that effort is related positively to the hourly wage. Measured in efficiency units, it would not be so clear that a rise in k would worsen the marginal cost of an hour relative to a worker because of offsetting hourly effort. This particular issue is explored in more depth in section 3.4.

Team working

One circumstance in which effort is difficult to monitor and control, is where individuals work in organised work teams in which interactive skills are important. Monitoring individual effort and performance may be particularly costly in these circumstances.

The overtime decision would be expected to relate directly to team working. Hours of overtime may relate negatively to the degree of coordination among the activities of individual team members. In part, overtime may be employed to meet shortfalls in task completion times resulting from inefficiencies linked to work rigidities, variations in worker productivities and work commitments, and lack of co-ordination among interrelated work tasks. Coordination of work groups – involving designated team leaders, team briefing, job rotation and multiple job tasking – may help to overcome related inefficiencies and thereby reduce the need for overtime working. Limited evidence of this tendency is provided in a study of the effects of introducing team working into a British aluminium smelter plant (Wright and Edwards, 1998).

Make-to-order production

The foregoing modelling approaches abstract from the specific nature of how the firm schedules output in order to meet customer demand. Researchers in production economics stress the importance of delineating between two broad methods. First, in so-called 'make-to-stock' companies the product is generally made in anticipation of customer orders. When orders arrive at the firm, they are supplied from stock. Second, 'make-to-order' companies supply products in direct response to customer orders; some or all of the production is undertaken after the order has been received. Overtime scheduling, and associated cost minimisation, would be expected to feature strongly in this case (Yura, 1994; Kingsman *et al.*, 1996; Özdamar and Yazgaç, 1997; Dellaert and Melo, 1998). Empirical versions of the foregoing demand models of overtime are perhaps best geared to tackling this latter type of activity.

---

[19] Actually, the results here may be modified if it is considered that there may be fixed set-up costs of increasing the number of shifts.

In make-to-order companies, the need for production flexibility designed to meet unforeseen events is a clear priority. An important aspect of company reputation in this sector is the customer assessment of delivery performance in relation to declared delivery times. Overtime, and/or sub-contracting, offer important means of buffering against unforeseen increases in demand and production bottlenecks. In essence, future capacity requirements are uncertain and overtime allows extensions of planned capacity 'norms'. There is a downside to the use of overtime in this context. Relative performance is also dependent on bid prices for customer orders in relation to subsequent costs. If unplanned overtime scheduling is required *ex post* then the bid price may turn out to have been unrealistically low.

3.3   Non-overtime and overtime workers

So far, the discussion of demand has proceeded under the somewhat convenient assumption that all workers in the firm work the same daily or weekly hours. This may represent a fair approximation to reality where team working and the use of interactive skills and inputs are important. But, as emphasised in section 2.2, we would expect that only a proportion of employees would work overtime with the remainder classified as non-overtime workers. The latter might consist of individuals who work the maximum number of daily or weekly standard hours and/or those who are working part-time. This distinction would be expected to be especially prevalent in firms where overtime is a voluntary activity. Retaining the demand approach to workers-hours allocation, the firm's optimisation problem is more complicated. It must decide not only the mix of workers and hours but also the mix of non-overtime and overtime workers.

Assuming that all workers must work given standard hours, h_s, average hours in the firm are $h = h_s + \mu(h - h_s)$ where μ is the proportion of workers choosing to work overtime and $0 \leq \mu \leq 1$. The standard model dichotomises between polar cases $\mu = 0$ and $\mu = 1$. What factors might stimulated the decision to work overtime? In an important extension to the standard model, Santamäki (1984) proposes that the proportion of overtime workers is functionally related to the (given) overtime premium and the (given) length of standard hours, thus $\mu = \mu(k, h_s)$, with $\mu_k > 0$, $\mu_{hs} < 0$ (see also the discussion in Bell, 1988). As noted in section 3.1, a rise in the overtime premium is likely to induce a stronger substitution than income effect on a worker's preference for overtime working. For a given premium, the shorter are the required standard hours, h_s, then the higher would be the worker's preference to work additional hours – given diminishing marginal utility of leisure – in order to restore lost income.

Modifying the standard cost minimisation problem in (3.5), the new problem becomes

$$\min_{h,N} C = \{w[h_s + k(h - h_s)\mu(k, h_s)] + z\}N \quad h > h_s \tag{3.31}$$

$$\text{subject to } F[N, h, h_s; \mu(k, h_s)] = \overline{L}.$$

Note that incorporating the choice of overtime or no-overtime requires that both h and h_s are explicitly differentiated in the production function. Assume positive, non-increasing marginal products of factor inputs N and h as well as positive cross-marginal products.

Santamäki (1984) shows that the solution to the problem in (3.31) involves two important differences compared to earlier outcomes:

(1) In the standard model, it is established in (3.14) that $\partial h/\partial k < 0$ and $\partial N/\partial k > 0$; a rise in the overtime premium causes workers-hours substitution. This occurs because costs on the intensive margin rise more than proportionately to costs on the extensive margin. In the problem in (3.31) both of these signs are ambiguous. As before, a rise in the premium increases the marginal cost of an hour and the marginal (weighted) cost of a worker. But, additionally, a rise in the premium directly increases labour input (and, therefore, output) since, through the assumption incorporated in (3.31), it entices a higher rate of overtime participation. In turn, this affects the marginal products of hours and employment. The net effects preclude unambiguous N and h outcomes unless specific functional forms are introduced and simulated with respect to selected values of the variables.

(2) As shown in (3.15), the standard model also produces $\partial h/\partial h_s < 0$ and $\partial N/\partial h_s > 0$; a cut in standard hours is associated with hours-worker substitution. The hours-worker substitution arises for a very simple reason. All workers are assumed to work overtime and the marginal cost of hours is unaffected by the change. This contrasts to the marginal (weighted) cost of employment, which rises because a lower proportion of a worker's hours is compensated at the cheaper standard wage rate. In this extended model, the position is less straightforward. Through (3.31), a cut in h_s induces more workers to opt to participate in overtime. Per-person hours for those who remain as non-overtime workers fall by the amount of the cut in h_s. But the average number of hours of those accepting overtime working may or may not rise. Also, employment may or may not rise. Outcomes in these last two respects will depend on the relative cost to the firm of changing employment compared to changing total hours worked. As in the standard model, the cost on the extensive margin rises because fewer per-person standard hours are available. However, costs on the intensive margin also rise due to average hourly wage increases stemming from the higher proportion of the labour force receiving premium pay for overtime hours.[20] In summary, a cut in h_s in this model has ambiguous effects on both optimal hours and employment.

Santamäki's model abstracts from making a clear distinction between an overtime worker and a non-overtime worker. Individuals are homogeneous as production workers but unspecified supply-side differences cause them to react unevenly to exogenous changes in the overtime wage and the length of hours after which overtime is paid. More structural insights may be gained if we are able to distinguish between overtime and non-overtime workers in a simple and systematic way.

---

[20] Santamäki (1984) shows that in the case of a constant elasticity production function with homogeneous hours input and constant μ, a reduction in h_s increases both employment and average hours of those opting to work overtime. With a production function specification in which the marginal products of standard and overtime hours are allowed to differ, however, the results are found to be nearer to those of the standard model. In this latter case, a reduction in h_s increases average hours of those working overtime while producing ambiguous employment effects; in fact, it is found that a negative employment outcome is more likely.

FitzRoy and Hart (1986) consider the case of a firm employing a mix of (homogeneous) part-time and (homogeneous) full-time workers. It is assumed that the former group works less than the maximum weekly standard hours while the latter works overtime in equilibrium. For simplicity, no one works exactly maximum standard hours. Labour services, L, are given by $L = L(h, n, H, N)$ where lower-case letters refer, respectively, to part-time hours and workers and upper-case letters to full-time hours and workers. Given overtime is worked by full-timers, $H = h_s + (H - h_s)$ where h_s denotes standard hours. Marginal products are assumed to be positive and decreasing while marginal products of full-time (part-time) labour decline with part-time (full-time) inputs. In order to avoid problems of firm size, fixed capital costs and number of firms, the convenient assumptions of constant returns to total employment $(n + N)$ and capital (K) are adopted. Using a Cobb–Douglas formulation production is given by $Q = K^{1-\beta\gamma}\hat{L}^\gamma$ with $\hat{L} = h^\alpha n^\beta H^\varepsilon N^\beta$. It is assumed that $0 < \alpha, \beta, \gamma, \varepsilon < 1$ and that, in order to satisfy the sufficiency conditions, that $\alpha < \beta$ and $\gamma < \varepsilon$.[21] The firm maximises profit, π, given by the expression

$$\max_{K,h,n,H,N} \pi = Q - rK - whn - nz - [WH_s + kW(H - H_s)]N - NZ \quad (3.32)$$

where r is the capital rental, w is the part-time standard hourly wage, W is the full-time standard hourly wage, k is the overtime premium, z is part-time fixed cost and Z is full-time fixed cost.

While a number of well-known results derive from the problem in (3.32) – such as rises in the fixed costs of one or other group of worker causes its utilisation to rise – the main new interest derives from cross-price effects. Thus, for example, a *ceteris paribus* rise in the fixed costs of part-timers – perhaps stemming from government employment protection legislation – leads to an hours substitution effect among part-timers and a full-time–part-time employment substitution effect. Perhaps the key result from a working time perspective is that an exogenous cut in the maximum number of standard hours now carries two repercussions. First, in line with the standard model, it leads to overtime-employment substitution among full-time workers. Second, it leads the firm to increase the ratio of part-time to full-time employees given a relative cost increase in the latter group. Therefore, the ability of firms to vary the mix of part-time and full-time workers may serve to mitigate a tendency to increase average overtime hours given a shortened standard workweek.

Leslie (1991) suggests that low-productivity workers in a given occupation may receive relatively low standard wage rates and may need to work longer weekly hours in order to reduce their earnings differentials.[22] It is also assumed that hours-independent costs may differ between the two types of worker, but this is somewhat more difficult to motivate. To simplify matters, a constraint is imposed that fixes the total hours of an overtime worker

---

[21] While the Cobb–Douglas specification serves greatly to simplify the ensuing solutions, it clearly entails the significant drawback of vulnerability to corner solutions as one or other labour input reduces to zero.

[22] Using the British NES for 1988, Leslie (1991) notes that the gross earnings (including overtime) of 41 per cent of male manual workers fell as hours increased. Using the 1998 NES, Bell and Hart (2003a) also find a strong negative association between standard hourly wages and the length of weekly overtime hours. Evidence is also presented in section 4.2.

at $h = \overline{h}$ and standard hours are given.[23] Therefore, under cost minimisation, a reduction in standard hours necessitates finding the optimal mix of non-overtime and overtime workers. Using N and O upper-case letters to denote these two respective groups, we have

$$\min_{N^N, N^O} C = w^N h_s N^N + [w^O h_s + k w^O (\overline{h} - h_s)] N^O + z^N N^N + z^O N^O$$

$$\overline{h} > h_s \quad (3.33)$$

$$\text{subject to } F(N^N, N^O) = \overline{L}$$

In parallel to the standard cost minimising model in (3.5), the first-order conditions to this problem establish an equilibrium whereby the ratio of the marginal costs of a non-overtime and an overtime worker is equal to the ratio of their respective marginal products.

Suppose, initially, that $w^N = w^O$ and $z^N = z^O$.[24] In this event, the first-order conditions establish unequivocally that the marginal product of an overtime worker exceeds that of a non-overtime worker. An exogenous cut in h_s will lead to a $N^N - N^O$ substitution because the marginal cost of an overtime worker would rise relative to a non-overtime worker. Given the relative marginal products, and recalling that output is given, total employment would *rise* in this event. This latter result is at odds with the standard model although it is important to add that it is predicated on several very special assumptions.

What if it is assumed that $w^N \neq w^O$ and $z^N \neq z^O$? Unambiguous outcomes with respect to total employment, i.e. $N = N^N + N^O$, are now more difficult to come by for the simple reason that relative sizes of marginal products cannot be inferred from the first-order conditions. A rise in k, for example, will lead to an $N^N - N^O$ substitution. But, unlike the standard model, the net effect on employment is ambiguous. If the marginal product of N^N workers is lower then N^O workers then N will rise in line with the standard model. If the marginal product of N^N workers is higher then N^O workers then N will fall in contradiction to the standard model.

Despite the imposed strictures with regards to hours' constraints,[25] these results contain an important message concerning the limitations of the standard model. Where workers are qualitatively different, and where such differences impinge on the desire to work overtime, net employment effects of changes in premium (and other) wage rates are probably far less than clear-cut. Although perhaps limited in its empirical importance, it might be added that the standard model has at least one comparative advantage. The assumption of labour homogeneity underscores the feasibility of employment-hours substitution far more readily than assigning qualitative differences among workers. If, for example, overtime is a phenomenon among relative low-productivity workers then this may involve severe

---

[23] Without the total hours constraint, the optimising problem becomes much more complex. In this event, the production function would need to demarcate among non-overtime and overtime workers, overtime hours and the proportion of workers working overtime. This contrasts, with the production constraint in Leslie's model (see (3.33)) in which only the two types of worker need to be considered.

[24] Although wage and non-wage equality for the two types of worker is somewhat difficult to defend in this set-up since, *a priori*, division into non-overtime and overtime worker is motivated by wage (i.e. quality) differences.

[25] In fact, when Leslie allows total hours, total employment and the proportion of workers working overtime as choice variables the tractability of the model is severely reduced. But, of course, this does not detract from the central message that the results of the standard model may well be quite sensitive to extensions that attempt to model the overtime participation decision.

constraints on the firm's short-run willingness to respond to price signals. A potential change in the quality mix of the workforce may have significant ramifications for the capital and organisational structure of the firm.

Andrews, Schank and Simmons (2002) also differentiate between N^N and N^O-type workers with respective w^N, w^O wages and z^N, z^O fixed costs. Both types of worker work h_s hours while overtime workers work $h^O - h_s > 0$ overtime hours. The productivity of overtime hours is allowed to differ from standard hours. Thus, the two types of workers and weekly hours enter both cost and revenue functions. The firm is assumed to be a profit maximiser and so scale effects are incorporated. The objective is to select optimum values of N^N, N^O and h^O for given standard hours, wages and fixed costs.

What if h_s is reduced in this set-up? Three reaction channels are identified. First, the cut in h_s serves to alter the marginal cost of an N^N worker, inducing a $N^N - N^O$ substitution effect as well as a positive scale effect on both types of worker. Second, the cut changes the marginal cost of an N^O worker, inducing a $N^N - N^O$ substitution effect but now a negative scale effect on both types of worker. The smaller the proportion of overtime workers, the more likely that the work sharing (substitution) effects of these outcomes offset the negative scale effects from the second outcome. Under both outcomes, however, the standard hours cut serves to reduce the proportion of overtime workers. The third outcome concerns the effect of a cut in h_s within the revenue function. This leads to a reduction in standard time workers while the effect on their overtime colleagues is ambiguous.

This last result is interesting and relates back to the discussion on pp. 55–7 concerning the fact that the outcome $\partial h / \partial h_s < 0$ in the standard demand model is at odds to the common empirical observation $\partial h / \partial h_s > 0$. In the current model, $\partial h / \partial h_s$ is decomposed into an average overtime hours' effect and a participation effect. The former is negative in the current model, in line with the standard model. However, the participation effect is likely to be positively related to standard hours changes and can more than offset the average overtime effect. Therefore, as with the rising overtime schedule possibility – outlined on p. 56 – we have an explanation of the common empirical finding that $\partial h / \partial h_s > 0$.

3.4 Overtime and effort

So far, labour input on the firm's intensive margin has concentrated solely on hours of work. Worker productivity has been represented by the hours function (3.3) that allows average productivity to vary over the working day. Coupled with this, the wage rate has been treated as a given variable. A shortcoming with this approach is that no allowance has been made for the firm to *intervene* in order to encourage more effort per hour. As has long been recognised in the efficiency wage literature, such a goal may be achieved through higher wage income (e.g. Arnott, Hosios and Stiglitz, 1988). Following Bell and Hart (1991) (see also Schmidt-Sørensen, 1991), we explore here implications for earlier key overtime results of regarding the wage as a choice variable with the role of optimising worker effort.

Supply-side considerations enter indirectly into this type of wage-hours framework through an assumed maxim understood by the firm. If workers enjoy higher levels of utility they will expend greater effort. This conditions the firm's optimising behaviour since it recognises that it can influence utility through changes in wage income. This is the core idea behind efficiency wage models of shirking. However, most of these models represent wage income as the hourly rate of pay. More generally, a worker's utility derives from the hourly wage rate *and* the daily number of hours of work.

Retaining fixed capital, let the firm's production function by represented as

$$Q = G\{e[y(w, h), h]h, N\} \qquad (3.34)$$

where Q is output, e is average daily effort and y is daily wage income. Assume $G > 0$, $G' > 0$ and $G'' < 0$. The function $e(\cdot)$ translates hours of work into efficiency units,[26] with $e_1 > 0$ and $e_2 < 0$. For the latter restriction, we might assume that effort increases in hours over the early part of the working day and then declines, with marginal hours operating in the second segment.

Labour costs are given by

$$C = C[y(w, h) + z]N. \qquad (3.35)$$

The firm chooses w, h and N to maximise profits, that is

$$\max_{w,h,N} \pi = G(\cdot) - C. \qquad (3.36)$$

From the first-order conditions, we obtain the simple result

$$\frac{e}{h} = -e_2. \qquad (3.37)$$

The firm increases hours of work to the point where the marginal product stemming from the physical effect of hours on effort equals average hourly effort. This implies that average hours are set within the diminishing returns segment of efficiency hours.[27]

The full solution of the model provides several intuitively plausible results. For example, $\partial h/\partial k$ cannot be signed *a priori*. In the standard model, which effectively holds effort as given, a rise in the overtime premium leads unambiguously to fewer total hours. There is a workers-hours substitution due to relatively higher costs on the intensive margin. Of course, this same effect carries over to the present model. But the substitution effect is offset by an increase in effort due to higher wage income. Measured in efficiency terms, unit costs may reduce on the intensive margin with total hours responding positively to an increased premium. In similar fashion, sign $\partial h/\partial h_s$ is also ambiguous. Again, the simple substitution effect in the standard model no longer holds.

---

[26] In Bell and Hart (1991), workers are also translated into quality units, q, via training expenditures – i.e. $q(z)N$ in (3.34), with z regarded as a choice variable in optimisation. For an extensive use of this transformation, see Hart and Moutos (1995).

[27] Equation (3.37) is equivalent to the 'Solow condition'. In the one-input factor case, labour is hired to the point where marginal product, measured in efficiency units, is equal to the real wage. Lin and Lai (1997) develop an efficiency wage model that distinguishes among wage, effort and overtime working. Their prime aim is to show that introducing overtime serves to modify the 'Solow condition' of a unitary effort-wage elasticity.

3.5   Hours in traditional demand and supply models[28]

It is not the intention at this stage to speculate further on why many working time studies have focused on *either* supply *or* demand aspects of the subject.[29] Nor will it be particularly illuminating to most students of labour markets to recount the limitations of emphasising one side of the market or the other. Suffice it to record that many working time contracts reflect the outcomes of at least two parties reaching agreements against the backgrounds of differing economic perspectives. Accordingly, we require equilibrium approaches that reflect both sides' interests.

As we will see in section 3.6, attempts to introduce bargaining into optimal hours decisions have not yet met with a great deal of success. Future modelling innovations will come along that take us further down the road of combining supply and demand interests along traditional lines. However, it is worth first reflecting on what exactly firms and employees care about when attempting to determine their joint hours requirements. Both supply- and demand- side models make, perhaps, somewhat special assumptions in this respect. Thus, they proceed 'as if' the employer cared only about total working hours rather than how hours are scheduled. In reality, the firm may seek to employ workers who are willing to supply daily hours of given length, as dictated by its technical, organisational and business trading constraints. Individual suppliers of labour services may focus on obtaining job length/wage earnings combinations that provide maximum utility. The wage becomes, in effect, the price that has to be paid to match both sides' work scheduling preferences.

If employers and workers mainly care about work schedules – as represented in its simplest form by hours per day – then traditional supply and demand approaches have more limited appeal. They are more concerned with highly divisible hours that can be fine-tuned to meet optimal workers-hours combinations. In fact, when supply and demand are treated in this traditional way, then it is difficult to achieve helpful equilibrium insights. As pointed out by Trejo (2003) for the case of overtime working, integrating supply and demand analysis is somewhat challenging. In section 3.1, we have seen that a rise in the overtime premium is likely to lead workers to supply more overtime hours. Yet such a rise on the demand side in section 3.2 induces firms to reduce average overtime hours.

If, by contrast, the two parties are mainly concerned to match preferences with respect to work schedules then agreements are likely to be reached in which *indivisible* hours along with associated wage earnings and the workforce size are the variables of prime concern. Then, as we shall see in section 3.7, equilibrium working time is more readily, and perhaps more meaningfully, established.

3.6   Bargaining

Integrating workers and average hours of work within a bargaining framework, as well as allowing for workers-hours substitution, turns out to lead to quite intractable modelling

---

[28] This section, together with the related discussion on pp. 70–2, benefited greatly from correspondence with Stephen Trejo. Any remaining errors and misconceptions are my own.

[29] Some interesting reflections on this topic, though in a wider labour supply and demand perspective, are provided in Hamermesh (1993, chapter 1).

unless special assumptions are made. One relatively simple approach is to assume that the firm may undertake workers-hours optimisation subject to the binding constraint that changes in exogenous events leave the level of workers' utility at or above the position before the changes took place (see FitzRoy and Hart, 1985; Hart and Moutos, 1995). But allowing for more explicit and structured hours' bargaining is not a simple task.

An overwhelming majority of firm-union bargaining papers concentrate on two key variables, the wage rate and the level of employment. The two dominant representations of union-firm bargaining are efficient contract and the right-to-manage models.[30] Efficient bargaining involves the parties jointly negotiating the wage rate and employment level. The optimal solution requires that the marginal rate of substitution between wages and employment of one party is equal to its equivalent measure for the other (McDonald and Solow, 1981). The sequential contract under right-to-manage typically entails the parties jointly determining the wage while leaving the firm unilaterally to determine the level of employment. A special variant within the latter class of model, the so-called 'monopoly union model', entails the union setting the wage unilaterally in order to maximise its utility given the firm's demand for labour. Expanding these models to embrace bargaining over working time produces exponential increases in conceptual and technical difficulties.

We will concentrate our discussion on the efficient contract and the right-to-manage model in which the parties jointly agree the wage. It should be noted, however, that the monopoly union framework of Booth and Schiantarelli (1988), incorporating hours, has perhaps gone furthest in deriving complete sets of results (see also Contensou and Vranceanu, 2000, chapter 10). This work concentrates on the issue of employment effects of cuts in the standard workweek. However, even in this relatively simple structure, the incorporation of endogenous overtime into the problem leads to such complexity as to force the authors to obtain insights into model performance by assigning plausible ranges of numerical values to various parameters. They find that, for all simulations satisfying utility maximisation, a cut in the standard workweek leads to negative employment effects. This, of course, is exactly in line with the outcomes of the labour demand models highlighted in section 3.2. As pointed out by Andrews and Simmons (2001), the union model constrains the solution to the firm's demand function and so perhaps unsurprisingly reflects the pure demand findings.

As a representation of an efficient bargain with flexible hours, let the firm's profit be given by

$$\pi(N, h, w) = pF(N, h) - w(h)N - zN \tag{3.38}$$

where p is product price and where the remaining variables relate to earlier models. We leave the wage schedule, $w(h)$, unspecified although it could incorporate the familiar overtime expression incorporated in (3.4) and elsewhere.

The union's rent from an employment relationship is given by

$$V - \overline{U} = N[w(h) - g(h) - b] \tag{3.39}$$

where $\overline{U}$ is utility if no bargain is struck and so $V - \overline{U}$ is rent. Further $g(h)$ is the disutility of hours worked (with $g_h > 0$ and $g_{hh} > 0$) and b is unemployment benefit.

---

[30] See Ulph and Ulph (1990) for a review of union bargaining models which includes an extension to incorporate hours of work into the negotiation.

Adopting the familiar Nash bargaining solution concept, we have

$$\max_{N,h,w} J^* = \pi(N, h, w)^{1-\alpha}(V - \overline{U})^{\alpha} \tag{3.40}$$

where α represents relative union strength, with $0 \leq \alpha \leq 1$.

Hart and Moutos (1995) analyse this bargain for the simple case of a single hourly wage rate (see also Earle and Pencavel, 1990 and Pencavel, 1991). Even with the added simplification of Cobb–Douglas technology, it proves to be difficult to obtain other than ambiguous employment and hours effects of changes in the exogenous variables, while income (wh) was found to respond positively to union power and to unemployment benefit. Incorporating a more elaborate $w(h)$ schedule that includes overtime payments will clearly not improve matters. These results do not merely reflect the technical set-up of the model but are probably indicative of actual complications involved in comprehensive wage-hours-employment contracts. For both parties in the bargaining process, hours pull in two opposing directions. A rise in hours increases revenue and cost to the firm and also increases wage earnings and disutility to the worker. Negotiating an agreed equilibrium against the background of these various forces is not a trivial task.

It would seem reasonable, therefore, to suppose that the parties might be eager to resolve contractual issues under a simpler bargaining agenda. On first reflection, it appears sensible to think in terms of right-to-manage scenarios. In the simpler wage-employment bargains, right-to-manage contracts are an attractive option (Nickell and Andrews, 1983). Allowing the firm to set the level of employment after joint wage negotiation may serve to reduce risks of negotiation failure due to the transaction costs of information communication and verification. It also may permit greater flexibility to adjust to unforeseen events during the course of the contract. On further thought, however, parallels are not easily established when flexible hours are included. The reason is that it is no longer possible to dichotomise between compensation and employment decisions. If the union abrogates the right to influence employment, this effectively means that the firm sets *both* workforce size and hours per worker. But hours also form part of wage income in (3.39) and it is difficult to imagine the union being willing to allow the firm unilaterally to determine employment as well as an important element of take-home pay. So what if the parties were to bargain jointly over the wage and hours, leaving the firm to set employment? Here, the firm may be unhappy because the union would have an impact on labour cost and on the intensive margin part of total employment.

Unlike the simpler wage-employment world, there is no natural partition of the sequential bargain when hours are included.[31] This does not mean that such bargains will not take place but, rather, that it is difficult to generalise about their structure. Usefully, Andrews and Simmons (2001) examine four such bargains, arguing that they serve as first approximations to labour market idiosyncrasies found in Britain and Europe. In all four cases, the firm determines the workforce size. In two models, there is no overtime and the parties negotiate a single hourly wage rate, w. They are differentiated by the fact that in one case hours

---

[31] This does not mean, of course, that the wage-employment bargaining models are somehow superior to extended wage-hours-employment models. Either implicitly or explicitly, firms and workers bargain over employment *and* working time and not just employment. In important respects, adding hours of work into the structure reveals a potential weakness of right-to-manage approaches.

are also bargained over while, in the other, hours are exogenously determined. In the other two models, there are overtime hours that are determined by the firm. Here, one model allows for the parties to bargain over the hourly wage rate and standard hours while the other treats such hours as exogenous. In common with many papers, these authors are interested to find out if work sharing results from reductions in standard hours. As in pure demand models, work sharing is most likely where no overtime is undertaken. The impact is reduced, however, because hours cuts are accompanied by a negotiated wage increase and this tends to lessen the employment effects. Where overtime takes place, work sharing outcomes generally require wage concessions – perhaps not realistic in a union setting – before work-generating effects are found.

The complexity of arriving at employment and pay decisions involving workers, standard hours and overtime hours as well as embracing both the firm's and workers' objective functions are not merely a problem for economic modellers. They certainly create potential bargaining intractability within the workplace itself. For this sort of reason, we advance the notion, in section 4.2, that the parties may well resort to established custom and practice in order to simplify decision making concerning overtime pay.

3.7   Joint-hours preferences and overtime regulation

Indivisible hours and earnings-hours preferences

In the conventional supply and demand models considered so far, individuals and firms treat working hours as highly divisible. Ignore overtime working. The supply and demand problems take the hourly wage as a given that is independent of hours of work. On the supply side, a change in the hourly wage will induce the individual to lengthen or shorten the daily supply of hours with outcomes dependent on relative sizes of income and substitution effects. On the demand side, a wage change will induce the firm to change average hours and the size of the workforce with outcomes dependent on relative directions and strengths of scale and substitution effects. By contrast, might it be more realistic to treat the per-period length of working hours as a job attribute, with workers and firms signalling preferences for one job length or another? A complete labour market would offer many job length-earnings combinations arising from heterogeneous consumption-leisure aspirations among households and diverse technologies and organisational configurations among firms. Market equilibrium would occur when the utilities of both sides were jointly satisfied over the complete distributions of preferences. The seminal work of Lewis (1969a) is essentially concerned with understanding the joint determination of daily pay and hours when hours and earnings are treated in these ways.

For the purposes of developing arguments related to our main concern, overtime aspects of working hours, it will suffice to give a few key features of the Lewis approach and then to highlight work where extensions and generalisations can be found. Therefore, for simplicity, we concentrate on bargaining between a representative worker and a single firm.

Let job lengths be defined in terms of the working day, with y representing daily earnings and h daily working hours. The worker's utility is given by the quasi-concave function

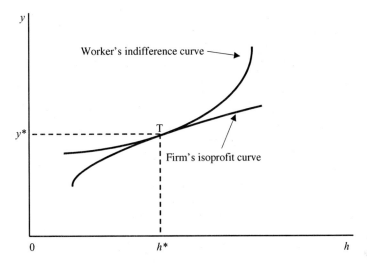

Figure 3.4 Indifference and isoprofit curves

$U(y, h)$, with $U_y > 0$, $U_h < 0$. An associated indifference curve is shown in figure 3.4, with $dy/dh = -(dU/dh)/(dU/dy)$. With output prices set to unity, the firm's profit is given by

$$\pi = F(N, h) - y(h)N - zN \qquad (3.41)$$

where N is workforce size and z is fixed employment cost. Isoprofit curves are increasing functions of working hours and one such curve is illustrated in the (y, h) space of figure 3.4.[32]

Conveniently, the illustrated indifference and isoprofit curves have a tangency point, T. How might we interpret T as representing a mutually agreed earnings-hours combination at y^*, h^*? Take two simple scenarios. Suppose the isoprofit curve represents that of a firm facing a zero profit constraint in a competitive product market. Then the indifference curve can be interpreted as representing the worker's utility maximising (y, h) combination subject to the firm satisfying its constraint. Alternatively, suppose the indifference curve represents the worker's reservation utility defined in terms of the next best opportunity in alternative employment. Then the isoprofit curve would be the firm's profit maximising (y, h) combination subject to meeting employees' reservation utility. In between these end-points, there are a continuum of (y^*, h^*) combinations, lying along a contract curve, that represent efficient contracts. A particular equilibrium outcome will depend on the relative bargaining strengths of the parties.

Of course, this bargaining description is very restrictive. A general representation would describe a labour market consisting of workers with heterogeneous preferences and firms with heterogeneous production technologies. Then we would need to describe a hedonic locus – labelled by Lewis the 'market equalising wage curve' – that reflects the joint

[32] From the profit maximising conditions to (3.41) we obtain $dy(h)/dh = (1/N)F_h$. This is positive given $F_h > 0$. Concavity of the isoprofit curve, as drawn in figure 3.4, requires $F_{hh} < 0$. See Kinoshita (1987, pp. 1267–9) for fuller details. Borjas (2000, pp. 209–13) provides a useful introduction to hedonic wage functions.

preferences of employees and employers who are brought together in equilibrium with labour demand equal to labour supply at all job lengths. Lewis (1969a) sets out to piece together the economics of this complete structure. His ideas clearly influenced the well-known work of Rosen (1974) on hedonic prices. Kinoshita (1987) translates Lewis' ideas along the lines developed by Rosen and produces a very accessible version of the complete structure (see also Barzel, 1973).

Implications for overtime regulation

Trejo (1991, 2003) provides a significant step forward by realising that the Lewis method of analysing the determination of working time has potentially profound implications for the existing studies on overtime working. We know from earlier discussion that the payments for daily hours may not be wholly under the control of employers and employees. What if maximum daily standard hours and minimum rates of the premium applying to overtime pay were exogenously determined by government? For example, optimal h^* in figure 3.4 might contain mandatory overtime hours and so y^* would consist of standard and overtime components of pay.

To start with, assume that there are no mandatory overtime rules and that the process depicted in figure 3.4 generates equilibrium weekly earnings $y^* = w^*h^*$, where w^* is the standard hourly wage rate consistent with the optimal (y^*, h^*) combination. The government then imposes maximum standard hours, h_s and a minimum premium, k $(k > 1)$. If $h^* \leq h_s$, the earnings–hours agreement within the firm is unaffected. However if $h^* > h_s$ then, ceteris paribus, average weekly earnings, $\hat{y}$, would exceed y^* since part of the week is compensated at the premium rate; that is $\hat{y} = w^*h_s + w^*k(h^* - h_s) > y^*$. Earnings-hours preferences would cease to be jointly satisfied. But, trivially, the parties could stick to their original agreement by setting a new standard wage, $\hat{w}$ such that $\hat{w}h_s + \hat{w}k(h^* - h_s) = w^*h^* = y^*$. The hourly wage is adjusted downwards by sufficient to ensure that the add-on cost due to the mandatory overtime rules is neutralised. Hourly wage flexibility would ensure that the parties adhere to the original terms of their contract.[33]

This idea has potentially major consequences for policy initiatives by governments to alter the price of labour input through overtime regulation. In the 'pure' case discussed above, where a change in the mandatory premium would be completely countered by a change in the standard wage, changes in overtime premium payments would have no effect on the firm's mix of workers and hours. Even where there existed short-run constraints on the degree that wage rates could be adjusted in the short term, some degree of wage flexibility may serve seriously to influence empirical workers-hours reactions. We return to this topic in section 7.1.

Standard wage flexibility has equally interesting implications in relation to exogenous cuts in the number of standard weekly hours. Suppose a firm works $h^* > h_s$ and pays

---

[33] In fact, offsetting adjustments to exogenous changes in the cost of overtime is not limited to the standard wage. Ehrenberg and Schumann (1982a) emphasise that *both* wages and fringe benefits may serve this purpose. Non-statutory fringe benefits are an important component of labour remuneration and offer enhanced flexibility within total compensation packages.

w^* for hours h_s and w^*k for $h - h_s$ $(k > 1)$. Suppose that h_s is reduced by mandate. In order to meet its output constraint the firm, at least in the short run, will be forced to extend overtime working. *Ceteris paribus*, average hourly wages would rise given a higher proportion of premium to total pay. But workers would not object to a cut in the standard wage as long as their original agreement over total weekly pay and hours was adhered to.

So, Trejo's insight offers a major challenge to predictions arising from the earlier literature on workers-hours demand models.

More on overtime regulation

What if there is limited scope for short-run standard wage changes? Moving away from the Lewis framework, the wage rate may represent the outcome of a more complicated agreement and the parties may be highly risk averse about renegotiation over the course of a contract period. Or the authorities may have introduced measures that attempt to prevent contemporaneous changes in standard hours contracts (Owen, 1989). There is another way of circumventing changes in overtime regulation, and this is illustrated via a slightly different initial scenario.

Prior to the government intervention, assume that the firm's employees worked agreed $h^* - h$ hours of overtime. Overtime is remunerated at the rate of $w^*k^*(h^* - h)$ where k^* $(k^* > 1)$ denotes an internally agreed premium. Now, as before, the government mandates h_s and k. Suppose that $h < h_s$ and $k^* < k$. There is a problem. While the parties are happy to work at the rate of w^*k^* for $h_s - h$ hours, the rate of w^*k for $h^* - h_s$ hours is too high.

The solution involves non-compliance with the regulation.[34] Here, the parties agree to maintain the prior negotiated wage, w^*, but to reach an implicit agreement over the organisation of overtime. For example, this may be an attractive short-term course to follow if the firm and its workers are locked into an existing wage contract. One such agreement along these lines is illustrated in figure 3.5. Here, the parties agree to work paid and unpaid hours in period 2 that solves

$$k^*w^*(h^* - h) = (h_s - h)k^*w^* + kw^*h_p + 0h_u \qquad (3.42)$$

where h_p is paid-for and h_u is unpaid-for hours. Under this arrangement, the firm pays for hours in excess of h standard time hours and up to h_s at the optimal premium rate and tackles the problem of $k > k^*$ by manipulation of the length of unpaid overtime. This latter exercise determines h_p and h_u as

$$h_p = \frac{k^*}{k}(h^* - h) \quad \text{and} \quad h_u = \left(1 - \frac{k^*}{k}\right)(h^* - h).$$

---

[34] Non-compliance certainly does not eliminate interest in the case. For example, Ehrenberg and Schumann (1982a, chapter 5) indicate that a 10 per cent rate of non-compliance with the US FLSA regulations would constitute a conservative estimate (see also Trejo, 1993). Further, Ehrenberg and Schumann (1982b) provide a costbenefit analysis of firms' decisions on whether or not to comply with the FLSA regulations.

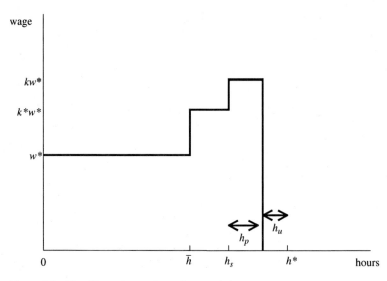

Figure 3.5   Unpaid overtime and overtime regulation

3.8   Unpaid overtime[35]

Looking at the type of occupations in which paid overtime is an important phenomenon (see table 2.1, p. 20), it is clear that many of the associated job tasks would be relatively easy to monitor and to verify. For most manual and lower-level white-collar jobs, a task duration time is either controlled by technology or can be easily established by reference to many previous occasions on which the same, or a very similar, task has been performed. Suppose that the actual time necessary to complete a given job task, h, is distributed with $h \sim f(\bar{h}, \sigma_h^2)$. Assume that f is some probability distribution that both the employer and the employee agree on. Let the employer's estimate of the time necessary be h_e while that of the worker is h_w. For simple tasks, we might expect $\bar{h} \cong h_w \cong h_e$ and $\sigma_h^2 = 0$. We might then think of the standard workweek as defining the time needed to perform an agreed number of repetitions of the job task over a 5-day period. Examples may include the number of delivery journeys of given length in a transport firm or the number of specified operations performed on car units passing down a production line of given speed. Where more repetitions of the task are required then the length of overtime required can also be readily agreed between the parties, with a contractually established premium acting to compensate for loss of (normal) leisure.

However, the above distribution may be non-degenerate, indicating a degree of uncertainty on the part of both parties about the length of the task. This may occur for non-repetitive tasks with an absence of historical information or for highly specialised tasks involving strong elements of specific human capital. For simplicity, we assume that the

---

[35] The discussion in this section is based on Bell and Hart (1999).

parties agree on the shape of the hours' distribution.[36] They bargain as to how much work time should be assigned to the task and, therefore, for how much time the worker will be paid. *Ex post* bargaining over divergences between paid-for and actual hours worked may be ruled out due to costly re-negotiation and unanticipated fluctuations in labour costs and wage income.

In some cases more information may be available on the going rate of pay for an individual with a given set of skills than on the time required to complete tasks associated with those skills. The market monthly or annual remuneration package for hiring a senior software engineer may be well known but the time needed, say, to achieve full operational capability of a new computer system in a client firm may be less certain. The estimated length of time to completion may be the main *ex ante* variable which both the principal and agent need to determine in order to proceed with the contract.

The problem is illustrated in a simple, stylised, way. A worker bargains with a profit maximising employer over the length of time needed to complete a given job task. The worker's utility is negatively related to the intensity of work and the alternative opportunity involves a lower wage. The rationale strategy is for the worker to claim hours (h_w) that are as long as possible while still meeting the constraint that the employer derives a surplus from the task. The employer seeks to keep costs low by assigning as few paid-for hours (h_e) as possible, while meeting the constraint that the worker is still prepared to participate. Thus, we might expect that the bargaining outcome regarding the length of time to be assigned to the task to be such that $h_e < h^* < h_w$.

Profit is given by

$$\pi = t - wh \tag{3.43}$$

where t is the value of the task and the w is the going hourly wage rate associated with the required skills. The employer has knowledge of both of these variables.

The value of the task is given by

$$q = (w - d)h - (\overline{w} - \overline{d})\overline{h} \tag{3.44}$$

where d is the hourly disutility of work and where $\overline{w}$ and $\overline{d}$ are the hourly values of the outside opportunity and disutility, respectively. The worker knows the values of these variables.

The problem is to agree on a contractual value for h. The employer will offer the task only if $h < t/w$. The employee will accept the task only if $h > (\overline{w} - \overline{d})\overline{h}/w - d$. Participation by both parties requires that the *ex ante* contractual value of h lies between these constraints. The particular outcome will depend, in part, on the relative bargaining strengths of the two parties.[37] Suppose the outcome, as illustrated in figure 3.6, is h^*. In this event,

---

[36] Possibilities of asymmetric information over the hours' distribution and associated problems of transaction costs and moral hazard are not considered. However, in parallel with the wage literature, the fact that the parties may have access to different sources of information on length of task completion times is a potentially interesting avenue to explore.

[37] This suggests a simple two-person Nash bargain along the lines of the discussion in section 3.4. However, other bargaining models may be relevant. For example, in a rank tournament setting with employees competing for promotion, 'optimistic' h_ws may be offered by workers in order to signal ability and effort commitment. This

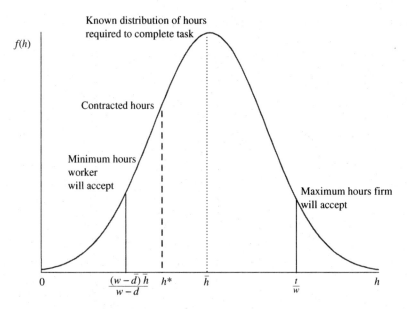

Figure 3.6   Known distribution of hours required to complete task
Source: Bell and Hart (1999).

$\text{Prob}(h > h^*) = \int_{h^*}^{\infty} f(h)dh$ is the probability that the worker works unpaid hours. The expected number of unpaid hours, given unpaid work is undertaken, is given by

$$E(h - h^*|h - h^* > 0) = \frac{\int_{h^*}^{\infty} hf(h)dh}{\int_{h^*}^{\infty} f(h)dh} - h^*.$$

Of course, the worker may also be 'overpaid' in this scenario, with probability given by $\text{Prob}(h < h^*) = \int_{-\infty}^{h^*} hf(h)dh$.

The size of the gap between h_e and h_w – and, therefore, the probability of a significant mismatch between paid-for and actual worked hours – is likely to be positively related to such factors as the degree of task complexity and the scope for individual worker initiative. Accordingly, we might expect higher incidences of professional and managerial workers who claim to undertake unpaid hours in excess of those implicitly or explicitly agreed in the terms of their contracts. In effect, such hours would be regarded as unpaid overtime.

Bell and Hart (1999) present other economic scenarios that could lead to unpaid overtime. These include (i) auction bids over the allocation of job tasks, (ii) divergent individual productivities within interactive work teams and (iii) additional hours provided by workers as part of a 'gift exchange' with the employer.

More recent emphasis behind the motivation for undertaking unpaid overtime has concerned deferred benefits. The 'premium' for undertaking such activity may be seen by

may be a particularly important effect in a hierarchical organisation and could explain cases where bargained hours are systematically lower than the mean actual hours required for task completion.

employers and employees as accelerated pay and promotion at some future date. A fuller discussion of this work is provided in section 5.6.

3.9   Summary

It is useful to highlight the main findings of work on the overtime decision.

- From the viewpoint of household labour supply, the imposition of a standard workday may lead to an individual working more hours than her/his unconstrained optimal working hours. This may create a tendency to *absenteeism* and the introduction of an overtime premium may serve to alleviate this tendency.
- Alternatively, the standard workday may produce *underemployment*, or fewer paid-for hours than desired. The firm may attempt to offset accompanying low worker morale and intensified job search by using an overtime schedule. Or underemployment may persist and the firm may employ a larger workforce. In effect, this is a form of worksharing.
- Within a pure demand framework, where the firm employs overtime hours in equilibrium, cost minimisation produces *work sharing outcomes* for changes in exogenous variables. Overtime tends to increase and employment to fall given (a) a fall in the overtime premium, (b) a rise in fixed employment costs and (c) a cut in standard hours.
- *Employment effects* of changes in the overtime premium are ambiguous when the objective of profit maximisation replaces cost minimisation.
- Most demand models predict that a fall in standard hours will increase total hours when in fact the common empirical finding is that a rise in overtime *only partially offsets the fall*. Introducing an overtime schedule that rises in hours or models that allow for both overtime and non-overtime workers helps overcome this problem.
- Developing the standard demand model to allow for individual decisions on *whether or not to participate in overtime* modifies standard results. Generally, employment implications of changes in exogenous variables are less straightforwardly determined.
- Dividing the firm's workforce into *overtime and non-overtime workers* also allows theoretical derivation of the empirical observation that a fall in standard hours is accompanied by a rise in overtime hours that only partially compensates the total hours' reduction.
- Extending the intensive margin to accommodate *wage-induced fluctuations in effort* also creates employment and hours ambiguities compared to the simpler models.
- *Demand and supply working time models* have the potential limitation of concentrating on total working hours within the firm rather than on the preferred lengths of work schedules.
- It is difficult to make unambiguous predictions when overtime is examined within an *efficient contract firm-union bargaining structure*.
- Results are more forthcoming in *right-to-manage* settings but the formulation of the sequential bargaining is hard to determine on *a priori* grounds.
- Allowing employers and employees to reach wage-hours agreements that represent *mutual preferences over job lengths* offers a radically different approach from the workers-hours demand model.

- Where *remuneration is linked to job length by* a priori *agreement*, mandatory changes in the maximum length of standard hours or in overtime premium rates may have no effect on the hours-worker allocation.
- Uncertainty over the *length of job completion times* – together with other labour market conditions – may lead to the claim by some workers that they are working hours in excess of the paid hours stipulated in their contracts.

Appendix 3.1   Cost minimisation and an exogenous increase in the overtime premium

It is helpful to illustrate the result in (3.14) graphically in terms of isoquants and isocosts.

An isoquant in this context is the locus of points of N-h combinations that provide the same amount of labour service. Using the labour services expression in (3.11), its slope is given by

$$\frac{dN}{dh} = -\frac{\partial L}{\partial h} \Big/ \frac{\partial L}{\partial N} = \frac{-\beta N}{\alpha(h - \tau)} < 0. \tag{3A.1}$$

Differentiating (3A.1) with respect to h gives $d(dN/dh)/dh > 0$ and so the locus is convex to the origin. The isoquant for $L = L_0$ is illustrated in figure 3A.1.

In the main text, we consider the isocost only in the region $h > h_s$. Allowing hours to be shorter than, equal to, and greater than h_s produces a kink in the isocost at h_s. The isocost kink is shown in figure 3A.1 at point e for illustrative purposes. The shape of the isocost above e differs from that below e because the underlying cost expression for the former does not contain overtime. Both isocosts are convex to the origin.

In line with the main text, we concentrate only on the overtime region. For given c in (3.4), the slope of the isocost in this region is given by

$$\frac{dN}{dh} = \frac{-wkN}{c} < 0. \tag{3A.2}$$

The curve is convex to the origin since $d(dN/dh)/dh > 0$. Thus, there is a diminishing marginal rate of substitution between N and h. The isocost $C = C_0$ in figure 3A.1 is at a tangent with $L = L_0$ at point f. This provides the cost minimising combination of workers and hours (N_0^*, h_0^*) that produces L_0. Note that the existence of such a tangency point – given the convexity of the two curves – requires that the second-order optimisation condition in (3.12) is satisfied which effectively requires that returns to workers exceed returns to hours of work.

What happens if the overtime premium (k) is increased? The isoquant is clearly unaffected but the isocost contains k and so changes slope. Differentiating (3A.2) with respect to k gives

$$\frac{\partial(dN/dh)}{\partial k} = \frac{wN[wk(h - h_s) - c]}{c^2} < 0,$$

or the slope of the isocost steepens (i.e. becomes more negative) for a rise in k. This is illustrated by $C = C_0'$ in figure 3A.1. However, satisfying the labour services constraint now involves higher labour cost. Isocost $C = C_1$ represents the steeper cost curve (i.e given

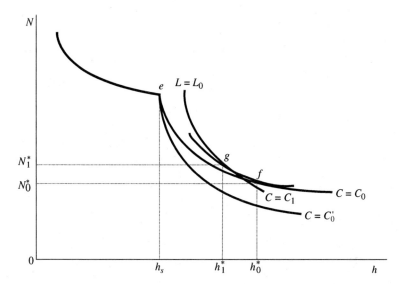

Figure 3A.1   Cost minimisation and a rise in the overtime premium

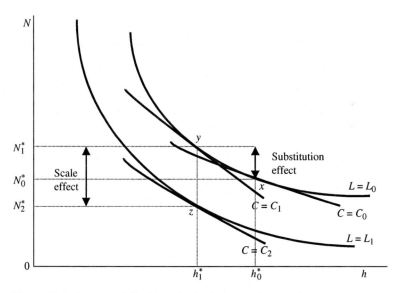

Figure 3A.2   Profit maximisation and a rise in the overtime premium

the rise in k) for required labour services at the new cost minimising tangency point g. The workers-hours combination N_1^*, h_1^* results from a substitution of a larger workforce for lower average hours per worker.

Workers-hours effects of changes in w, z, h_s and τ can be illustrated in similar fashion.

Appendix 3.2   Profit maximisation and an exogenous increase in the overtime premium

As in the cost minimisation case, the firm is in initial equilibrium at point x in figure 3A.2, employing N_0^*, h_0^* combination of workers and hours. (For convenience, we now ignore the kink point, concentrating attention purely in the overtime region.) A rise in k now has two effects. First, as in the cost minimisation case, the *substitution effect* – the vertical distance between x and y – leads to a reduction in overtime hours (h_0^* to h_1^*) and an increase in employment (N_0^* to N_1^*). Second, the rise in total labour cost produces a *scale effect* that affects employment but not hours. The isoquant shifts down from $L = L_0$ to $L = L_1$ and the new equilibrium point z represents a fall in employment from N_1^* to N_2^*. Note that while there is a net reduction in employment (i.e. $N_2^* < N_0^*$) depicted in figure 3A.2, the scale effect may have involved a less-than-offsetting fall in employment.

4   The overtime premium

Why do firms pay an overtime premium? Several straightforward reasons spring readily to mind. In the first place, governments may attempt to reduce health and social costs of excessive work demands by imposing high labour costs on firms' marginal daily or weekly hours beyond acceptable norms. Second, in the absence of such intervention, labour unions may require high marginal rates as compensation for the potential adverse effects on their members' welfare. Third, in order to satisfy unanticipated increases in product demand while minimising hiring and firing costs – especially in make-to-order production (see pp. 60–1) – firms may pay a premium to compensate workers for unexpected interruptions of leisure activity.

On more reflection, however, such explanations for the payment of a premium are not altogether satisfactory. Consider, for example, the problem of negative health and social repercussions of working long hours. If we were to tackle the question of why overtime firms paid a premium during the first half of the twentieth century, then it is probable we would think first and foremost in terms of additional pay to compensate for the socially detrimental effects of excessive working hours. At this time, long standard workweeks were typical. For example, in British engineering in the inter-war period (see section 6.3), the standard workweek was 47 hours. Additional and significant levels of regular overtime working – a feature of many engineering sectors – could well have implied the risk of impaired health as well as being socially detrimental to personal development and family well being. But concerns over such negative impacts become far less potent when set against the background in most countries, and particularly in Europe, of secular reductions in the standard workweek. Over the post-war period, these have amounted to, on average, more than a day-equivalent of working hours.

As for product demand fluctuations, it is difficult to reject the notion that firms use overtime working as a short-run adjustment response to economic shocks. In this event, the premium may reflect the 'call option' on workers' leisure time. But, as we shall see in section 5.4 in relation to job match effects in overtime working, this falls well short of providing a complete explanation of the recourse to overtime working.

While additional payments for marginal daily/weekly hours to meet health and social welfare objectives may have originated in an earlier era, the resulting premia may nevertheless retain considerable relevance to *current* payments practices. Once overtime premium rates have been established – within an industry or trade union or geographical labour market – it may well prove to be in the interests of firms and workers to regard them as constituting laid-down custom and practice. Designing and updating efficient employment contracts to cover both standard and overtime pay and hours may be regarded by the bargaining parties as too complex a task. It might well be in their interests to anchor premium rates to earlier norms – that perhaps have resulted from constraints and conditions that no longer pertain to the firm – in order to circumvent more or less indeterminate bargaining outcomes. Competitive average wage earnings can be achieved by manipulation of the standard hourly wage rate.

One reasonably uncontroversial explanation of premium pay for overtime work relates to its imposition by an outside agency with the aim of altering the marginal cost of labour input to the firm. Government objectives to encourage work sharing by increasing the relative costs of existing compared to new labour come most readily to mind in this context (see section 7.1). While it has been argued that firms and workers are able to formulate implicit contracts that can neutralise labour cost consequences of mandatory payments interventions (see section 3.7), there is as yet no overwhelming evidence that this happens extensively. In any event, as long as politicians (and voters) perceive potential employment creation resulting from such strategies – often regarded as possessing the additional appeal of carrying relatively neutral government budgetary implications – then the fact remains that policies to encourage job creation may well provide an important explanation for premium pay.

Rather than endeavour to neutralise the cost effects of mandatory overtime rules, some firms and labour unions might perceive benefits arising from allowing exogenously imposed premium rates to bite in times of increased demand. Mandatory rules over the timing and remuneration of overtime hours help bargaining parties to avoid potentially frequent and costly re-contracting over marginal rates in the face of demand fluctuations. Even though they may not view the imposed payments as representing a fair cost/reward in all economic eventualities, they may be regarded as offering the net advantages of achieving speedy and transparent compensation responses to the changing economic climate.

Of course, payment of an overtime premium does not necessarily arise from earlier established custom and practice or from the imposition of mandatory rules. We have already considered several partial equilibrium models in chapter 3 that give rise to the necessity of premium pay for overtime hours. Overtime outcomes tend to rely on the fact that, *a priori*, the firm and the worker face an exogenously given standard workweek. From a supply-side perspective, the firm might find it cost effective to pay a premium for overtime hours because, otherwise, imposed standard hours that are longer than desired hours under a single rate pay structure may encourage absenteeism (see figure 3.1 and the related discussion). On the demand side, where there is worker discretion to participate in overtime, and where the firm faces heterogeneous preferences among workers, overtime pay may act to 'find' those workers willing to supply extra hours at given premium rates. There are clear advantages in attempting to combine demand and supply overtime considerations given the problem of worker heterogeneity.

There may also be an incentive-compatible explanation for the premium. In the agency work of Lazear (1979), workers are compensated by less than their marginal product in the earlier years of tenure with the firm and more in later years. The prospect of high returns in later years of tenure serves to discourage poor work performance since it increases the cost to the worker of job loss due to dismissal. Now suppose that overtime working is offered on a permanent basis to a proportion of the firm's workforce. For those workers whose leisure preferences lead them to desire to work such overtime, the firm may impose an incentive-compatible payment system in the spirit of the Lazear structure. By paying a premium rate of pay above marginal product for overtime hours and standard pay below marginal product, the firm may be able to ensure better effort levels over the whole of the working day.

4.1 Institutional compensation rules

Work sharing

Let us start with a simple and irrefutable explanation of the reasoning behind the payment of an overtime premium. It is imposed by government mandate as an overt device to promote work sharing. For example, one of the goals of FLSA regulations, introduced in 1938, was 'to increase employment by spreading the amount of available work' (Costa, 2000). Especially in the pure demand models of chapter 3, we have seen that an exogenous increase in the premium encourages the optimising firm to trade off fewer average hours for a larger workforce. It is an appealing policy device because it appears to combine a notion of social fairness with a form of active labour market intervention that involves little exchequer cost. At best, however, it provides a very partial explanation:

(1) Theoretical derivations of unambiguous work sharing outcomes are predicated on special assumptions that play down such features as variable capital, efficiency wages, partial workforce overtime participation and rising overtime schedules.
(2) The payment of a premium is widespread among firms not subject to mandatory rules.
(3) There is mixed empirical evidence that obligatory premium payments do in fact have work sharing associations (see section 7.1).
(4) Policy effectiveness may be severely reduced if management and workers agree to manipulate straight-time wage rates in response to changes in overtime regulations (see section 3.7).

Interestingly, through less direct routes, the payment of a premium may serve to *reduce* the impact of policy initiatives designed to encourage work sharing. Suppose these took the form of enforced reductions in standard weekly hours. We have seen, especially in section 3.2, that the existence of an overtime schedule may contribute to hours-worker substitution given mandatory hours cuts. This contrasts, for example, with the case of a cost minimising firm that employs no overtime; at least in the short run, a cut in the workweek is likely to require an increase in workforce size.

Approximately efficient contracts

Commonly, the overtime premium comprises part of a long-term contractual compensation rule. The rate of hourly premium pay for hours worked beyond the maximum stipulated standard hours represents an explicit compensation agreement. One consequence is that the rule serves to relate marginal hourly pay directly to product demand. As product and labour demand increase, average hourly pay rises because a higher proportion of an individual worker's total hours is compensated at the premium rate. Demand rises often reflect increased macroeconomic activity. In such a climate, outside job opportunities and earnings would typically be improving. This suggests a role for the overtime premium. It may be designed to reflect workers' opportunity cost of supplying labour services. In other words, it may serve to capture the fact of higher forgone earnings in alternative employment as aggregate demand rises. Symmetrically, as demand falls and average hours shorten reduced opportunity cost is reflected in lower proportions of hours worked at the premium rate.

Opportunity cost in the foregoing scenario refers to earnings forgone in alternative employment.[1] Why might there be mutual advantages to workers and management in mechanistically accommodating fluctuations in such cost within collective bargaining agreements? One answer is that this may provide a realistic way of dealing with information asymmetries.

Suppose that, under a collective bargaining framework, a profit maximising firm and a union seek to strike an efficient bargain with respect to the level of labour input, L, and the wage, w. Ignore other labour costs and assume that capital is fixed. The firm's profit is $\pi = R(L) - B$ where $B = wL$ is the wage bill. Union members' income net of the opportunity cost of supplying L amount of labour, $V(L)$, is $Y = B - V(L)$. The bargain will be efficient if the agreed level of labour input is $L = L^*$, where L^* is the set of points at which the firm's marginal revenue is equal to the labour's marginal opportunity cost of work, i.e. $R'(L) = V'(L)$. If, by chance, $V'(L)$ equalled the average wage, $w = B/L$, then an efficient bargain would be equivalent to profit maximising subject to this wage. Generally, this would not be the case (Leontief, 1946).

Hall and Lilien (1979) suggest that contracts may more reliably achieve efficiency if the wage bill is designed to be a function of labour input, $B(L)$ with $B'(L) > 0$. Profits are now $\pi = R(L) - B(L)$ and workers' net income $Y = B(L) - V(L)$. Both parties would agree to a compensation rule $B(L)$ that equates marginal labour cost $B'(L)$ to marginal opportunity cost of labour $V'(L)$ and that lets the profit maximising firm unilaterally chose the efficient level of employment, L^*.

The problem is that both revenue and opportunity costs are subject to random shocks. The revenue function is more realistically written as $R(L, x)$ where x represents demand fluctuations. Comparably, the opportunity cost of employment becomes $V(L, z)$ where z captures fluctuations in outside wages and in the cost of living. For given values of x and z, the equation of marginal revenue and marginal cost defines L^* as a function of x and z, that is $L^*(x, z)$. In order to maintain L^* the parties may attempt to draw up contracts that

---

[1] Opportunity cost may also relate to consumer surplus forgone in diverting leisure to work. A rise in this latter cost may result from an unexpected rise in the cost of living. To cover this event, contracts may contain agreed escalator provisions.

are contingent on agreed values of x and z. To achieve this, they would require a contingent compensation rule $B(x, z)$. In other words, labour input would be dependent on the parties reaching *ex post* agreements on the values of random shifts in x and z. One potentially major problem is that informational asymmetries over fluctuations in demand and outside wages may lead to problems of moral hazard. For example, if $B(x, z)$ was sensitive to x and if management were deemed to have more information about the state of demand then it would be in the management's interest to play down labour input by falsely understating sales prospects.

Realising that these sorts of problems may well lead to bargaining breakdowns and costly disputes, what if bargainers agree to make compensation contingent only on the level of labour input and not on outside variables? Now, the firm's profit becomes $\pi = R(L, x) - B(L)$ and the union's net income is given by $Y = B(L) - V(L, z)$. As before, $L^*(x, z)$ defines the efficient level of employment. For all x and z, the quantity of labour demanded by the firm is derived from its optimising rule, $\partial R(L, x)/\partial L = B'(L)$, while the union would supply labour according to the rule, $\partial V(L, z)/\partial L = B'(L)$. This contract would automatically lead to an agreed efficient level of employment if the parties could agree how to share monopoly profit. Herein lies a snag. Since the compensation rule is not contingent on outside variables, the parties have no means of allocating profit as between demand and supply influences.

This leads Hall and Lilien (1979) to consider a contract with a less than ideal compensation rule but one that is approximately efficient. Suppose that the parties make *a priori* agreements about reducing supply-side uncertainties, to the extent that they are willing to make the contract contingent only on the demand side.[2] The ideal compensation rule satisfies $\partial R(L, x)/\partial L = B'(x)$ for all x and $V'(L) = B'(L)$. Here, the firm internalises marginal opportunity cost by paying an equivalent amount as marginal labour cost. Hall and Lilien suggest the payment rule $B(L) = B_0 + V(L)$ where the fixed cash payment, B_0, can be any chosen amount and covers the well being of the union.[3] When this guaranteed amount is agreed, the union is indifferent to the level of employment that is unilaterally set by the firm and determined by its assessment of x.

What sort of institutional framework lends itself to this form of contract? In the first place, it would seem unlikely that the union would allow potential large fluctuations in labour input without safeguards to members' long-term employment prospects. One possibility might be to envisage variable annual utilisation rates among a fixed, or 'permanent' workforce. For example, the notion of mutually agreed temporary layoffs (Feldstein, 1975, 1976, Lilien, 1980) would seem to fit more comfortably with this scheme of things. Second, the compensation rule must be such that marginal rates of compensation reflect keenly fluctuations in demand. Achieving required rises in labour input in response to upward demand fluctuations necessitates speedy and adequate rises in marginal rates of compensation that reflect the changing climate of opportunity cost. In the reverse direction, management will want the ability to reduce marginal rates. A contractual or mandatory obligation to pay an

---

[2] Hall and Lilien (1979) also deal with the case where supply shocks are dominant.
[3] The union's well being is $B(L) - V(L)$ which, under this compensation rule, is $B_0 + V(L) - V(L) = B_0$.

overtime premium matches this requirement. Average hourly earnings rise with increasing demand since proportionately more hours are paid at the premium. When demand falls, fewer premium-pay hours are worked and, if demand shrinks sufficiently, pay may also be reduced by agreement to receive unemployment benefit for short spells.

This is an appealing interpretation of the role of the overtime premium[4] but it does entail limitations when set in a wider context. Hall and Lilien (1979) advance it in the context of the US labour market. Here, most firms face the statutory rule of premium pay of 1.5 times the standard rate for weekly hours in excess of 40. Moreover, temporary spells of unemployment are not uncommon in the United States, thereby underpinning the notion that the attainment of contract efficiency through a rising payments schedule is best realised within a permanent workforce. As shown in table 2.4 (p. 31), however, mandatory rules covering overtime premia are not common to all major countries. Premium overtime rates vary considerably and it is improbable that these reflect, even approximately, international differences in perceived opportunity cost. Further, in Europe and elsewhere, a temporary spell of unemployment followed by re-employment in the same firm is a phenomenon that is far less common than in the United States. The force of the Hall–Lilien institutional interpretation of the role of the premium is reduced somewhat in this broader context.

4.2   Custom and practice

The United Kingdom is representative of an economy with no imposed rules governing the timing and payment of overtime hours. Overtime agreements tend to be undertaken at company level, with different companies offering different premium rates (Incomes Data Services, 1997). There appears to be little tendency for the marginal premium to vary directly with changing economic events, such as movements in the business cycle.[5] We know that significant elements of overtime hours represent individual fixed effects (see section 5.4). There are very plausible reasons for believing that these observations are consistent with the view that, to important degrees, rates of overtime premia simply reflect established custom and practice within individual sectors. The following arguments are based on Bell and Hart (2003a).

There is some British evidence (Brown et al., 1986[6]; Incomes Data Services, 1997) that the weekly payments schedule facing most individual overtime workers consists of either

---

[4] For example, the line of reasoning can be extended to offer an explanation for the fact that some firms in the United States pay the premium for weekly hours not covered by the FLSA rules. In specific instances, fine-tuning payments to match both firms' work organisation in a given industry and workers' opportunity costs may involve increasing payments schedules that occur earlier than the mandated 40 hours.

[5] There is some tendency, however. It is reasonably common for firms to pay higher overtime rates for weekend and public holiday working (Incomes Data Services, 1997). These higher rates will tend to operate more commonly during periods of peak demand. Note, however, that even if there are no cyclical movements in the marginal premium, the importance of overtime pay within total compensation is likely to be procyclical. If overtime workers undertake longer hours towards cyclical peaks, then the proportion of overtime to total pay will increase.

[6] This derives from a detailed study of 5,000 British workers carried out in 1980. The study revealed that the shapes of individuals' overtime premium schedules are varied. Some workers receive a single premium for all overtime hours worked. Others receive discrete rises in the marginal premium as the length of the working day/week increases. Far less common are payments schemes whereby workers receive less than the standard rate for the first hour of overtime. In general, an individual's marginal overtime premium can be expected to be either a constant or a rising step-function of overtime hours.

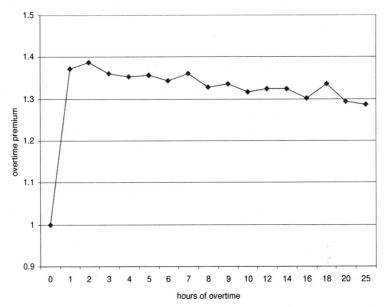

Figure 4.1   Average premium, by weekly hours of overtime (NES), 2001

a single premium rate for all overtime hours worked *or* a rising step-function. At a given point in time, how does the average premium relate to the length of weekly overtime hours? Figures 4.1–4.4 investigate key relationships for the year 2001. They repeat, and confirm, the results of Bell and Hart (2003a), who carried out the same exercise using 1998 data.

The (unconditional) shape of the average premium schedule for 2001 is shown in figure 4.1. The data refer to full-time non-managerial/professional male workers.[7] Between 1 and 2 hours, the schedule rises steeply to reach almost 1.4 times the standard rate. Thereafter, while dipping slightly, it declines very gently to 1.3 times the standard rate to 25 hours of overtime working.[8] This finding is in line with earlier estimates of Hart and Ruffell (1993).[9] Overtime workers are then divided into different bands of weekly overtime. These range from 1–4 hours to over 16 hours. Figure 4.2 shows the proportions of workers within each band. The proportions are very similar across the bands. Combining the findings of Figures 4.1 and 4.2, the overtime premium appears to be almost invariant to the number of weekly overtime hours.

---

[7] 'Full-time men' are defined as those who work at least 30 hours per week. Individuals with a recorded premium of greater than three times the standard rate are excluded. Individuals with a premium of less than unity are included, however.

[8] The graph in figure 4.1 is based on 17,285 male non-managerial workers. The slight downward slope is accounted for by the distribution of individuals who received a premium rate of one or less. There were 2,261 such individuals of whom 24 per cent worked 14 or more overtime hours per week. A partial explanation of this phenomenon is that many employers are willing to satisfy workers' preferences for long hours only at relatively low marginal pay rates in order to offset a perceived loss of productivity due to fatigue.

[9] Bell and Hart (2000) undertake a Tobit regression of the determinants of the average overtime premium so as to control for other potential influences. These include the standard wage, standard hours, collective bargaining

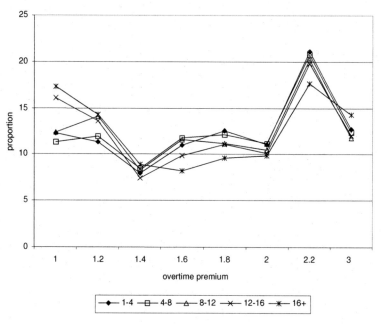

Figure 4.2   Proportions working overtime, by overtime premium (NES), 2001

Figures 4.3 and 4.4 show relationships between standard hourly wages and the premium. The former shows a predominantly negative relationship – workers with high premiums tend to average relatively low standard rates and vice versa. The latter again shows a breakdown into different length-bands of overtime. It reveals a negative relationship between the premium and the standard hourly wage.

How do these observations relate to arguments concerning custom and practice? Efficient long-term contracts require that agreements be reached with respect to both wage rates and hours of work. Suppose that the maximum length of standard hours is set exogenously, perhaps at industry or regional level. Firms requiring longer average hours than the maximum will employ overtime hours. Contract efficiency in these circumstances implies that the overtime premia are indeterminate. We would expect, therefore, that there would be no systematic patterns in the premia. However, we have seen that the premia exhibit significant regularities. In fact, they involve three striking relationships. First, the level of the overtime premium is independent of the length of weekly overtime hours (figures 4.1 and 4.2). Second, there is a negative relationship between the premium and the standard hourly wage (figures 4.3 and 4.4). Third, there is a negative relationship between the standard hourly wage and the length of weekly overtime hours (figure 2.12). Combining these observations, there is strong UK evidence that average hourly wage earnings (i.e. including the effects of overtime) are constant with respect to the length of weekly overtime hours (figure 2.14).

agreements, public/private sector employment, etc. It is found that after conditioning with such controls, the shape of schedule shown in figure 4.1 is unaffected.

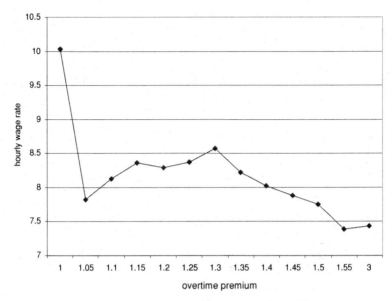

Figure 4.3   Standard hourly wage rate and the premium (NES), 2001

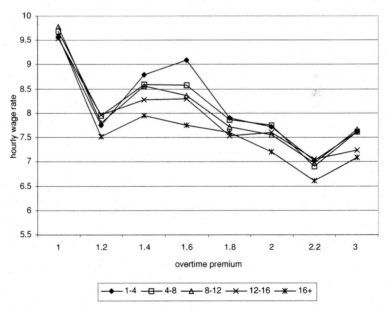

Figure 4.4   Standard hourly wage rate, by premium and overtime hours (NES), 2001

In order to circumvent the indeterminacy problem, firms and workers may agree to anchor premium rates at established 'norms'. Due to firm- or industry-specific historical circumstances – perhaps arising from working conditions, production requirements and collective bargaining arrangements – levels of premia will vary across firms. Whether a firm faces a relatively high or low premium is not dependent on its contracted length of overtime hours. The average overtime premium will tend to be independent of overtime hours. However, contract efficiency will demand that in competitive markets firms facing the practice of paying high premium rates and/or employing long average overtime hours will tend to have offsetting low standard wage rates. For given overtime hours, low standard rates will occur in firms that face relative high premiums. For given premium rates, the cost of long overtime hours would also be offset by a lower standard wage. In effect, the standard wage rate is adjusted to achieve a competitive average hourly (total) wage in much the same way as represented in the Lewis fixed-job model (see section 3.7). This is consistent with the profiles displayed in figures 4.3 and 4.4.

What are the implications of this approach to setting wages and hours? Rather than attempting to set the optimal marginal wage that 'encourages' individuals to work required hours, firms may set the same competitive average hourly wage and let workers select the hours on offer at that wage so as to match their work/leisure preferences. This may be labelled the *constant average wage model*. As shown in figure 2.14, average hourly earnings by hours of overtime are more or less constant in British data. In effect, it implies that both workers and firms are not making marginal hours decisions. The model offers two potential advantages. First, it avoids transaction costs associated with reaching individually tailored wage-hours contracts. Second, and relatedly, it bypasses problems of information asymmetries between the parties concerning their working time preferences.

4.3   Heterogeneous worker preferences

Workers express a broad range of reasons for their decision to work overtime. Take, for example, replies to questions in the 1998 British Workplace Employee Relations Survey (WERS). The survey covers around 26,000 employees and table 4.1 presents a summary of their main reasons for working overtime or extra hours.[10]

One-fifth of workers report that their main reason for working overtime is because they need the money.[11] An even larger percentage of respondents (24 per cent) report that they work overtime because their job requires them so to do. In fact, these workers report the joint-longest average weekly overtime (5.5 hours).[12] A comparable percentage of respondents

[10] As is made clear elsewhere in the survey, 'extra hours' are meant to include unpaid overtime.
[11] WERS asks the question: 'How satisfied are you with the amount of pay you receive?' Cross-tabulating we find that 30 per cent of those claiming that, primarily, they need the money are either dissatisfied or very dissatisfied with their pay. Unsurprisingly, this is a far higher percentage than any other group classified in table 4.1.
[12] Despite indicating that overtime is a job requirement, such workers are, in general, favourably disposed towards important aspects of their jobs. Cross-tabulating with other WERS questions, we find that such workers are satisfied or very satisfied with (a) the amount of their job influence (61 per cent), (b) their sense of achievement derived from work (67 per cent), (c) respect they get from their supervisors/line managers (53 per cent). By contrast, only 38 per cent are satisfied/very satisfied with the amount of pay they receive.

Table 4.1 *If you do work overtime or extra hours, what would you say is the main reason you do this? (WERS, 1998)*

	Frequency	Percentage	Average weekly paid and unpaid overtime or extra hours (standard deviation)
I never work overtime or overtime or extra hours	3,136	11.8	–
I enjoy my work	1,191	4.5	4.8 (6.4)
I need the money	5,289	20.0	4.9 (6.1)
I don't want to let down the people I work with	2,658	10.0	2.9 (4.7)
So that I can get all my work done	6,476	24.5	5.4 (6.4)
Its required as part of my job	6,264	23.7	5.5 (6.9)
Some other reason	1,464	5.5	2.2 (4.1)
Total	26,478	100.0	

claim that their job demands are such that they need to work overtime. At somewhat smaller levels, 10 per cent of the sample claim to work overtime so as not to let their work colleagues down and 5 per cent appear to work overtime because they like the job they do.

Of course, this is an individual-based survey and so we should be cautious about making inferences concerning work groups within the workplace. But several reasonable inferences can be made. We might imagine that a few of these responses may be representative of entire work groups within a given firm. For example, if the workforce belongs to a low-paid occupation or sector, than we would not be surprised to find that the 'I need the money' response is all pervading. Similarly, overtime that is required as part of the job may be expected to be the common response by all workers within some firms. More generally, however, it is quite likely that one response holds for a part of a firm's workforce, another response for another part, and so on. Low-productive workers in a given firm may find the need to undertake more overtime so as not to let down their work colleagues with respect to joint production goals. Others may chose not to work overtime while some may want to work extra hours because they derive high levels of job satisfaction. Even within relatively highly paid jobs, some individuals are likely to give as their main reason for working overtime the need to attain higher earnings. This may derive from high costs associated with maintaining a large family or more than one family or sick relatives or a high consumption life style.

If overtime is a voluntary activity, heterogeneous preferences across the workforce may result in a range of responses from a desire to work no overtime whatsoever to that of working as many hours as is physically possible to cope with. Herein lies a fundamental

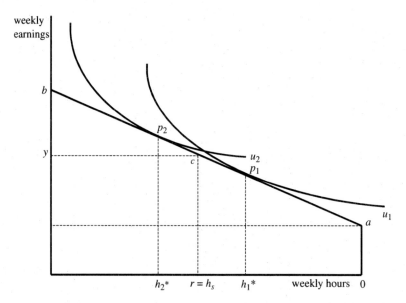

Figure 4.5   Income and leisure preferences

problem. Heterogeneity with respect to workers' supply preferences may clash with a demand for homogeneous hours' provision by firms. In many work environments, technical and organisational constraints impose the need for a high degree of uniformity in workers' provision of hours of work. Service sector activities within communication, transport, education, retailing and health care often entail regularised daily hours that are designed to meet prescribed work schedules and consumer provision. In the manufacturing sector, line production requires work synchronisation across teams of workers because of a dependency on interactive inputs. An industry- or national-level contractual agreement between employers' representatives and unions may formally impose the length and timing of weekly hours across occupational groups in member firms.

The most common means of ensuring that these and other demand-side constraints are met is to impose a *standardised workweek* on all workers within the firm or enterprise (e.g. 5 working weekdays of 7 hours per day). Problems may arise, however, if the goal of achieving hours uniformity is set against a background of heterogeneous consumption/leisure preferences across workers. As we have seen in section 3.1, some workers may regard themselves as being in a state of overemployment if imposed standard hours exceed their unconstrained hours' preference at the given wage rate. Others will regard themselves as underemployed since they would be willing to supply more than standard hours at the given rate.

Moses (1962) has considered several implications of introducing overtime schedules for workers who regard themselves as overemployed or underemployed in relation to prescribed standard hours and given wages. Leslie (1982) has suggested an interesting implication of this work that provides an explanation of the payment of an overtime premium.

Figure 4.5 depicts two workers in a firm that are representative of different consumption/leisure preferences. The budget line $0\text{-}a\text{-}b$ represents non-wage income together with

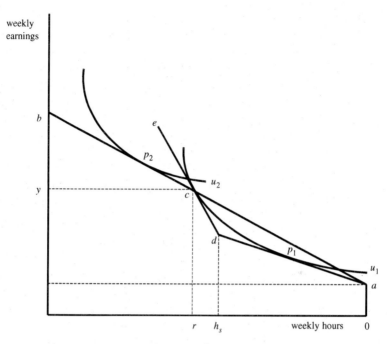

Figure 4.6 Overtime and income/leisure preferences

the payment of a single hourly wage rate for daily hours worked. Suppose that the firm faces a strict production, collective bargaining or organisational constraint that requires each worker to work r daily hours. Accordingly, it unilaterally sets the standard workday at $h_s = r$. For the given wage, this is equivalent to daily earnings of y. Worker 1 is overemployed since he prefers to work $h_1^* < h_s$ hours, i.e. coinciding with the optimal p_1, u_1 tangency point. Worker 2 is underemployed, with $h_2^* > h_s$ at the p_2, u_2 point. What are the potential costs of the imbalance between the firm's hours' requirements and the workers' preferences? Worker 1 may be encouraged to take spells of absenteeism in order to attempt to bring actual and preferred average hours more into line. (See also discussion in relation to figure 3.1, p. 47). Worker 2's work performance may be impaired because of a loss of job satisfaction entailed with a shortfall of actual compared to desired weekly hours (see also figure 3.2, p. 49). Can the firm design a wage structure that discourages these tendencies?

The firm can pay y earnings for required h_s hours via a range of compensation schemes. For example, as shown in figure 4.6, it could cut standard hours, so that $h_s < r$, and pay a reduced standard hourly wage rate. Then, between required hours r and standard hours h_s it could pay an overtime wage consisting of the new lower standard rate times a premium in excess of unity. The premium could be chosen so that $h_s + r$ hours are compensated at y earnings as before. The new budget line is given by 0-a-d-e. In effect, the firm would be offering permanent overtime hours at a guaranteed overtime premium. What are the advantages of this alternative scheme? Note that worker 1's utility is tangential at two points – that is at p_1 on a-d and at c on d-e. The worker is indifferent between working short hours at standard pay and working overtime so as to meet the firm's r-hours constraint. The new wage structure has removed the propensity to be absent from work. In effect, compared to the conventional linear wage schedule in figure 4.5, the overtime ratchet in figure 4.6 has served to increase the marginal cost to the worker of working standard workdays. As for worker 2, the alternative wage, like the conventional wage, will have no effect on the state of underemployment.

In general terms, a permanent overtime wage structure might serve to curb absences among two groups of workers. First, as portrayed in figure 4.6, some workers will gain about the same utility working to the hours' requirement as the unconstrained alternative to be derived from a shorter working day. Second, some workers will be able to achieve the same utility at r hours compared to shorter hours, *despite not being at the tangency point of the utility curve*. This would occur in figure 4.6 if the budget line segment, d–e, cut through the utility curve, u_1; in other words, if the slope of the utility curve at point c was less than that of the d–e overtime schedule.[13] While these workers would not militate to work fewer hours – because they have at least achieved their highest potential utility of short-time working – they would prefer to work *more* overtime than that guaranteed. In effect, they would be underemployed.

The positions of two additional groups would not be altered by the imposition of guaranteed overtime. First, as with worker 2 in figure 4.6, those overemployed workers whose utility tangency points lie along c–b would be unaffected by the overtime schedule. Second, some overemployed workers with tangency points along a–d would remain better off if they could work shorter hours. They would feel that an imposed r hours represented lower utility if the slope of their utility curve that is a tangent along a–d was greater than the slope of the d–e overtime schedule at point c.

Therefore, while there may be advantages to certain firms in imposing an overtime schedule as part of regular remuneration, such a scheme is clearly not a panacea for removing the threat of absenteeism due to overemployment or the dissatisfaction associated with underemployment. What factors might serve to accentuate the gains from this use of overtime thereby encouraging firms to incorporate overtime as a regular facet of worker remuneration? First, the degree to which the firm views a fixed daily or weekly hours' requirement as a necessary condition for meeting technological, organisational or collective bargaining constraints. Second, where fixed capital and fixed labour costs are high so that disruptions due to absences or poor work performance are seen as particularly costly. Third, where there is a large positive gap between actual and desired hours of work for significant numbers of workers.

4.4   Hours preferences, productivity and industrial relations

Section 4.3 addressed the issue of workers who have different lengths of preferred working hours within a single firm. Survey evidence, combined with the fact that we know that firms employ a mix of overtime and non-overtime workers in the same occupation, lends

---

[13] For these workers the marginal rate of substitution between income and leisure at point c is less than the premium overtime rate that converts leisure into earnings.

support to the need to confront this issue. The problem discussed so far involves workers with different hours' preferences being required by the firm to work the *same* per-period hours. What if a single firm offers two or more jobs of *different* daily lengths? Further, what if the jobs are held by workers with the same skills and productive performance but with different preferences with respect to job length? The firm's technical and organisational set-up may lead managers to want to fill more than one job-length requirement. For example, they may wish to gear towards more daytime production during weekdays and less evening and weekend production.[14]

This raises a potential difficulty for the wage-hours compensating differential model linked to the work of Lewis. How does the firm pay different hourly rates of pay to individuals who perform equivalent job tasks and provide similar levels of hourly productive performance but who work different job lengths? Potentially, this would lead to industrial relations difficulties.

Suppose the firm employs two types of worker. Type 1 work long daily hours, h_1 for daily pay y_1. Type 2 work shorter daily hours, h_2 for daily pay y_2. Suppose that those working long daily hours are compensated by higher average hourly wages, in part reflecting adverse social costs. How can the firm design a wage package to meet $w_1 > w_2$ while also attempting to avoid adverse reactions among Type 2 workers? Perhaps the introduction of an overtime schedule, along the lines suggested by Hart and Ma (2003), may help to provide a solution. Recall that $h_1 > h_2$ due to differential work preferences. The firm could classify h_2 hours as 'standard' for which it pays a standard wage; that is $w_s = w_2$ and $h_s = h_2$. Thus, wage earnings of Type 2 workers are given by

$$y_2 = w_2 h_2 = w_s h_s. \tag{4.1}$$

Type 1 workers also receive w_s for h_s and so the two types of worker receive the same rate of pay for their overlapping hours. Type 1 workers receive additionally an overtime package (k, h_0) designed such that

$$k = \frac{w_1 h_1 - y_2}{w_2 h_1 - y_2} \quad \text{and} \quad h_0 = h_1 - h_2 > 0. \tag{4.2}$$

The premium, k, represents the total daily earnings difference between the two types of workers as a proportion of the difference if Type 1 workers were paid the same hourly rate as Type 2 workers. The earnings schedule of Type 1 workers is then given by the one-step schedule familiar to the working time literature (see, for example (3.4), p. 51), that is

$$y_1 = w_1 h_1 = w_s h_s + k w_s h_0. \tag{4.3}$$

There are several obvious objections to this 'solution'. First, it is not at all clear that the market equalising wage curve (Lewis, 1969a) – that links equilibrium daily earnings and hours – is upward sloping. It is quite feasible that the relationship between earnings and

---

[14] Lower production and business activity outside of weekdays may relate to fixed costs of operation. Firms may not find it cost effective to provide such items as heating and lighting as well as administrative back-up during evenings and weekends on a scale equivalent to the standard workday. But they may find it advantageous to operate at partial utilisation of plant/premises at these marginal times.

hours is negative, in which case the payments structure above would not be appropriate.[15] Second, it is not clear that the value of k in (4.2) would accord with empirically observed values, like time and a quarter, etc. Third, if mandatory overtime rules pertained, it is unlikely that optimal k in (4.2) would correspond with the legislated value.

Even if there were an internal arrangement along the above lines, this still leaves difficulties for this kind of endogenous overtime solution. Assume an economy like the United States with mandatory overtime legislation. Suppose that long-hours workers within the firm work marginal overtime hours at a premium while short-hours workers work only standard time. Both sets of workers receive the same standard wage. Suppose the government intervenes to raise the mandatory overtime premium. Would it then be claimed that overtime workers would receive a lower standard wage than their non-overtime worker equivalents in order to offset an increased average hourly wage differential that has been created for non-economic reasons? Flexible standard hourly wages are not so feasible when workers with interactive skills work differing lengths of daily hours within the same firm.

Hart and Ma (2003) have constructed an efficient contract model involving different hours' preferences among workers within the same firm. Again, there are two types of worker. Type 1 workers have a small disutility of work per hour, d_1, and a high hourly reservation utility, $\bar{u}_1$. Type 2 workers have a high hourly disutility of work, d_2 and low hourly reservation utility, $\bar{u}_2$. The model solution provides the intuitive result that $h_1 > h_2$ because $d_1 < d_2$, or workers with smaller disutility of work will work longer hours. Again, as with the Lewis model, it cannot be established with certainty whether $w_1 > w_2$ or vice versa. The schedules (4.2) and (4.3) might provide solutions in special circumstances.

As discussed in section 3.3, attempts have been made to integrate different length of working time into the workers-hours demand model. It is clear that future work needs to accommodate within-firm heterogeneous hours' preferences as an aspect of the wage-hours compensating differential modelling structure.

4.5 The premium, marginal product and work incentive

We know that many firms employ both overtime and non-overtime workers in the same occupation (see table 2.3, p. 24) and, more generally, a significant proportion of firms employ a mix of such workers (Andrews, Schank and Simmons, 2002). Workers may self-select into overtime jobs and/or the firm may attempt to assess individuals' suitability for working long hours. Some workers may attempt to obtain the take-home pay associated with long hours but without providing an adequate increment of increased daily or weekly effort. Employers may insist that the ability to work overtime is conditional on a regular attendance record[16] as well as a sustained work rate throughout the working day.

Brown (1999) has studied the practice of imposing a ban on overtime for some specified period of time for those individuals with an 'unacceptable' history of absence. The rationale is to circumvent the tendency, where overtime is freely available, for employees to take spells

---

[15] Nor do estimates of such a wage locus underscore a predominantly positive slope (see Kahn and Lang, 1996)

[16] Overtime plays a potentially interesting role within a range of policies adopted by firms designed directly to prevent absenteeism (see Dalton and Mesch, 1992 for general references).

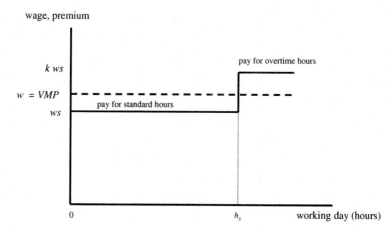

wage, premium

$k\,ws$

$w\ =VMP$

ws

pay for overtime hours

pay for standard hours

0

h_s

working day (hours)

Figure 4.7   Wage profile of an overtime worker

of absenteeism and then to make up the loss of earnings by increasing overtime hours in future time periods.[17] Brown uses discrete panel data derived from the work histories of individuals working in a British manufacturing firm. If an employee takes two unauthorised absences in any 5-week period in this firm then s/he is banned from working overtime for the next 4 weeks. It is found that the ban significantly *raises* the probability of absence. This perverse outcome seems to derive from the fact that once a ban has been incurred the overlapping nature of the scheme means that the marginal cost to the individual of future absence declines. For this reason, Brown recommends a scheme whereby bans are accumulated consecutively.

What other actions can the firm take in order to ensure satisfactory work commitment from overtime workers? Imagine a firm in an unregulated competitive labour market in which all, or almost all, employees undertake overtime. (This covers 23 per cent of British establishments reported in table 2.3.) Suppose that the firm pays its overtime workers a wage equal to the value of marginal product, $w = VMP$. Its problem is that it cannot select, *a priori*, overtime workers who will provide satisfactory work. Following the practice identified by Brown, suppose that it threatens an overtime ban over a specified period of time if poor work attendance and/or other specified forms of work shirking are observed.

Monitoring work performance involves cost. A way to reduce such cost is to design an overtime schedule that provides incentives to work application and effort. Suppose, the firm pays a standard hourly wage $w_s < VMP$ and an overtime wage $kw_s > VMP$ (see figure 4.7), where k is the overtime premium. The average hourly daily wage is $w = VMP$. Provided that marginal product does not change drastically over the working day, this may well represent the wage/marginal product relationship for many overtime workers. Its advantage to the firm is that it increases the cost to the worker of being discovered to be providing poor

[17] The studies of Gowler (1969) and Martin (1971) emphasise the association between absenteeism and overtime in work environments with limited job mobility and where large demand fluctuations caused frequent use of overtime.

work performance and, therefore, of having to face an overtime ban over a given period. An additional benefit is that the firm may feel less need to invest heavily in monitoring individual performance. If work involves interactive, or team, activity then workers themselves would welcome a penalty imposed on their less productive colleagues. Of course, the worker may quit because the standard wage is below marginal product. However, the cost of finding a replacement is offset by the return of losing a sub-standard worker.

4.6   Summary

This chapter began by asking why firms pay an overtime premium. In important aspects of overtime incidence, this question has been largely unanswered in the literature. In part, this reflects the fact that firms in a number of economies are predominantly governed by regulation over their allocations and payments of overtime hours (see table 2.4). Where this occurs, some firms may perceive advantages. While the timing and amount of mandated premium pay for long daily/weekly hours may not match equivalent terms derived under privately negotiated efficient contracts they may provide a reasonable approximation. Their advantage is that they help to eliminate the potentially high costs of negotiating standard and overtime pay scales as well as the hours for which overtime rates apply.

We know, however, that overtime working is also an important labour market phenomenon in economies with either weak or non-existent overtime regulation. Even under the relatively strong regulation in the United States, which imposes high marginal rates of overtime pay, up to 20 per cent of workers receive a premium *before* maximum standard workweek hours are achieved (see Trejo, 1993, table 2). A simple, but potentially powerful, explanation of the payment of an overtime premium in unregulated markets is that firms find it convenient to follow established custom and practice. Suppose that the length of standard hours is treated as a given variable by the firm. Certainly in a European context, many firms adhere to industry/regional/public sector norms over the length of the standard workweek. How are wages determined for working time requirements in excess of standard hours? So long as there is freedom to negotiate standard pay, firms and workers may be happy to circumvent indeterminacy problems by paying premiums based on custom and practice. Competitive average hourly wages may be achieved through firms with traditionally high premium rates paying relatively low standard rates and firms with low premium rates paying relatively high standard rates. In effect, for a given hourly wage, workers select into jobs of varying lengths so as to satisfy their working time preferences. To the extent that this system operates, overtime may well be observed to contain significant elements of permanent, or guaranteed, working time.

The supply-side literature offers an explanation of the payment of an overtime premium as a means of averting absenteeism among those workers who, in a flat-rate compensation scheme, would prefer to work fewer than prescribed standard hours. Solutions generally depict all workers in the firm – whether initially desiring to work more or fewer hours – being required to supply the same daily length of hours. Potential difficulties arise when the firm employs workers to perform similar job tasks for different lengths of per-period hours. In special situations, an overtime premium may allow the payment of a higher average hourly wage to long-hours workers while all workers receive the same standard wage. In general, however, heterogeneous preferences over job lengths within the same firm produces difficulties for the wage-hours compensating differential model.

Finally, heterogeneous work attitudes among individual workers who wish to work long hours may lead the firm to impose overtime penalties on poor timekeepers and shirkers. Monitoring costs may be allayed if the firm is able to introduce an overtime schedule in which marginal daily hours are compensated at above marginal product and standard hours at below marginal product.

5 Overtime hours and empirical studies

5.1 Individual-based studies of overtime

Much of the micro evidence on factors affecting the incidence and the number of hours of overtime working is based on two contrasting labour markets. At one end of the spectrum, the US market is highly regulated in that, for most firms, the hours eligible for premium payments and the minimum level of the premium are set by legislation. At the other, the UK market is unregulated as far as overtime practices are concerned. Here, we concentrate attention on these two markets along with a third, the German labour market. Germany has not experienced legislation with the coverage of the United States. However, recent governments as well as large unions have adopted much more interventionist working time approaches than their UK counterparts.

Taking the lead from the work by Trejo (1993) for the United States, two additional studies provide micro evidence on the incidence and hours of overtime working. Bauer and Zimmermann (1999) report findings for Germany while Bell and Hart (2000) study the United Kingdom. The effects of several key explanatory variables on the numbers of overtime hours worked are provided by the Tobit estimates shown in column (1) under each labour market in table 5.1.[1] Columns (2) and (3) contain the decomposition proposed by McDonald and Moffitt (1980). This shows the effects of each explanatory variable on the probability of overtime incidence and on the expected number of overtime hours of those working overtime.

For the United Kingdom, the standard hourly wage is found to exert a negative influence on overtime hours. This is consistent with an income effect on the supply side, with decreasing marginal productivity of overtime hours on the demand, or some combination of these effects (perhaps as the outcome of the bargaining process).[2] Trejo (1993) finds a significant substitution effect of overtime hours with respect to the standard wage for the United States. This contrasting UK/US finding may be indicative of differences between regulated and unregulated markets with respect to overtime working. An increase in the standard wage rate in the United States may induce many workers to seek to forgo leisure in order to take advantage of a relatively high mandatory overtime premium of 1.5 times the standard rate.

---

[1] All three studies additionally report results of a probit model of the incidence of overtime working.
[2] Bell and Hart (1999) corroborate this result on another British data set, the Labour Force Survey (LFS).

100

The UK results indicate that standard weekly hours are negatively related to overtime. When combined with the standard wage findings, this may indicate an income effect on the supply side; thus, low standard earnings induce more overtime working thereby producing an offsetting increase in total weekly earnings. It may also reflect the demand-side effect emphasised in chapter 3. For given output, lower standard hours increase the cost of labour on the extensive margin (i.e. employment) relative to the intensive margin (overtime working) and thereby lead the firm to substitute in the direction of longer average overtime hours. This finding is not replicated in the German study. Here, it is found that standard hours relate positively to overtime hours. The effects are very small, however. Actually, this finding is at odds with another German study of overtime that uses the first wave of the GSOEP in 1984 (Hübler, 1989). Here, it is found that the probability of working overtime decreases with increasing standard hours.[3]

We also have micro evidence from Finland on the effects of standard wages and hours on overtime. Using individual-level manufacturing data from 1989 to 1995 – supplied by the Confederation of Finnish Industry – Böckerman (2002) obtains estimates that are in line with the above UK findings. Reductions in the standard wage and standard hours are found to exert a negative influence on overtime hours.

Collective agreements are significantly positively associated with overtime hours in the United Kingdom. Bell and Hart find that being covered by a collective bargaining agreement over pay and conditions increases by 4.5 percentage points the probability of an individual, with sample mean characteristics, working overtime. Coverage increases expected overtime working hours for those working overtime. For an individual with mean characteristics, coverage increases the conditional mean of weekly overtime by 30 minutes. The joint effect of coverage on overtime participation and overtime hours given participation is to increase unconditional mean overtime hours by just over 8 per cent. Of this latter figure, 70 per cent of the rise is accounted for by increased overtime among those workers working overtime. The finding of a positive association between collective bargaining agreements and overtime also holds in the United Kingdom between 'belonging to a union' and overtime. This is shown in Bell and Hart (1999) using the British Labour Force Survey (BLFS). However, these results are at odds with the US findings in table 5.1, where union coverage reduces overtime hours. Trejo finds that, at the sample means, unionisation lowers the conditional mean of weekly overtime by 5 per cent (25 minutes) and the unconditional mean – embracing union effects on participating in overtime and overtime hours given participation – by over 20 percent. Of the total effect, 78 per cent is accounted for by the union effect on overtime incidence.

As for establishment-level characteristics, Bauer and Zimmermann (1999) find in their German study that working for a small firm is associated with an overall increase of 10.7 per cent in overtime hours, and a 6.5 per cent increase among those already working overtime. Böckerman (2002) also reports a modest increase in overtime hours within smaller-sized Finnish establishments.

---

[3] In general, Hübler's paper finds that overtime effects are in line with the core predictions arising from labour demand analysis. Overtime is positively related to fixed non-wage labour costs and decreases in the wage rate and standard hours.

Table 5.1 *Determinants of overtime hours in Germany, the United Kingdom and the United States (Tobit equations)*

Variable	Germany (Bauer and Zimmermann, 1997) Coefficient (1)	Effect on Pr(p_h > 0) (2)	Effect on E(p_h | p_h > 0) (3)	United Kingdom (Bell and Hart, 2000) Coefficient (1)	Effect on Pr(p_h > 0) (2)	Effect on E(p_h | p_h > 0) (3)	United States (Trejo, 1993) Coefficient (1)	Effect on Pr(p_h > 0) (2)	Effect on E(p_h | p_h > 0) (3)
Standard hourly wage	–			-0.631* (0.034)	-0.024	-0.274	0.356* (0.095)	0.007	0.081
Standard weekly hours	0.034** (0.020)	0.002	0.013	-0.202* (0.022)	-0.008	-0.087	–		
Collective agreement	–			1.160* (0.228)	0.045	0.503	–		
Union coverage	–			–			-1.840** (0.845)	-0.035	-0.407
Skilled blue-collar	0.508* (0.189)	0.029	0.187	–			–		
Unskilled white-collar	1.860* (0.303)	0.108	0.686	–			–		
Skilled white-collar	2.572* (0.206)	0.149	0.949	–			–		
σ				9.933* (0.062)			14.997* (0.398)		

Additional explanatory variables			
Age	Yes	Yes	Yes
Education	Yes	No	Yes
Married	Yes	No	Yes
Industry and occupation	Yes	Yes	No
Other	Tenure, firm size, time trend, output growth	Private/public sectors, geographical regions	Ethnic; cities/regions
Log likelihood	−35,162.3	−61923.6	−5,292.2
Source; time period; reference group; sample size	GSOEP; pooled cross-sections 1984–97 (exc. 1987); male (non-civil servants); 17,332	NES; 1996; males (non-managerial, not self-employed); 24,621	Current Population Survey; 1985; individuals aged 18–61 (not self-employed and non-agricultural jobs; 4,429

Note:

* Statistically significant at the 0.01 level (two-tailed test); ** Statistically significant at the 0.05 level (two-tailed test).

5.2   Establishment-based studies of overtime

A major problem with household-based studies is that overtime decisions are primarily taken at the level of the establishment and not the individual. Paid overtime is largely a voluntary decision and the individual is usually offered the choice of whether or not to work additional, non-standard, hours. But this choice is conditional on the demand for such hours within the workplace. Individual-level data tell us little or nothing about workplace variables. These may have considerable bearing on working time arrangements in general and the use of overtime in particular. What type of products is the establishment producing? Does it employ batch- or flow-production methods? Is it a capital- or labour-intensive operation? What percentage of the workforce undertakes shift working? What percentage of the shop floor is unionised? Is it prone to lose working days due to absenteeism and/or sickness?

If an individual registers no overtime working within a household questionnaire, we usually have no information about demand constraints and this may lead to misleading inferences. Does this response signify a straightforward choice not to work overtime or does it result from the fact that overtime would have been undertaken but that overtime hours are not available? Unfortunately, questions on desired hours in most existing data sources are insufficiently detailed to allow us to find out if the individual would like to work overtime hours but is prevented from doing so because of demand constraints. Ideally, combined establishment-household data are needed to capture the full overtime decision. However, if it has to be an either/or choice then establishment-level information is to be preferred. This view is reinforced by the fact that policy questions involving overtime are dominated by demand-side labour market economics.

The limited amount of establishment-based empirical research on overtime working has been dominated by the question – uppermost within the European working time debates – of the effects of cuts in standard working time on the demand for workers and hours.[4] From the cost minimisation theory of labour demand (see pp. 51–3) we know that – if we have an interior solution with overtime – a cut in standard hours induces the firm to substitute more overtime hours for *less* employment. In general, of course, we may start with an interior solution involving short-time working or a corner solution where the maximum standard hours are undertaken.[5] In Europe, the corner solution and the interior solution with overtime cover the vast bulk of firms' experience. If a reduction in standard hours moves a firm from one corner solution to another then employment will *increase* since the working time reduction is binding. If the reduction is large enough to move the firm from a corner solution to an interior solution with overtime then the employment effect is ambiguous. The critical point is that the employment effects of a cut in the standard workweek are critically dependent on whether or not the firm initially works overtime. Consequently, at least as a first approximation, it becomes important to differentiate between overtime and non-overtime establishments.

[4] Additionally, establishment-level empirics have been directed on the question of the relative returns to workers and hours, as discussed in section 5.3.

[5] The full cost minimising problem is analysed by Brechling (1965), Calmfors and Hoel (1988), Andrews, Schank and Simmons (2002) and Bhattacharya, DeLeire and MaCurdy (2001).

Hart and Wilson (1988) investigate the foregoing issues based on estimated conditional factor demand schedules. Their data consist of a random sample of 52 UK metal working establishments for the years 1978–82. They are able to control for type of product, market conditions and market structure, production methods, the nature of the production process and technology as well as labour-related variables. Of the 52 establishments, 43 employed overtime in one or more years of the sample period and 9 employed none at all. Using the total sample, it is estimated that the elasticity of total average hours with respect to standard hours is about 0.8; a fall in standard hours produces a less than proportionate fall in total hours.[6] To the extent that firms are faced with a production constraint, this would suggest that overtime hours would rise to compensate for the loss in total hours. This is also confirmed in the estimation. By contrast, the effect of standard hours on employment is not well determined in the full sample. However, as argued above, establishments that work overtime would be expected to react differently to changes in standard hours from those that do not work overtime. Separate estimation on these two types of establishment was therefore undertaken. This yielded elasticities of employment with respect to standard hours of 0.41 among overtime firms and −0.49 among non-overtime firms. These findings are consistent with the underlying theory.

A limitation of the Hart and Wilson study is the imposed strict dichotomy between establishments working some and those working zero overtime.[7] A very important added dimension, as we have seen in the theoretical discussion in section 3.3, is to distinguish *within* establishments between non-overtime and overtime workers. The work of Andrews, Schank and Simmons (2002) and Schank (2001, 2003) develops this dimension along both theoretical and empirical lines. Their Establishment Panel Data Set provides information on 8,250 plants in the former West Germany for 1993 and 1995–9 and on 7,000 plants in the former East Germany since 1996.[8] The data permit demarcation among plants where (i) all employees work overtime, (ii) none works overtime and (iii) a proportion of employees works overtime.

These authors investigate the effects of cuts in standard hours via differenced workers-hours demand equations in order to remove scale effects associated with plant size. They also employ a logit model that decomposes plants into the foregoing three overtime regimes. They find that reductions in standard hours have no effect on employment in the West. In the East, there is a negative employment trade off in the agricultural/manufacturing sector; a 2-hour cut in standard hours is associated with an employment rise of about 4 per cent. On the hours side, reduced standard time appears to translate into reduced total hours with no offsetting overtime increase. Their key result, however, is new to the literature. They find, in line with labour demand theory, that standard hours are positively associated with the proportion of employees working overtime. A 10 per cent cut in standard hours is estimated to increase the number of purely standard time plants by roughly 5.5 with an equivalent

---

[6] This contradicts the standard cost minimising theory in which a fall in standard hours is predicted to increase average total hours – see the result in (3.15). This topic is further discussed in sections 3.2 and 3.3.

[7] Actually four establishments with extremely low overtime working were re-classified as non-overtime regimes, with no substantive effect on the overall results.

[8] The sampling frame of this work over represents large plants (more than 5,000 employees) so that while their survey covers 0.4 per cent of all German plants it represent 8 per cent of the workforce.

reduction in purely overtime plants. The estimated elasticity of demand for a standard time worker (overtime worker) with respect to a change in standard hours is −0.44 (0.43).

5.3   Returns to workers and hours

As we have seen in the demand analysis of chapter 3, optimising outcomes arising from model specifications are critically dependent on the relative sizes of the returns to workers and hours. The history of attempts to estimate the returns to these labour inputs has been long and chequered. The work has been dominated by aggregative (industry-or national-level) time-series studies, although more micro-based work has started to appear. A core issue derives from the fact that average per-period hours almost invariably include overtime at the margin.

The popular estimating equation is Cobb–Douglas which, for industry i at time t, may be expressed:

$$\ln Q_{it} = \alpha \ln N_{it} + \beta \ln h_{it} + \gamma \ln K_{it} + \delta \ln U_{Kit} + \text{other variables} \qquad (5.1)$$

where Q is output, N is employment, h is average hours, K is capital stock, U_K is capacity utilisation and where α, β, γ and δ are parameters. Other variables may include measures designed to account for cyclical and time variations. It is particularly necessary to capture these latter effects in the present context because of the strong possibility that estimated returns to hours may exaggerate 'true' returns because of firms' propensities to hoard labour during economic downturns.

Perhaps the most critical problem concerns the fact that the optimising equilibrium conditions from the underlying labour demand theory require $\alpha > \beta$. (See, for example, the discussion on p. 52 in respect of cost minimisation: this requirement also holds for profit maximisation.) Schank (2001) summarises results from nine studies devoted to estimating equations similar to (5.1). Returns to workers are found to be in the region of 0.7 while returns to hours exhibit wide fluctuations, between 0.64 and 1.92. A particularly influential early study is by Feldstein (1967) who obtains elasticities for workers and hours of 0.76 and 1.90, respectively. While attempting to estimate functions such as (5.1) is clearly superior to ignoring completely the hours' dimension, typical results are critically at odds with underlying workers-hours theoretical derivations.

As suggested by the range of the estimated returns to hours, findings of increasing returns are common. A major contributory factor in this respect has been the absence of a measure of capacity utilisation in estimating equations. *A priori*, we would expect that fluctuations in hours of work would be highly correlated with production volume per unit of time, which in turn reflects, for example, the intensity of the use of capital equipment, organisational efficiency and line speed. Omitting measurement of capacity utilisation may well serve to bias upwards the estimated returns to hours of work. Using West German data, Hart and McGregor (1988) have estimated a number of variations of (5.1) from the literature both with and without capacity utilisation and find that increasing returns occur when the utilisation variable is omitted.

Nevertheless, after correcting for capacity utilisation, Hart and McGregor still find in their full specification that, generally, the estimated returns to hours exceed those of workers. This is also the finding of the study of Anxo and Bingsten (1989), which also controls for capital stock and capacity utilisation, using data on 8 Swedish industries from 1980 to 1983. Only Ilmakunnas (1994), using Finnish data on 5 industries between 1968 and 1986, has found returns to workers (at 0.73) to exceed returns to hours (at 0.60) with this extended production specification. The stubbornness of the higher-returns-to-hours-than-workers outcome has increasingly been taken to signify a fundamental weakness in the underlying demand theory. Fortunately for demand-side work, it has recently been shown that aggregation bias may well provide an explanation of this 'wrong' direction of relative returns.

There has been a general failure to differentiate among industries – let alone establishments – when formulating the production process. Estimation has been carried out 'as if' all industries face a common set of production relationships. Returns to hours of work are unlikely to be independent of technological and organisational make-up of the type of firms that predominate in given industrial aggregates. For example, we know from standard demand theory that firms with relatively high *per capita* specific investments are likely to require workers to undertake relatively long per-period hours. Higher fixed costs associated with such investments induce more intensive utilisation of the labour input. Generalising, firms with higher factor fixity will tend to utilise their factors of production more intensively. Now, if firms with relatively high specific investments expend more resources on improving the efficient organisation of their hours' schedules then returns to hours in (5.1) may simply reflect such inter-firm differences. Indeed, Leslie and Wise (1980) conjecture that firms with longer hours tend to be more efficient. Based on a study of 28 British industries they 'remove' these productivity effects by incorporating dummies and different time trends for each industry. They estimate returns to hours of 0.64, the lower bound of the range quoted above. In fact, estimated hours' returns are identical to worker returns in this study.

What is the nature of the aggregation bias under the Leslie and Wise conjecture? DeBeaumont and Singell (1999) have explored this issue in more detail. Imagine two firms in different industries with fixed worker and capital stocks. They face the same exogenously imposed real wage and profit maximisation occurs where the wage equals the marginal product of an hour. Suppose, as illustrated in figure 5.1, that average and marginal product are higher in Firm 2 than in Firm 1. Accordingly, Firm 2 demands higher average hours than Firm 1, or $h_2 > h_1$. Fitting a common production function to Q_i, h_i combinations would produce a regression line that exceeds the actual returns to hours in each of the two firms. Moreover, removing the fixed effects represented by the difference in the firms' intercepts would be insufficient to eliminate the source of the bias, given the assumed differences in marginal product (i.e. slopes) at the optimal points.

Controlling for capital stock and cyclical factors as well as for state or sub-industry fixed effects, DeBeaumont and Singell (1999) estimate (two-digit) industry-by-industry estimates of (5.1). They use two US manufacturing data sets relating to industry-specific data by state for 1972–8 and four-digit industry data from 1958 to 1994. Estimates from both are consistent. In general, they reveal returns to hours that are less than unity and which

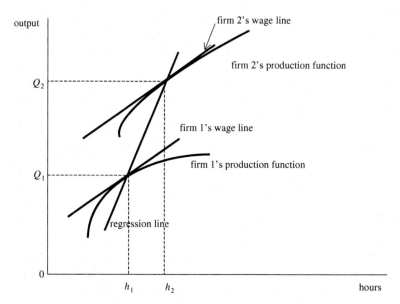

Figure 5.1   Aggregation bias and returns to hours
(*Source:* DeBeaumont and Singell (1999).

are less than returns to workers. When they impose a common production structure on their data – a constraint common to much of the earlier work – estimated returns to hours are in excess of unity and exceed (in two out of three versions tested) returns to workers.

The work by Leslie and Wise and by DeBeaumont and Singell is apparently reassuring for the standard theory of labour demand. Relaxing the heroic assumption of a common production structure across sectors, industry-by-industry estimation produces outcomes that are largely supportive of returns to workers being in excess of returns to average hours. However, these studies are by no means the final word on this topic. While pointing researchers in a potentially rewarding direction, they continue to provide highly aggregative, industry-level, estimates. The work on German establishments of Schank (2001, 2003), at the establishment level, underlines the need to exercise extreme caution. Here, returns to workers and hours are estimated after differentiating between establishments that do and do not work overtime. It is quite apparent that accounting for unobserved plant characteristics is an important consideration, with a differenced version of (5.1) being the preferred specification. Returns to workers are found to be in the order of 0.25 in standard time plants and 0.46 for overtime plants. However, returns to hours in both types of plant are largely found to be insignificant.

The driving force behind the DeBeaumont and Singell explanation of typical estimates of relative returns is the conjecture that hourly productivity is greater in firms with longer average hours. It would seem reasonable to surmise that such firms are more likely to work overtime. Might this suggest higher returns to overtime hours compared to standard hours? At least, the question arises as to whether the returns to overtime hours are necessarily the same as those to standard hours. In an attempt to investigate this issue, Hart and McGregor (1988) propose the following labour services function:

$$L = N^{\alpha}[h_s + \lambda v]^{\beta} \tag{5.2}$$

where $v = h - h_s$ and λ – a parameter that converts overtime hours into standard hour equivalents – represents the relative productivity of an overtime hour.[9] If $\lambda = 1$, the two types of hours are equally productive while if $\lambda > 1$ ($\lambda < 1$), overtime hours are more (less) productive than standard hours.

Hart and McGregor's West German estimates of (5.1), incorporating (5.2) as the specification of the labour input, proved to be disappointing. The estimated λ is insignificant while the scaling term, β, does not deviate significantly from the coefficient on average total hours in the straightforward estimation of (5.1). Either overtime hours play no productive role or they are completely obscured by a very close correlation with capacity utilisation. Ilmakunnas (1994) attempts to overcome this latter possibility by combining the capital stock and capacity utilisation variables in (5.1) to form $K.U_K$ in his Finnish data set. Returns to workers (0.73) are found to exceed returns to hours, with returns to overtime hours (0.69) being slightly greater than those to standard hours (0.59).

5.4 Dynamic adjustment and job-match effects

In traditional time-series analyses of hours of work, overtime is viewed as offering firms the ability to effect relatively speedy labour responses to unforeseen short-run product demand fluctuations. Not only can overtime hours offer a direct labour reaction to given shocks but may additionally provide a temporary buffer against the problem of relative sluggishness of employment and capital responses (e.g. Nadiri and Rosen, 1973; Nakamura, 1993). For example, a firm may require considerable time to recruit, hire and train appropriate labour to meet an unexpected increase in sales but may, in the meantime, meet demand through existing workers undertaking more overtime. Of course, overtime may not offer the only short-run adjustment response. For example, a firm may be able to weigh up the relative costs of changing overtime and changing inventories above or below planned levels (Topel, 1982). Overtime working has also featured prominently in dynamic general equilibrium models of the real business cycle (Hansen and Sargent, 1988; Hall, 1996). This work focuses on the role of overtime in helping firms adjust to output shocks in the face of labour market rigidities.

Understanding the dynamic adjustment of overtime hours involves a potential major complication, however. Sections 3.7 and 4.2 highlight another role of overtime that derives from the ideas of Lewis (1969a). This emphasises the joint determination of wages and hours that within long-run contractual agreements. Suppose that a US firm negotiates wage earnings under such a contract that involves relatively long daily hours. Since the maximum length of standard weekly hours is mandated, the contract may well involve a permanent

---

[9] If we incorporate the labour services function (5.2) into the cost minimisation framework of section 5.3, then the second-order condition requires that $\beta < \alpha$.

element of overtime working. Moreover, such overtime may not be affected by changes in the overtime premium, the minimum level of which is also mandated, since the parties can agree to adjust the standard wage rate so as to leave contractual earning intact (Trejo, 1991). Bell and Hart (2003a) extend these ideas to a British context, where no overtime regulation applies. As discussed in section 4.2, overtime premia are seen as being determined largely by custom and practice. For many non-management/professional workers, labour market competition produces fairly constant average hourly wages among overtime workers. For example, firms with a tradition of paying high premiums offset these with low standard wage rates while low premiums and high standard rates coexist in other firms. Workers have some control of weekly earnings, however. They can select into long- or short-hours jobs, depending on supply-side preferences.

It may well be the case, therefore, that overtime working involves significant job-match effects. In the absence of appropriate estimation of dynamic overtime equations, such effects would serve to obfuscate estimates of adjustment speeds. Based on British NESPD, Bell and Hart (2003b) investigate this problem for the period 1990–6. Their estimating equation is given by

$$v_{it} = c_t + \alpha v_{i,t-1} + \beta \mathbf{x_{it}} + (\lambda_i + \varepsilon_{it}) \tag{5.3}$$

where, for individual i at time t, v_{it} is weekly overtime hours, c_t is a year-specific intercept to account for common cyclical or trend components, $v_{i,t-1}$ is the overtime observation on the same individual in the previous period, x_{it} is a vector of current and lagged values of additional explanatory variables, α and β are constants, λ_i is an unobserved job-match effect and ε_{it} is a disturbance term. The length of weekly standard hours, the lagged standard hourly wage rate and industry dummies are included in x. This hours specification nests a traditional demand-side model of hours determination where the coefficient α is taken to measure the speed of response of actual to desired hours input.

If there are job-match effects in overtime then OLS estimates of (5.3) will be inconsistent because of their correlation with lagged overtime. In fact, the estimates are likely to be upward biased due to the omitted variable problem. In turn, this would produce an underestimation of the speed of adjustment of overtime hours. This is captured by the estimate of α.

Bell and Hart (2003b) construct a test to determine that such job-match effects are important in the context of this dynamic panel model.[10] They also investigate the implications for adjustment speed of incorporating an estimator that tackles the above econometric problem. The methodology is detailed in Arellano and Bond (1991) and Arellano and Bover (1995) and incorporates the Generalised Method of Moments (GMM) estimator (Hansen, 1982).

Estimation is based on between 26,000 and 45,000 full-time males over the period 1990–6. These years cover a recession at the beginning of the 1990s followed by a period of sustained growth. Therefore, the influence of changes in product demand emanating from business cycle fluctuations is by no means suppressed over this sample period. The OLS

---

[10] The joint significance of the individual effects is examined via a test of the null hypothesis var$(\lambda_i) = 0$ against the alternative var$(\lambda_i) > 0$.

estimate of the coefficient on lagged overtime is 0.48. This implies that only 52 per cent of desired changes in overtime hours are undertaken within a 1-year period. It is difficult to envisage why firms are able to achieve only such modest intensive margin reaction. However, OLS would tend to underestimate this adjustment speed because it is confounding job-match effects with adjustment processes. These effects are fixed components of individuals' habitual working time patterns. They are integral to the job match and not conditioned by demand-side shocks. The GMM method, by contrast, yields an estimate of 0.07 on lagged overtime. Much more realistically, this implies a 93 per cent annual adjustment of overtime towards the desired levels. The test for individual effects is significant at the 20 per cent level.

5.5 Actual and desired hours

In many instances, workers will not be in a position to match exactly their preferred numbers of weekly hours with the actual number they are contracted to work. Constraints stemming from such considerations as work organisation, production scheduling, inter-company trading and just-in-time (JIT) delivery may lead to gaps between actual and desired hours of work. Might we expect overtime workers to experience different gaps from non-overtime workers?

One consideration relates to the discussion in section 4.5. Suppose that the average hourly wage of overtime workers is equal to marginal product but with overtime hours above and standard hours below marginal product. Non-overtime workers receive hourly pay equal to marginal product. *Ceteris paribus*, we might expect that overtime workers would desire to work longer hours given advantageous marginal rates. Non-overtime workers, by contrast, would be more content with their actual hours. But we have also seen, in relation to figure 4.1 (p. 87), that relatively large proportions of employees who work long overtime hours receive relatively low premia. Given the combination of high social costs and low hourly pay, we would not be surprised to observe overtime working expressing concern about actual hours.

Using the German GSOEP, Hunt (1998) casts some light on the relationship between actual and desired hours of workers by length of weekly hours for Germany. British evidence in respect of workers who report that they work overtime, at least occasionally, or who never work overtime can be obtained from the BHPS.

Results are reported in table 5.2. Among those workers whose hours preferences were recorded in the 1997 BHPS, most were clearly satisfied that actual and desired hours were more or less in line. The most satisfied in this respect were males who worked no overtime. Two-thirds of these reported no desired change, this compared with around 55 per cent of males working overtime. Among this latter group there was a higher proportion expressing the wish to work fewer hours. Note that this relatively strong desire to work fewer hours is even more marked among female overtime workers. While much smaller proportions of males and females indicate a wish to work more hours, there is no great difference in this direction between overtime and non-overtime workers. Hunt's data, for the years 1985 and 1994, distinguish among ranges of weekly hours rather than by overtime or no overtime.

Table 5.2 *Proportions of British and German workers desiring to work more/same/less than their actual working hours*

	Year	More	Same	Less	Sample size
British (BHPS)					
Males (zero overtime)	1997				
Manufacturing		8.5	62.8	28.6	234
Non-manufacturing		4.7	64.5	30.8	234
Service		6.4	66.3	27.3	267
Males (overtime)	1997				
Manufacturing		4.3	53.0	42.6	462
Non-manufacturing		7.2	58.0	34.8	362
Service		5.4	54.6	40.1	392
Females (zero overtime)	1997				
Manufacturing		4.2	57.1	38.7	119
Non-manufacturing		6.8	59.6	33.6	146
Service		3.2	56.1	40.7	408
Females (overtime)	1997				
Manufacturing		1.7	47.7	50.5	107
Non-manufacturing		7.0	47.9	45.1	142
Service		2.8	48.6	48.6	428
German (GSOEP[a])					
Less than 40 hours	1985	64.2	14.1	21.8	187
	1994	28.8	39.0	32.2	517
Exactly 40 hours	1985	6.0	69.7	24.3	749
	1994	3.7	55.5	40.9	227
More than 40 hours	1985	7.4	6.1	86.5	428
	1994	6.2	8.2	85.6	200

Note:
[a] GSOEP results are taken from Hunt (1998).

For those workers on relatively short workweeks (less than 40 hours) there is a considerable expression of support for more hours, especially in the earlier period. By contrast, among those working more than 40 hours, around 86 per cent of respondents indicate a desire to work fewer hours in both periods. As with the British data, relatively modest percentages of workers working 40 hours or more would like their working hours to be increased.

During Hunt's time frame, German standard, or contractual, hours were reduced (see figure 2.10, p. 27). Hunt proceeds to run fixed-effects regressions – incorporating firm size and industry dummies – to ascertain the impact of these reductions on the gap between actual hours and desired hours. A 1-hour reduction in standard hours on the absolute value of the difference is found to bring hourly paid manufacturing workers 0.25 hours nearer to their desired hours and hourly paid service workers 0.63 hours nearer.

We should be wary of making detailed inferences from these rather general, and largely uncontrolled, observations. However, the data do point to significantly less satisfaction with actual hours among overtime than non-overtime workers in both countries. This may detract to some extent from the wage-hours compensating differential model in which firms and workers are assumed to reach agreement over preferred lengths of per-period hours. Of course, we would anticipate many exceptions to hours' agreements formulated along these lines. We would not expect, perhaps, such large and systematic differences in actual/desired hours relationships as between workers holding relatively short jobs (non-overtime workers) and those holding relatively long jobs (overtime workers).

5.6 Returns to unpaid overtime

Empirical work on the phenomenon of unpaid overtime is a subject in its infancy. The emerging view is that we should be careful to distinguish between short-term and long-term reasons for individuals reporting to work such hours. We have seen in section 2.7 that the incidence of unpaid overtime is most marked among managers and professional workers. In the short run, a manager may feel the need to work unpaid overtime due to the nature of her/his labour market role. Suppose, for example, that an individual is managing a team of workers and that the team's progress in a given project is unexpectedly delayed compared to planned execution times. This may arise because of absence due to illness or an unexpected complexity of job tasks or lower than anticipated productivity potential among team members. The manager may feel that in order to help regain planned scheduling, she/he must personally provide extra hours of work. If these hours were greater than the contractual norm, then the manager would report working unpaid overtime hours.

But is this really unpaid work? It certainly would be in a short-run context. But what about the long run? Providing extra time to tackle unforeseen problems may be regarded favourably by the manager's peers. Such attitude to leadership and responsibility may be rewarded at some stage in the future by accelerated promotion and/or a higher than average growth in compensation. The manager's motivation for providing short-term unpaid working time may be the perceived potential for future improved job returns.

Pannenberg (2002) has cast most light to date on the longer-term earnings effects of working unpaid overtime. This German study uses data on full-time job stayers taken from GSOEP for the years 1988–2002. The descriptive, unconditioned, statistics reveal that workers who reported undertaking some unpaid overtime experienced the highest median wage growth over a 10-year period. In fact, it is estimated that those working unpaid overtime realised a real earnings increase that is at least 10 per cent higher than other types of worker. Two panel models of real monthly earnings growth[11] appear to corroborate these initial findings. For male job stayers, it is found that a once and for all increase of 1 weekly hour in unpaid work associates with a 2 per cent increase in real hourly earnings. Results for females are less certain due to a lack of robustness when unobserved individual characteristics on earnings growth are taken into account.

So, the returns to working 'unpaid' overtime hours may well be in the form of delayed compensation. Are other types of return linked to unpaid overtime? Several possibilities arise.

[11] The first is a fixed-effects model while the second additionally attempts to account for individual characteristics influencing the wage level and also the rate of earnings growth.

In the first place, high fliers may attempt to gain relatively scarce senior positions in a company by displaying work commitment and effort. It is perhaps easier to be noticed by one's peers through providing extra hours of work than by exerting more effort and application per hour. Undertaking extra hours for no pay is a particularly 'visible' signal. Bell *et al.* (2000) test the link between promotion and unpaid work for Germany (using GSOEP) and the United Kingdom (using BHPS). Despite testing a range of promotion measures, no association was found in the case of German workers. For the United Kingdom, the BHPS asks respondents to rank their perceived promotion prospects. Using a Logit model, controlling for a range of other possible influences on promotion, a significant positive association between unpaid overtime and anticipated promotion prospects is found.

Another return to unpaid overtime may occur at the other end of the ability spectrum. Less-productive workers may price themselves into jobs by their willingness to work beyond contractual hours. Suppose that the firm is indifferent to the hours that workers spend in the execution of job tasks. For simplicity, suppose that jobs are described by the estimated length of time to completion. These jobs are allocated by means of an auction in which workers make bids to undertake the prescribed work. Less-productive workers might win the auctions if they 'overbid' on time by providing additional unpaid hours. In effect, such hours serve to adjust the hourly pay of 'standard' productive workers into the pay of less-productive workers. In their cross-sectional study of unpaid overtime using the British Labour Force Survey (LFS), Bell and Hart (1999) proxy productivity by the deviation of an individual's standard hourly wage from the mean occupational wage. Their Tobit estimates reveal significant negative associations with unpaid hours.

Unpaid overtime may relate not so much to an attempt *a priori* to realise a better wage or to achieve a job promotion but rather a means of recognising the existence of already high returns in the form of existing favourable work conditions. The notion of 'gift exchange' would seem apposite in this respect. The value of the gift from the firm is the margin between the actual wage and the outside wage. The worker's gift is 'work in excess of the minimum standard' (Akerlof, 1982, p. 544). This may take the form of additional hours – i.e. in excess of contractual hours – without any change in work intensity.[12] Again, this would require that employers were indifferent to the number of hours actually worked. In this event, we might anticipate strong positive associations between standard wage rates and unpaid work and between job satisfaction and unpaid work. Firms that compensate well and/or provide attractive working environments, *ceteris paribus*, are likely to receive more unpaid work as a gift response from their workers. Using the GSOEP and BHPS panels over the period 1991–8 for West Germany and Britain, respectively, Pannenberg and Wagner (2001) estimate probit equations where the dependent variable is a 'satisfied' or 'otherwise' dummy. Workers are classified by their positions on the earnings distribution. Results are particularly strong in the case of Britain. No matter where placed on the distribution, individuals who report working persistent unpaid overtime are more satisfied overall than are those reporting

---

[12] The efficiency wage literature has usually interpreted the worker's gift as taking the form of a higher level of per-hour productivity. This may not always be possible, however. Such features as capital constraints on production flow and dependence on interactive inputs within work teams may serve to limit responses along these lines.

no overtime. Interestingly, at the lower end of the distribution, unpaid overtime appears to be associated with more job satisfaction than paid overtime.

What if workers' remuneration is tied up, at least in part, with company performance? A well-known rationale for linking pay to performance is to induce greater productive effort. On the downside, however, it may be prohibitively costly to monitor hourly effort (Alchian and Demsetz, 1972). Work organisation permitting, one way round this problem may be to improve transparency by measuring effort in terms of numbers of hours spent in the workplace each day rather than work rate per hour. At least, partially, this could act to counter the free-rider problem. In other words, if work groups operate in a culture where long hours – both paid and unpaid – become the norm then monitoring costs are reduced since enhanced performance is more visible. Both the GSOEP and the BHPS record whether or not an individual receives a part of total compensation in the form profit related pay and/or a performance bonus. For both Germany and the United Kingdom, Bell *et al.* (2000) tested equations that related profit sharing to previous commitments to undertake unpaid work. No associations were found between profit-related pay and unpaid work in the United Kingdom. For Germany, however, there is reasonably strong evidence to support a link.

5.7 Summary

At various stages throughout this text, we have emphasised the necessity of embracing the employer's participation in the overtime decision. Certainly this orientation is contained within the bulk of the theoretical work on which core policy debates have been conducted. Yet, there is a dearth of empirical research into the determination of overtime hours that makes use of establishment-based data. It is clear that, where micro-level establishment data have been looked at, an extended range of overtime-related questions opens up, leading to the formation of new theory and policy. At the forefront has been the recent emphasis on the need to separate non-overtime and overtime workers within the same establishment. As we have seen in earlier chapters, this dichotomy has important consequences for demand-side modelling as well as for models that emphasise the need to accommodate both demand- and supply-side preferences over the choice of job lengths.

The development of establishment-based studies to examine the relative returns to workers and hours should also be a highly fruitful avenue to explore. After numerous aggregate level papers on this subject – usually finding far higher returns to hours than to workers – the work of DeBeaumont and Singell (1999) shows that separating industries in the estimation of returns is the way to proceed. This work has provided a serious challenge over whether earlier studies found the correct direction of relative returns. It has also offered good news to demand theorists who have often relied on the outcome of higher returns to workers than to hours. Clearly, the logic of this work is to proceed further down the firm-level disaggregation.

As indicated in chapter 1, important time-series modelling of overtime hours – or, at least, total hours including overtime – has derived from interrelated factor demand models, and especially those models that have concentrated on short-term adjustments in input factors. Interestingly, overtime research that has developed along very different lines has potentially important implications for empirical investigations into the dynamic time-series behaviour of the overtime variable. If firms and workers have long-term preferences with respect to the per-period length of working hours then overtime is likely to contain strong elements of fixed job-match effects. To the extent that these are significant, then accounting for them econometrically has implications for the estimation of the speed of overtime adjustment. Recent work would suggest that these effects are indeed quantitatively important.

So, econometric results with respect to the dynamic micro behaviour of overtime hours perhaps give indirect support to theoretical approaches such as the workers-hours compensation model that emphasises the importance of fixed effects in overtime due to mutually agreed length of hours. To the extent that such agreements are prevalent, we would not expect to observe systematic differences in actual-desired hours gaps between overtime and non-overtime workers. Yet, at least for Germany and the United Kingdom, there is evidence that overtime workers are generally less satisfied with their actual hours of work than non-overtime workers, with an overwhelming majority wishing to work for fewer hours. Of course, this may simply mean that long-term contractual hours' agreements give a less than complete picture – a view that is supported in the policy literature (see section 7.1).

The most recent area of research activity into overtime hours has concerned the claim by many professional and managerial workers that they provide extra daily or weekly hours for no pay. Instinctively, labour economists would query the concept of working for nothing. Therefore, it is almost inevitable that early work has concentrated on the distinction between the short-term activity of providing extra hours for no pay and the longer-term returns to this 'sacrifice'. Early work would suggest that 'unpaid' overtime is in fact paid for in the form of *deferred compensation*.

6 Overtime pay and empirical studies

Interest in the pay aspect of overtime working stems largely from the fact that hourly wage rates that attach to overtime hours typically differ from standard rates. Most of the overtime wage literature has concerned itself with overtime rates that, due to a payment of an overtime premium, are in excess of standard rates. We have seen, however, that some workers receive lower-than-standard rates for overtime work while others claim to work overtime hours at a zero rate.

Three variables determine the relative importance of overtime pay within the firm's total payroll. The first is the average number of overtime hours employed by the firm. The second is the size of the hourly premium – or premia if the premium varies with the length of weekly hours – relative to the standard hourly wage rate. The third is the proportion of the firm's employees who are classified as overtime workers. The topic of wage earnings decomposition is clearly central to issues of overtime pay (see section 2.6) and we return briefly to it in section 6.1. This section also contains a discussion on the difficulties over interpreting the roles of wage rates and wage earnings in time-series analysis.

An unanticipated increase in the firm's product demand might be expected to impact positively on one or more of these three variables. This is especially likely if adjustment impediments were to prevent speedy responses in labour and capital stock. In turn, given premium payments, this would have implications for marginal wages and marginal employment costs. This sort of reasoning has led to overtime pay featuring prominently in the study of the cyclicality of wages. The topic of cyclicality also dominates our discussion of wages in relation to overtime pay. It embraces empirical studies carried out at three levels of aggregation – (i) individual, (ii) regional or local labour markets, (iii) industry or national. These three aggregates are discussed, respectively, in section 6.2, section 6.3, and section 6.4.

Overtime has also featured importantly in the literature on the behaviour of marginal cost and price over the business cycle. Not only do overtime payments comprise an important part of firms' total labour cost but also, as we have seen elsewhere, overtime itself may be more prone to vary with the cycle than many other cost elements. This topic is discussed in section 6.4.

In most studies of wage behaviour over the business cycle, the cycle itself is typically proxied by a single economic variable. The favourite choices relate either to output- or unemployment-based indicators. Yet different component parts of average earnings may respond to cycles of different lengths and timings. In this event, the use of a single cyclical representation would produce misleading results of comparative responsiveness across the components. In fact, there is no reason why a single component should not itself relate to more than one length of cycle. In section 6.5, we report on findings based on the analysis of the frequency domain of wage variables – rather than conventional time-series analysis – that allows us to unravel different, possibly multiple, cyclical influences on wage components.

If an overtime premium is paid, working longer daily or weekly paid-for overtime hours serves, *ceteris paribus*, to increase average hourly pay. If marginal overtime hours are undertaken for no pay, then longer hours will depress the hourly wage. We know from section 2.7 that there is a highly uneven incidence of unpaid hours of work; it is most prevalent among managerial and professional workers and – as a clearly associated variable – persons with a graduate education. One implication of these observations, which we explore in section 6.6, is that shapes of wage-experience profiles of these groups may be revised if actually hourly pay, including unpaid overtime, is considered to be the relevant remuneration variable.

6.1 Wage earnings or wage rates?

Average hourly wage earnings include both standard and overtime rates of pay. Hourly wage rates refer only to remuneration for standard hours. In empirical work on wage determination, the question often arises as to which measure it is more appropriate to adopt (see the discussion in Abraham and Haltiwanger, 1995). Unfortunately, as we now discuss, the answer is not straightforward. A useful backdrop to this discussion is to return to the topic of wage earnings decomposition (see section 2.6).

Suppose that an individual works h weekly hours, of which h_s are standard hours remunerated at the hourly standard wage, w. If $h > h_s$ then $(h - h_s)$ defines weekly overtime. Let overtime hours be remunerated at a fixed premium, $\overline{k}$ (where $\overline{k} > 1$) so that the hourly overtime rate of pay is $\overline{k}w$. If $h = h_s$ then the worker is employed for maximum standard hours, or for short-time hours, and all hours are compensated at w. Expressing an individual's average hourly earnings, e, as a geometric average, we have

$$e = w^\theta (\overline{k}w)^{(1-\theta)} \tag{6.1}$$

where $\theta = h_s/h$. Taking logs and re-arranging gives

$$\ln e = \ln w + (1 - \theta) \ln \overline{k}. \tag{6.2}$$

Earnings decompose into the standard wage rate, the proportion of weekly hours devoted to overtime and the overtime premium. If no overtime is undertaken, so that $\theta = 1$, e and w are the same.

Differentiating (6.2) with respect to time, we obtain

$$\frac{1}{e}\frac{de}{dt} = \frac{1}{w}\frac{dw}{dt} - k\frac{d\theta}{dt}. \tag{6.3}$$

So, proportional rates of changes in wage earnings and the standard wage are the same if the ratio of standard to total hours is constant through time. In general, however, changes in both w and θ influence changes in e. Clearly, *wage earnings can rise even if both the standard wage rate and the overtime premium remain constant.* Such a rise can occur because a higher proportion of total working time per week consists of (more expensive) overtime hours.[1]

Suppose that our main interest is to analyse the behaviour of the hourly wage over the business cycle. We might expect that *both* w and θ would display procyclical variations. This implies that, empirically, the cyclical behaviour of e is likely to differ from that of w. What if we want to confine our attention to the cyclical behaviour of the price of labour services? Then, maybe we might feel inclined to concentrate on analysing the movements of w rather than e since the latter variable also captures hours effects via the behaviour of θ. Unfortunately, this w or e choice is not so straightforward.

It may well be argued on the basis of (6.3) that using wage earnings as the basis for measuring pay cyclicality can lead to misleading outcomes because the measure of the wage is not independent of the length of working hours. However, Devereux (2001) raises an important point that relates to the Lewis model, discussed in chapters 1 and 3 (see section 3.7) and elsewhere.

For illustrative purposes, let us concentrate on an economy like that of the United States with mandatory overtime rules imposed on the remuneration and timing of overtime hours. Following the earlier discussion in section 3.7, suppose that overtime is worked in longer-hours' jobs because marginal contractual hours per period happen to be in excess of maximum mandated standard hours. The standard wage acts as a compensating differential to take account of job length. In this event, the average hourly wage measure should include overtime since using the base wage alone would inadequately represent the agreed *average* hourly wage settlement. In effect, the standard hourly wage would underestimate the utility derived from the actual contracted average hourly rate of pay since the latter embraces overtime hours and remuneration. But another interpretation of the determination of overtime hours would lead to different conclusions. What if the overtime premium represents a compensating differential to account for the unsocial effects of working long hours? Then the overtime component of hourly pay does not represent increased utility and so it would not matter if the standard hourly wage were used as the basis of analysis.

So we seem to be reduced to the question of whether the Lewis-type interpretation of average pay or the disutility-correcting explanation of the premium offer the principal explanation. This in itself is a very difficult issue to determine but, unfortunately, the problem is not confined to identifying the relative strengths of these two views. Compensation for unsocial hours may not be confined to the payment of an overtime premium. It may also be

---

[1] Abowd and Card (1989) are also interested in wage rate, earnings and hours distinctions in their analysis of the behaviour of the life-cycle labour supply model.

reflected in higher standard hourly wages or better fringe benefits, or both. Thus, the level of standard hourly pay may indirectly reflect the length of overtime working. Again, this would seem to suggest that hourly earnings rather than hourly standard rates should generally be taken as the basis of analysis. We have some evidence on this sort of possibility. Overtime linked to unsocial hours implicitly refers to mandatory rather than voluntary overtime within the firm. In some firms, the requirement to work regular overtime is signalled as part of the employment contract. For example, Ehrenberg and Schumann (1984) report that 16 per cent of individuals in the 1977 Michigan Quality of Employment Survey declared that overtime working was a mandatory workplace requirement, set unilaterally by the employer. Yet, these authors find no supporting empirical evidence that the standard wage acts to compensate such workers for this enforced activity.

From the foregoing arguments, it may seem to be appropriate to use average hourly earnings as the basis of empirical wage investigations. However, returning to (6.3), if average hours rise due to product demand effects and there is no offsetting compensation in the standard wage or the premium then – given a fixed production constraint – the average hourly wage would rise as a strict consequence of the hours effect. Now, it may be the case that sophisticated union leaders, or suppliers of labour in general, may understand that these hours' repercussions will indirectly benefit hourly wages if marginal premium rates apply. This has echoes of the subject of approximately efficient contracts discussed on pp. 84–6. But, more generally, there is a reasonably persuasive argument that in order to capture the effect of economic events on the unit price of labour services the standard wage should be adopted as the dependent variable.

It is extremely difficult, therefore, to come down on one side or the other regarding the appropriate wage measure to adopt. The pragmatic approach is to carry out estimation using both wage rates and wage earnings. If results differ radically then it may well be worth investigating more deeply the reasons for the disparity.

6.2 Longitudinal micro studies

The first insight into the potential importance of overtime working in the study of wage determination relates to US wage determination work based on longitudinal micro data (see, especially Bils, 1985; Solon, Barsky and Parker, 1994). A prime objective in these studies is to investigate wage cyclicality using unbalanced individual-based panels. Typically, micro studies differentiate between job stayers and job movers. Solon, Barsky and Parker (1994) develop a statistical model of real wage change. The real wage is expressed as a function of a quadratic time trend, the deviation of the unemployment rate from its own quadratic trend, individual fixed effects, a cubic in workers' years of work experience and the interaction of experience and fixed effects. First differencing removes the influence of individual (and company) heterogeneity. For individual i in job j at time t, the differenced within-job estimating equation (i.e. *job stayers*) is given by

$$\Delta \log w_{ijt} = \alpha_0 + \alpha_1 X_{ijt} + \alpha_2 T_{ijt} + \alpha_3 \Delta U_t + \alpha_4 Year_t + v_i + \varepsilon_{ijt} \qquad (6.4)$$

where w_{ijt} is the real hourly wage rate, X_{ijt} (T_{ijt}) is a cubic in labour market experience (job tenure), U_t is the national unemployment rate, v_i is an error that represents persistent differences in rates of growth across individuals and ε_{ijt} is a random error term.[2]

The types of models represented by (6.4) reveal that wage cyclicality, as represented by wage-unemployment interactions, is considerably greater than previously found in aggregate macro studies. A typical finding is that a one-point increase in the rate of unemployment is associated with a 1 per cent decrease in the wage.[3]

How does overtime enter this picture? Following the discussion of section 6.1, an issue might arise if the wage measure refers to real hourly earnings (including overtime) as opposed to real hourly standard wages. This issue is investigated by Devereux (2001) on the basis of a regression equation similar to (6.4) and using the Panel Study of Income Dynamics (PSID) from 1970 to 1991. Since overtime is pro-cyclical (Bils, 1985) and since overtime hours in the United States command a premium of 1.5 times the standard rate, then we would expect *a priori* that hourly wage rates would be less procyclical than the hourly earnings. For hourly paid workers, Devereux produces very different estimates for the hourly wage and for hourly wage earnings. The former is found to be virtually acyclical while the latter is highly procyclical. In fact, the estimated coefficient on the change in the unemployment rate is 10 times larger when hourly earnings replace the hourly wage. A one-point decrease in unemployment is associated with 1.1 per cent increase in hourly earnings but only a 0.1 per cent increase in the hourly wage. An implied role of overtime is given in Devereux's summary that the evidence points to 'a response to the business cycle that involves adjustments in hours worked at relatively constant hourly wages'. In further regressions using salaried workers, Devereux concludes that bonus and overtime payments are the main source of wage procyclicality, rather than variations in salaries themselves.

British longitudinal data does not produce the same stark differences between w and e results. Hart (2003b) estimates a version of (6.4) for job stayers using the NESPD between 1980 and 2001. These data allow us to distinguish between non-overtime and overtime workers. It is found that a one-point increase in unemployment is associated with a 1.2 per cent fall in the standard real hourly wage of non-overtime workers as well as in average real hourly earnings of overtime workers. Further, it is found that the cyclicality of the standard wage of non-overtime workers is slightly greater than that of overtime workers. Very tentatively this may point to the possibility that, as a compensating differential for the larger cyclical variability of overtime pay, overtime workers receive more stable basic wage payments. This study is also able to measure the cyclicality of the average overtime premium as given by (2.2) (p. 30). For example, if workers receive multiple

---

[2] Solon, Barsky and Parker (1994) recognise that there is a potential problem of regressing individual-level wages on single annual rates of unemployment. They adopt a two-step estimation method to get round the problem that this is likely to result in OLS underestimating the standard errors (Moulton, 1986).

[3] Findings of relatively strong wage cyclicality in micro studies contrast markedly with findings of weak procyclical, or acyclical, wages in more aggregated studies. See Abraham and Haltiwanger (1995) for a review. This work also deals indirectly with the role of overtime through its distinctions between wage earnings and wage rates.

wage premiums that vary with the length of the working week – for example, weekday, Saturday and Sunday rates – then the average premium may be expected to be procyclical in line with weekly hours. However, the evidence points firmly to an acyclical average premium.

6.3   Regional wage curves

Another application of the w and e distinction concerns the estimation of wage curves based on local labour market or regional unemployment rates observed through time (see Blanchflower and Oswald, 1994a, 1994b). The main issue is that, as illustrated by (6.3), average hourly earnings contain both an hours and a wage rate dimension.[4] Overtime hours are critical to this distinction. *Both* wage rates and weekly hours of work would be expected to relate negatively to unemployment rates – in both time and cross-section dimensions – and so wage rate-unemployment elasticities cannot be deduced from an equation that measures the wage in terms of average hourly earnings. Models developing negative wage rate-unemployment relationships derive from a very large literature. Appendix 6.1 provides a simple hours curve model of negative hours–unemployment association with respect to regional breakdowns.

Purely for illustrative purposes, let us take a bare-bones representation of the wage curve observed in respect of local labour markets through time. Let wages be given as averages over individuals in each market. Then, for market r in period t we have

$$\log w_{rt} = a \log u_{rt} + d_r + f_t + v_{rt} \tag{6.5}$$

where w_{rt} is the average standard wage, u_{rt} is the unemployment rate, d_r and f_t are sets of dummies for (respectively) markets and time and v_{rt} is an error term. Card (1995) and Card and Hyslop (1996) suggest an alternative specification that also provides a test of wage curve versus Phillips curve. First-differencing (6.5) eliminates fixed labour market effects, producing

$$\Delta \log w_{rt} = b_1 \log u_{rt} + b_2 \log u_{rt-1} + g_t + \Delta v_{rt} \tag{6.6}$$

where g_t are the reformulated dummies after differencing.

If in (6.6) b_1 is found to be significant and b_2 insignificant then this provides empirical support for the Phillips curve. Alternatively, if estimates of b_1 and b_2 reveal equal-sized parameters with opposite signs then the wage curve is supported.

Rather than incorporating the standard hourly wage in (6.5) and (6.6), we might alternatively define the dependent variable as average hourly earnings, e. Equation (6.6) becomes

---

[4] The idea that the e-w distinction may have a bearing on the wage curve estimation relates to an earlier argument by Card (1995) along similar lines. This concerns annual earnings – the principal measure used by Blanchflower and Oswald (1994a) in their estimation of US wage curves. Card points out that these are the product of annual hours and hourly wages. It becomes important to understand the extent to which estimated elasticities represent wage effects and hours' effects. Breaking earnings into standard wage and overtime components offers a parallel problem.

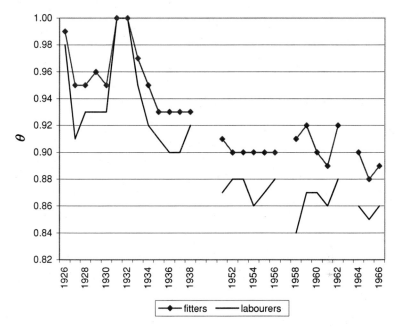

Figure 6.1 Pre- and post-war movements in θ: fitters and labourers in the British engineering industry, 1926–1966
Source: Hart (2003a).

$$\Delta \log e_{rt} = c_1 \log u_{rt} + c_2 \log u_{rt-1} + h_t + \Delta v_{rt}. \tag{6.7}$$

Suppose that, comparable to the US FLSA system, all overtime workers in all labour markets are paid the same premium rate. As illustrated in (6.3), estimates of (6.6) and (6.7) can still differ if the proportions of average standard to average total hours vary. Such variation would be accentuated if the average marginal overtime premium were to rise in overtime hours.

Hart (2003a) has explored the performances of equations similar to (6.6) and (6.7) for two homogeneous occupations – skilled fitters and unskilled labourers – in the British engineering industry in the pre- and post-war periods. The data refer to a panel of 28 local labour markets in England and Scotland and cover the years 1928–38 and 1952–66.[5] Consider the variable θ in (6.1), the ratio of standard to total hours. Averaged across all labour markets, annual movements in θ are illustrated in figure 6.1. In the pre-war period, θ ranges from $0.93 \leq \theta \leq 1$ for fitters and $0.90 \leq \theta \leq 1$ for labourers. The value of $\theta = 1$ for both occupations in 1931 and 1932 represents the fact that, on average, short-time hours

---

[5] These data implicitly control rigorously for education and training. They also benefit from the fact that the rules governing the timing and payment of overtime in engineering were simple. First, maximum weekly standard hours were fixed throughout the industry by national agreement. Second, the overtime premium was also fixed throughout the industry, with an overwhelmingly dominant rate of 1.5 times the basic hourly rate.

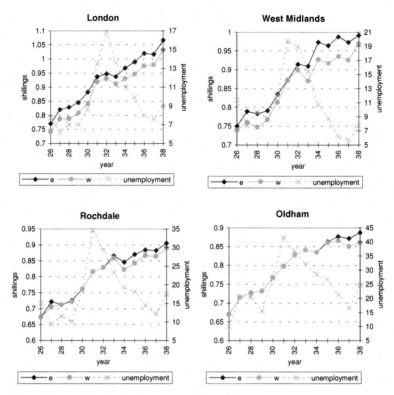

Figure 6.2   Real wage rates, real wage earnings and unemployment in four local labour markets, 1928–1938 (fitters on time-rates)
Source: Hart (2001).
Note: Shillings: Pre-decimal UK curency in use before 1971.

were worked in the industry.[6] In the post-war period, values of θ were in the narrower bands of $0.88 \leq \theta \leq 0.92$ for fitters and $0.84 \leq \theta \leq 0.88$ for labourers.

In the light of these observations, and given the e-decomposition shown in (6.2), it is unsurprising that e and w diverged considerably in some local labour markets. Four of these are illustrated in figure 6.2. In London and the West Midlands, overtime was always positive but reduced in the depression years. Accordingly, such hours' movements serve to narrow appreciably the real e-w gaps. By contrast, in a labour market such as Oldham in the north of England where short-time working was the norm, this influence on the hourly rate of compensation was not so important; e and w coincide in values for much of

---

[6] Between 1929 to their peak in 1932, unemployment rates, averaged across the 29 labour markets, more than doubled (from 11.7 per cent to 25.3 per cent). The standard workweek was 47 hours throughout the industry in the inter-war period. In 1929, weekly hours of timeworking fitters averaged 49.2. These reduced by 7 per cent in the next two years – to a trough of 45.8 hours in 1931 – and then recovered slightly to 46.2 in 1932. Therefore, short time was worked on average in engineering in these last two years. By 1931, about one-quarter of labour markets – mainly in Scotland and the North of England – experienced short-time working which averaged more than 3 hours below weekly standard hours.

the period. Rochdale, also in the north, shows a similar though less extreme e-w relationship. Black, Chapman and Chatterji (1993) also emphasise the distinction between wage rates and earnings in their evaluation of UK regional earnings growth between 1974 and 1991.

Inter-war estimates based on equations such as (6.6) and (6.7) and using weighted least squares (WLS) are presented in Hart (2001) while ordinary least squares (OLS) estimates are provided in Hart (2003a).[7] These two sets of findings are broadly similar. Wage rate results are generally weak, with no support for either a wage curve or a Phillips curve. A wage curve construct is supported when, as in (6.7) compared to (6.6), earnings replace wage rates. In terms of (6.3), the conclusion is that these latter findings owe more to associations between θ and unemployment than between w and unemployment. Post-war OLS estimates are presented in Hart (2003a). These not only serve to reinforce the inter-war findings they also provide a stronger contrast between w- and e-estimates. Estimated e-unemployment elasticities are three times larger than their w-unemployment equivalents.[8]

Undoubtedly, the foregoing findings owe a great deal to the fact that overtime working is an important phenomenon among blue-collar workers in British engineering. Can we draw more general conclusions about the effect of earnings decomposition on estimated wage curves? Two additional studies provide contrasting evidence.

In the first study to investigate the role of overtime in wage curve estimation, Black and FitzRoy (2000), also find that e-type compensation specifications differ radically from w-type. These authors concentrate on British full-time manual workers in a panel of 56 British counties between 1980 and 1995. They set out to distinguish between traditional Phillips curve and wage curve effects. They postulate that a prime role for overtime is to provide a rapid adjustment response of hours to demand shocks. In this event, estimating an earnings equation such as (6.7) would tend to support a wage curve formulation because the overtime influence is likely to be reflected in a relatively strong association with *current* unemployment. Removing overtime from the analysis, as in (6.5), will allow the identification of standard wages that might be more reflective of this slower response and be more likely to support the more traditional Phillips curve formulation. In general Black and FitzRoy's empirical results lend support to these arguments.

A second study also investigates the implications of overtime for wage curve formulation and performance but arrives at somewhat different conclusions. Using the first three waves of the IAB Establishment Panel, Bellmann and Blien (2001) attempt to account for the role of overtime in their German establishment-level study. Their measure of the average wage is the 'computed sum of gross wages divided by the number of employees'. In their wage curve regressions, they incorporate an overtime dummy to account for paid overtime. The dummy

---

[7] There is something of a 'debate' as to whether OLS or WLS are appropriate estimators for these types of equations. For example, Blanchflower and Oswald (1994b) use OLS while Blanchard and Katz (1997) use WLS. Deaton (1997) discusses the econometric arguments for and against each approach.

[8] Given the greater time-wise variations in θ during the inter- compared to the post-war period, we might have expected weaker difference between w- and e-based regressions in the latter period. However, during the depth of the Great Depression many labour markets experienced short-time working thereby reducing the overtime influence on earnings movements.

is significantly positive but appears to have no effect on their estimated wage-unemployment elasticities.[9]

There may be a compositional problem in studies that incorporate wages that are aggregated over a number of occupations. The argument runs parallel to the role of overtime in general and the payment of a premium in particular. If different occupations within the same establishment (or region) are paid at different hourly standard rates and *work different numbers of weekly paid-for hours* then relative time-wise movements and cross-sectional differences in hours across occupations could systematically affect the wage measure. In other words, the need to separate hours and (standard) wages in wage curve studies remains.

6.4   Marginal cost and price over the cycle

Understanding the behaviour of labour compensation over the business cycle is clearly of key interest to bargaining parties in wage negotiations as well as to governments in their attempts to enact countercyclical fiscal and monetary policies. As far as firm-level or industrial competitive performance is concerned, a more broadly related subject is the relationship between marginal cost and price over the cycle. Since the wage is only one component of the firm's total costs, it may appear that the role of hours in general, and overtime hours in particular, is of far less concern in this wider context. In fact, due primarily to the contribution of Bils (1987), this is not the case.

A cost minimising firm seeks to equate relative marginal costs of inputs to respective marginal products. Suppose that inputs are chosen to satisfy this optimum requirement. Then, the marginal cost of a change in output can be measured in terms of the cost of changing a given input, *ceteris paribus*. Bils focused attention on the firm's intensive margin, selecting average hours of work as the representative input. Other inputs are held constant at their optimum levels. Here, we highlight a slightly modified version of Bils' approach (see Hart and Malley, 2000).

A convenient way of separating the hours input from other production inputs is to make use of a homothetic function, highly popular among labour market economists since its adoption by Ehrenberg (1971a). This may be written as $Y = h^{\alpha} F(N, \ldots)$, where Y is output, h is average hours and N is the number of workers (highlighted from a list of other inputs). Hours-related costs of employment are expressed $C = W(h)hN$ where $w(h)$ is the wage schedule. Let w be a monotonic function of h with $W'(h) > 0$. We can now express the marginal cost of output in relation to the selected hours input. This is given by $dC/dY = (dC/dh) \times (dh/dY)$ which, combining production and cost expressions, is given by

$$\frac{dC}{dY} = \left(\frac{1}{\alpha}\right)\left(\frac{h^* N^*}{Y^*}\right)\widetilde{W}(h^*) \tag{6.8}$$

where $\widetilde{W}(h^*) = [W(h^*) + W'(h^*)h^*]$ is the marginal wage schedule and asterisks denote optimal values of inputs.

---

[9] The estimated elasticities turn out to be in the region of -0.10, in line with Blanchflower and Oswald's findings.

Studies of marginal cost and price over the cycle are typically conducted at the industry level of aggregation. At this level, employees average positive overtime hours. Potentially, overtime affects marginal wage costs along two routes. First, the proportion of overtime hours per period varies positively with average hours. Average hourly costs will rise because overtime hours involve hourly premia that, on average, exceed basic hourly rates. Second, additional overtime hours might be obtained only at increased marginal costs; the average marginal overtime premium might itself vary positively with average overtime hours (see sections 2.5 and 3.2). These overtime effects can be captured by the wage schedule

$$W(h) = w \left[1 + p(v) \left(\frac{v}{h} \right) \right] \tag{6.9}$$

where w is the standard wage, $p(v)$ is the mean marginal overtime premium function with $p'(v) > 0$, and v is the average number of overtime hours per worker. The marginal wage with respect to an increase in working time is given by

$$\frac{dW}{dh} = w \left[1 + \left(p(v) + v \frac{\partial p}{\partial v} \right) \frac{\partial v}{\partial h} \right]. \tag{6.10}$$

As suggested, at the industry level the term, $\partial v / \partial h$ would be expected to be increasing in h.[10] At any given time, we would expect variations in the number of overtime hours worked per worker and in the proportions of workers working overtime. As average hours rise from the trough of a cycle and labour dishoarding takes place, the proportion of workers working overtime and average overtime hours per worker will increase relatively modestly, with much of the response resulting from workers working longer basic hours. As the upturn progresses, both of these dimensions of overtime working will increase at an increasing rate.

The empirical strategy is to obtain estimable expressions for the right-hand side components of the marginal cost expression (6.10). Full details are given in Bils (1987) and Hart and Malley (2000). It turns out that marginal cost can be broken down into the standard hourly wage, (the inverse of) hourly productivity and an expression for movements along the marginal wage schedule. This last measure captures the overtime effects. These components are then regressed on measures of the business cycle. The relationship between marginal cost and price is simply taken to be the mark-up, that is the difference between the change in producer price and the change in (total) marginal cost.

In Bils' study, using two-digit US manufacturing data from 1956 to the early 1980s, it is found that a 10 per cent increase in production worker employment is associated with an increase in marginal cost of 2.4 per cent. Most of the cost increase is due to overtime payments, resulting from a higher proportion of total hours compensated at the premium rate. Hart and Malley undertake their work for Japan and the United States, also on the basis of two-digit industry data (from the late 1950s to the early 1990s). They also find that the marginal wage schedules display the expected positive association with the cycle measure. The two countries exhibit similar magnitudes of response. Two countervailing effects help to explain these outcomes. On the one hand, during the upturn of the cycle, a given rise in the proportion of workers working overtime will lead to higher rises in average hourly costs

---

[10] If all workers work the same hours per period then we would expect $\partial v / \partial h = 0$ when average hours are below the level for which overtime rates apply and $\partial v / \partial h = 1$ in the overtime regime.

in the United States compared to Japan because the overtime premium is higher. On the other hand, there is a greater tendency in Japan for the average rate of premium pay to rise as average overtime increases (see figures 2.16a and 2.16b, p. 35). Unlike Bils, however, Hart and Malley find that the productivity component of marginal cost plays the most important role.[11]

In both countries, therefore, we find that marginal cost and price are countercyclical. In Japan, the price changes over the cycle are offset to a large degree by marginal cost changes. The net outcome leaves price/marginal cost margins as exhibiting significant, though relatively mild, procyclical fluctuations. The price effects are much smaller than the marginal cost effects in the United States, with the result that movements in price/marginal cost margins are both significantly procyclical and much larger than comparable Japanese results. A 10 percentage point increase in real output is associated with a 6.9 percentage point increase in the margin in the United States; this compares with a 1.3 percentage point increase in the Japanese margin.

6.5   The frequency domain and earnings decomposition

Assume that we are interested in the cyclicality of firm-level or industry-level real wage earnings. Section 2.6 contains a method of decomposing aggregate earnings into 3 parts – the standard wage, the proportion of overtime to total workers and the overtime premium mark-up. Understanding the cyclicality of the average earnings measure involves estimating the cyclicality of each of the component parts. However, a single representative indicator of the cycle may not be appropriate in this case. Let us take the example of the standard wage and the premium mark-up. The latter, as shown in (2.6), is determined by the number of overtime hours in relation to standard hours. If standard rates are negotiated at predetermined intervals – typically a year in Europe and 3 years in the United States – then at the aggregate level, standard wage outcomes would be expected to reflect economic conditions prevailing at all phases of the business cycle. Accordingly, economists have used indicators such as output and unemployment changes to reflect activity over the entire cycle. Changes in overtime, by contrast, may be most apparent in tight labour markets – that is, towards cyclical peaks. In fact, the extent to which firms increase their use of overtime may depend on the relative prices of alternative high-demand buffers. An example of the latter might involve a greater than planned rundown of inventories (Topel, 1982). So if overtime is used primarily to meet shortfalls in planned economic growth, overtime cycles may be relatively short and changes in inventories may provide an ideal cyclical indicator.

---

[11] Marginal cost is found to be markedly countercyclical in both countries. In large part, these outcomes derive from the dominant finding of strongly procyclical labour productivities. A 10 percentage point increase in real output in Japan is associated with a 6.2 percentage point decrease in Nh/Y and an even larger 8.1 percentage point decrease in the United States. These outcomes are generally consistent with findings of earlier empirical studies of the two countries. Hart and Malley's (2000) US results with respect to the cyclical behaviour of labour productivity run counter to the earlier findings of Bils. This almost certainly derives from the fact that Bils adopts an employment-based measure of the business cycle while Hart and Malley use an output-based measure.

The general conclusion is that different components of wage earnings may respond best to different cyclical indicators and, in fact, any one component may respond to more than one indicator.[12] One way of testing for multiple cyclical influences is to work in the frequency domain of the wage variable rather than the standard time series analysis (Hart, Malley and Woitek, 2003). A stationary time series can be broken down into constituent harmonic waves of varying phases and amplitudes. We can then test the extent to which influential constituent cycles of the earnings time series are explained by different cyclical indicators representing a range of cyclical lengths. We can also measure the degree to which significant associations are in phase with one another. For example, we might conclude that the standard wage is both significantly procyclical and in phase (or not in phase) with respect to a given measure of the business cycle.

Using Bureau of Labor Statistics (BLS) on US manufacturing earnings from 1959 to 1997, Hart, Malley and Woitek (2003) use four cyclical indicators – gross fixed capital formation ($GFCF$), output (Y), employment (N) and inventory investment (II). $GFCF$ is chosen to represent the longer end of the time spectrum; it is dominated by a long cycle in the 5–7-year range. The Y and N variables are most associated with a middle band of cycle in the 5–7-year range, while II principally represents the 3–5-year range. Four main groups of results are worth reporting. First, all components of the wage are found to be both significantly procyclical and largely in phase with their dominant cyclical indicators. Second, the overtime mark-up is the only wage component that associates significantly with the II indicator and, moreover, this accounts for easily the largest source of explained overtime variation. Third, the dominant cyclical influence on both consumption of production wages are middle time bands (5–7-year) although the former is also influenced significantly by the longest (7–10-year) band. Finally, each component measure displays significant covariations with more than one indicator. This leads to the conclusion that tests of wage cyclicality should embrace more than one measure of the cycle.

6.6 Paid-for and effective hourly wages

We know from the evidence presented in section 2.7 that managerial and professional workers claim that their contractual paid-for hours are, on average, significantly less than their actual hours. From a pay perspective, this translates into the notion that their actual hourly wage is less than their paid-for hourly wage. Since the incidence of unpaid overtime is far less marked among other workers then accounting for this phenomenon serves to narrow actual wage differentials. However, there is a potentially more interesting implication of the effects of unpaid overtime on hourly wages. It relates to the estimation of returns to schooling and experience (Mincer, 1974). For obvious reasons, the incidence of unpaid hours also correlates positively with educational attainment. Therefore, what happens to the wage profiles of, say, degree-level individuals if actual wages replace paid-for wages in the estimation of returns?

---

[12] For example, the cyclicality of the standard hourly rate may depend on the lengths of the wage contract, the business cycle and the firm's product cycle.

Table 6.1 *Simulated hourly earnings for metal goods industry at different levels of experience/tenure: workers with graduate education, not married and non-ethnic*

Hourly earnings	Years tenure/experience			
Males	0	10	20	30
Actual (£)	8.68	12.97	15.59	18.06
Paid-for (£)	9.46	14.62	17.95	20.98
% Diff.	8.2	11.3	13.1	13.9
Females	0	10	20	30
Actual (£)	9.44	12.54	13.48	14.35
Paid-for (£)	10.26	14.02	15.41	16.82
% Diff.	8.0	10.6	12.5	14.7

Source: Bell and Hart (1999)

Bell and Hart (1999) have examined this issue. Using individual-level British data for males and females taken from the 1993–4 Labour Force Survey (LFS), they estimate an equation of the form

$$\ln(w_{ij}) = a_0 + \mathbf{b}'\mathbf{x_i} + \mathbf{c}'\mathbf{z_i} + \varepsilon_i \quad (j = p, a) \tag{6.11}$$

where i indexes the individual and $\ln(w_{ij})$ is the logarithm of paid-for ($j = p$) or actual ($j = a$) standard hourly wages, the vector $\mathbf{x}$ consists of the human capital variables experience, tenure and pre-work qualifications,[13] $\mathbf{z}$ is a vector of other explanatory variables and, ε is a disturbance term. ($\mathbf{b}$ and $\mathbf{c}$ are coefficient vectors.) Variables in $\mathbf{z}$ include ethnic status, marital status, union status, firm size, industry and geographical location.

Three findings are of particular relevance to the current topic. First, estimated wage profiles are concave with respect to both the standard wage and its adjusted actual wage counterpart. Second, returns to pre-work education are highest for degree-level graduates, with increasingly wider differentials as educational attainment decreases. Third, adjusting wages to account for unpaid work serves to reduce significantly the coefficient sizes on all experience, tenure and education variables.

A simulation based on single non-ethnic males and females with a graduate education and employed in the metal goods industry was undertaken on the basis of these results. We assume that a 'typical' female or male graduate leaves university and immediately enters a firm in that industry and has unbroken employment until the age of retirement. In this event, experience and tenure are the same lengths over all years of employment. This allows simulation of the growth profiles of the two types of wage earnings. Results are shown in table 6.1. It is clear that the use of paid-for hourly earnings serves to overestimate the 'true' actual earnings figures. Paid-for hourly earnings are an estimated 8.2 per cent greater than

---

[13] Experience is measured as the current age minus age when completed full-time education including higher-order terms, tenure is the length of time in current job. These two variables are entered as quartic specifications. Pre-work qualifications covered five levels of educational attainment.

actual hourly earnings for males at 0 years of tenure; this grows to 11.3 per cent higher after 10 years, to 13.1 per cent after 20 years, and to 13.9 per cent after 30 years. The female profiles display quite similar outcomes.

Hübler (2002) provides an interesting application of these wage distinctions. This involves the use of personal computers by managers in Germany. In the first study of its type, Krueger (1993) (using Current Population Survey data) found that employees who use computers at work earn a 10–15 per cent higher wage rate. DiNardo and Pischke (1997) suggest that such increases may in part reflect a selection problem: computer users may differ in their characteristics from non-users. Hübler points out that in this type of study it is essential to distinguish between paid-for and effective wage rates. The critical point is that using computers involves a range of potential problems that cause delays in task execution times. Implementation problems, tracking down mistakes in computer programmes and misinterpretations of computer manuals are among a broader range of examples. Hübler develops a model in which the employer and employees jointly maximise profits and utility. Utility and the production function include unpaid overtime that is devoted to surmounting computer problems. The profit function, by contrast, concentrates on paid hours. The model solves to produce an unpaid overtime equation – found to be functionally related to standard hours, the standard wage, the use of a PC, and a variable that captures worker effort. The argument is that if unpaid hours are part of an implicit contract then hourly wages that include an allowance for unpaid hours – that is, *effective* hourly wage rates – should be associated with computer use. Using the GSOEP from 1991 to 1997, Hübler finds that PC use among managers has a positive and significant influence on the wage. This remains even when unobserved heterogeneity is allowed for. It is also found that PC use relates positively with unpaid work. When this additional unpaid work is accounted for in the wage, effective wage advantages of PC use among managers is found to be insignificantly different from zero.

6.7 Summary

We have found that the effects of overtime may have important bearings on observed wage and labour cost behaviour:

- Overtime working is critical to the distinction between *wage rates* and *wage earnings*.
- It is difficult to evaluate, *a priori*, whether it is more appropriate to use *hourly earnings* or *hourly rates* in studies of time-series behaviour of wage movements.
- US micro panel studies of real hourly wage behaviour over the business cycle find significantly different behaviour as between *rates* and *earnings*.
- There is evidence of significant differences between these two measures of the wage in *regional wage curve studies*.
- In several studies of marginal cost and price over the cycle, measuring changes in *marginal cost* has been undertaken in respect of firms' intensive labour margins with overtime found to play a prominent role.
- Different components of wage earnings are found to relate to different *cyclical indicators*, with overtime components responding to cycles of relatively short duration.

- *Unpaid overtime* drives a wedge between actual and paid-for hourly wages.
- Given an unequal incidence of unpaid overtime hours, it is found that graduate male and female wage growth with respect to tenure and experience are exaggerated if *paid-for* rather than actual hourly wages are used as the basis of analysis.

Appendix 6.1   Hours curves

Here, a simple example is provided that motivates the idea of hours curves within the spatial study of hours-unemployment relationships.

Let a firm's total wage bill consist of a wage rate w for h per-period hours paid to a homogenous workforce, N: thus

$$W = whN. \tag{6A.1}$$

The workforce also incurs fixed (or hours-independent) labour costs, given by

$$Z = (z + tq)N \tag{6A.2}$$

where Z is total fixed cost, z is (exogenous) non-human capital fixed cost, t is training cost and q is the quit rate. For simplicity, training standards are laid down at industry level and so, together with occupational homogeneity, training cost is treated as an exogenously determined constant. The quit rate is assumed to depend on

(1) the firm's w relative to the rate in other firms in the local market, w^*, and
(2) the unemployment rate which represents the (inverse of the) probability of finding alternative employment in the market (see Schlicht, 1978; Salop, 1979; Hoel and Vale, 1986).

Thus

$$q = q(r, u) \quad \text{where } r = w/w^* \tag{6A.3}$$

with $q_r < 0$, $q_u < 0$. Low intra-market information and mobility costs – together with important elements of national and district elements of wage setting – are assumed to ensure that $r = 1$ (i.e. $w = w^*$). Therefore, a special case of (6A.3) is given by

$$q = q(1, u). \tag{6A.4}$$

Setting output price to unity, the Lagrangian function, L, for the firm's cost minimising problem is expressed

$$\min L(N, h, \lambda) = Z + W + \lambda[Q - F(N, h)] \tag{6A.5}$$

where Q is the firm's output, and λ is a Lagrangian multiplier. It is assumed that $F_i > 0$, $F_{ii} < 0$ and $F_{ij} > 0$. From the first-order conditions, we obtain

$$\frac{wN^*}{z + tq + wh^*} = \frac{\partial F/\partial h}{\partial F/\partial N} \tag{6A.6}$$

where N^* and h^* denote equilibrium values of the decision variables. Thus, the firm equates the ratio of marginal costs on the intensive (hours) and extensive (employment) margins to their respective marginal products. This model produces the equilibrium hours demand function

$$h^* = h^*(w, z, u, Q). \qquad (6A.7)$$

Totally differentiating the first-order conditions and solving the h (and N) variables establishes in (3A.7) that $h_1^* < 0$, $h_2^* > 0$, $h_3^* < 0$ and $h_4^* > 0$. The first three conditions derive from the fact that a rise in hours-independent relative to variable costs induces hours-worker substitution. It is noted that $\partial h^*/\partial Q = 0$ in in (6A.7) if there is an underlying homothetic (e.g. Cobb–Douglas) production technology.

The variable of particular interest is the rate of unemployment. Its role in (6A.7) stems from the result that rises in fixed labour costs cause hours-worker substitution in the cost minimising firm. As unemployment increases, the quit rate reduces due to falls in alternative employment opportunities. Accordingly, fixed costs associated with labour turnover are reduced. *Ceteris paribus*, starting from an equilibrium position, the cost minimising firm reacts to falls in fixed to total labour costs by reducing the variable labour input, hours of work.

7   Policy issues

7.1   Work sharing and mandatory overtime rules

At industry or national level, work sharing is usually taken to mean spreading the available work more thinly across more workers. It may occur because firms voluntarily re-structure towards the use of more part-time employees, split jobs and flexible working time arrangements. Such actions probably account for relatively minor employment changes and may not mean, necessarily, that there is a net increase in workforce size. In order to achieve a sizeable employment impact, and often with an eye towards alleviating unemployment, some governments have taken the view that significant shifts towards more work sharing require direct and systematic labour market intervention. Overtime working is usually at the centre of such initiatives. The reason has as much to do with social and political concerns as with economic ones. Why should sections of the workforce work hours beyond their standard contractual commitment, the argument proceeds, when others are unemployed or working involuntary short-time hours? While this line of reasoning has potent political appeal, policy makers in Europe and the United States have adopted radically different approaches to work sharing in general and to its overtime dimension in particular.

Europeans have concentrated on manipulating the length of contractual hours. In this context, overtime plays a generally misunderstood role. It is typically argued that, for given production requirements, a cut in contractual hours will lead to new hires because the main alternative, increased overtime hours, involves premium rates of pay. There are three main arguments against this line of reasoning.

First, the demand analysis of chapter 3 offers the best-known, but perhaps not the most compelling, argument against this contention. Suppose a firm works initial overtime in equilibrium. For a given production requirement and a *given* premium, mandatory cuts in the standard workweek increase the marginal cost of new hires – because new workers work proportionately fewer standard hours – relative to the cost of extending overtime. Recall from the analysis presented on pp. 53–5 that such hours' reductions lead to negative employment effects via *both* substitution and scale impacts. So, the policy can have the opposite effect to that intended.

The force of the foregoing demand-side outcomes are greatly increased when combined with a second consideration. This concerns the issue of whether or not hours cuts are accompanied by upward wage rate adjustments designed to restore average hourly earnings. Where wage and hours levels are subject to collective bargaining agreements, we should not be surprised if workers seek compensation for their loss of earnings due to shorter weekly time schedules.[1] Where upward wage adjustments are significant then they would tend significantly to reinforce negative employment scale impacts of hours' reductions.

The third criticism of outside interventions to reduce contractual hours has been increasingly recognised as potentially the most persuasive. It relates to the model of Lewis (1969a), as discussed in section 3.7. Some firms and workers are tied into long-term contracts concerning hours and compensation. An outside agency cannot influence the agreed arrangements by simply changing one component of working time or earnings. For example, the bargaining parties can easily counteract a mandated reduction in standard hours. They can simply agree to extend overtime hours so as to maintain contractually agreed total weekly hours. As for compensation, they can allow for a downward adjustment of standard hourly pay in order to offset the added cost of proportionately more premium hours.[2]

The US work sharing debate has been dominated by considerations of the policy of manipulating the mandated overtime premium. While not without ambiguities – chiefly concerning negative employment scale effects – theoretical work into the effects of a rising premium on employment is generally more favourable to work sharing outcomes than is the case with standard hours' restrictions. Ignoring additional inputs, such as effort and capital, a *ceteris paribus* rise in the overtime premium reduces the relative cost of extensive to intensive margin labour input, thereby producing a workers-hours substitution effect.

Based on the cost minimisation framework of pp. 51–3, consider the following log-linear estimating equation of the demand for overtime,

$$\log v = b_0 + b_1 \log(z/\varpi) + \mathbf{b_2}\mathbf{X} + \varepsilon \tag{7.1}$$

where v is per-period overtime, z/ω is the ratio of fixed costs per employee to the overtime wage rate,[3] $\mathbf{X}$ is a vector of other variables that influence the demand for overtime, bs are constants and ε is a stochastic error term. From the theory outlined in section 3.2, we would

---

[1] For example, Hunt (1999) studies hours reductions – resulting from union/employer negotiations – in 30 (West) German manufacturing industries. A sequence of industrial reductions in standard hours occurred in metal working and printing industries between 1985 and 1994 and also took place in other industries at a later starting date. Using the German Socio-Economic Panel (GSOEP), it was estimated that hourly paid workers (*Arbeiter*) experienced a fall in total weekly hours between 0.88 and 1 hour given a 1-hour fall in standard hours. Wages for all full-time workers were then examined and in those sectors where standard hours were reduced it was found that the reductions associated with a 2–2.4 per cent increase in the standard wage. This finding tended to corroborate German union claims that they achieved full-wage compensation. Given that firms experiencing lower standard weekly hours were now faced with no fall in monthly wages, it is not surprising that Hunt estimated *lower* employment overall.

[2] It might be impractical, for contractual and other reasons, to effect short-term wage reductions. But the parties could adjust in the longer term by allowing price inflation rather than nominal wage reductions to bring about the required real wage offsets.

[3] From the basic theory, z/ω represents the ratio of fixed labour costs to the overtime wage (i.e. $\omega = wk$ in terms of our demand analysis in chapter 3). The fact that it is theoretically appropriate to enter these variables in ratio form can be deduced, for example, from the derived equilibrium hours' equation (3.13). For convenience, let the overtime premium k be a constant so that we can re-write (3.13) as $v = h - h_s = c_0(z/w) + c_1\tau + c_2 h_s$ where $c_0 = \beta/k(\alpha - \beta) > 0$, $c_1 = \alpha/(\alpha - \beta) > 0$, and $c_2 = (\beta - \alpha k)/(\alpha - \beta) < 0$. A rise in the ratio of fixed costs to the hourly wage rate increases overtime as does a rise in set-up time, τ. A cut in standard hours is associated with a rise in overtime.

expect that a fall in the ratio z/ω is likely to be associated with a reduction in v. A fall in fixed relative to variable labour costs represents a marginal cost advantage on the extensive relative to the intensive margin and leads the firm to employ more workers and fewer hours.[4]

Suppose we obtain data to estimate (7.1) for an economy with mandated overtime rules. Since k, the overtime premium, is incorporated within ω then it would be possible to use the estimates in order to simulate the effects of an exogenous increase in k on the demand for overtime. This, essentially, is the operational agenda of Ehrenberg and Schumann (hereafter, E–S) (1982a), based on the original derivations and empirical analysis of Ehrenberg (1971a, 1971b).

Using the 1976 Employer Expenditure for Employee Compensation (EEC) survey, E–S estimated (7.1) by OLS for 638 manufacturing establishments, all of which reported positive levels of overtime hours. Additionally, OLS regressions were undertaken for 658 non-manufacturing establishments with positive overtime and Tobit regressions for an extended sample of 878 non-manufacturing establishments that included over 200 cases where zero overtime was reported.[5] Equation (7.1) was also estimated by two-stage least squares (2SLS) in order to accommodate the possibility that z/ω and v might be simultaneously determined.[6] The principal measurement difficulty concerned the allocation of hours-independent and hours-related components of labour costs into z and ω, respectively.[7]

E–S calculate upper-bound estimates of the effects on overtime of a rise in the overtime premium from time and a half to double time. Their findings appear to lend considerable support to the potential work sharing benefits from this type of policy intervention. OLS produces estimates of employment gains between 0.5 and 1.5 per cent in manufacturing and between 1.0 and 2.3 per cent in non-manufacturing. Tobit estimates for non-manufacturing are similar to OLS. 2SLS estimates are considerably larger; they are between 2.0 and 3.0 times larger for manufacturing and 1.5–3.0 times larger for non-manufacturing. On first reflection, therefore, these results may suggest that employment creation through the manipulation of the premium may offer a useful policy tool.

---

[4] Hübler (1989) estimates a probit equation for Germany where a dummy for an overtime or a non-overtime worker replaces actual overtime hours worked. In line with the standard theory, he finds that overtime relates positively to non-wage costs and negatively with the basic wage rate and standard hours.

[5] The vector **X** includes a dummy variable for whether the standard workweek is 40 hours or less, the ratio of paid leave to total hours (to proxy absenteeism), the proportion of employees with less than 1 week of annual vacation (to proxy the experience distribution of the workforce), a dummy for union membership as well as establishment size and industry controls.

[6] Firms may attempt to lower the marginal cost of high levels of overtime hours by paying relatively high fringes (which enter z and w) and low hourly wage rates.

[7] Two further points need to be highlighted concerning the ratio z/ω in the context of actual estimation. First, a critical problem concerns the allocation of non-wage labour costs into fixed and variable components. Both statutory and social employer benefits contain elements of hours-independent and hours-related costs and published data often preclude exact separation. For a detailed examination of fixed and variable non-wage costs in Japan, the United States and the United Kingdom, see Hart (1984). Certain fringe benefits are hours-related and serve to extend the definition of the overtime 'wage'. In fact, E–S find it impossible with their data to separate rigorously fixed and variable labour costs and in fact carry out their estimation with three alternative definitions. Second, from a regression standpoint the ratio in (7.1) implies a restriction that if $\log z$ and $\log w$ were to be included as separate variables, their coefficients should be of equal size and opposite signs. E–S test this restriction. It is rejected in respect of their manufacturing establishment data and not rejected for non-manufacturing establishments. The problem with respect to manufacturing is a major factor leading the authors to be highly cautious over making policy prescriptions on the basis of their overall analysis.

The E–S monograph is notable not so much for providing the above employment magnitudes[8] but more for its careful labour market assessment of how wider considerations may lead to significant qualifications of the estimated net employment effects. From a starting point of finding reasonably large employment gains, their extended analysis leads them to revise downwards the impact of the overtime premium changes. In fact, they conclude by recommending that no such policy initiative be undertaken. Since these additional potential labour market repercussions are germane to a much wider set of related policy programmes, it is worth summarising them briefly.

E–S start by considering the consequences of relaxing the within-firm *constraints on the estimated employment effects* that are implicit in the derivation of (7.1). First, as discussed on p. 59, they relax the assumption – inherent to the cost minimising demand model – of completely inelastic wage elasticity of demand. Based on econometric evidence of the wage elasticity, they revise down their employment creation estimates by 0.25 per cent. Second, they consider the possibility that – through moonlighting (double job holding) – currently employed individuals may fill newly created job slots. This would serve to limit the policy impact on unemployment.[9] However, via simulations based on existing studies of moonlighting, E–S discount the quantitative impact of this effect. Third, production indivisibilities may represent a severe constraint on firms' abilities to substitute hours with workers. This may especially be the case in small firms where marginal reductions in overtime hours among a few employees may be insufficient to translate economically into full time job equivalents. In his earlier study, Ehrenberg (1971a) did not find evidence of the trade off between overtime hours and employment being systematically influenced by establishment size but, nevertheless, this line of argument remains persuasive. The fourth consideration is that of compensating adjustments of standard wages or fringe benefits to changes in the premium. This is potentially the most important limitation to employment effects. A later, and more detailed, study by Trejo (1991) suggests that only partial offsetting adjustments take place (see below).

Outside the firm, *skill mismatches of those working overtime and the unemployed* may also serve to limit the employment creation impact of mandated premium increases. Using data from the Current Population Survey (CPS), E–S estimate that at least 8.5 per cent of newly created jobs could not be filled by individuals with the requisite skills living in the same geographical area. Finally, *the non-compliance rate* under the FLSA regulations may also act to dampen employment impacts. At the time of the E–S study, it was estimated that between 10 and 20 per cent of overtime workers covered by the Act did not receive the minimum premium of time and a half. Clearly, full potential employment increases would be reduced by this rate if, as seems likely, firms continued not to comply after the premium was increased (see E–S, 1982b).

While E–S exercise considerable care to account for a wide range of possible economic effects that might lead them to revise their original estimates, the latter are nevertheless

---

[8] The E–S findings are reasonably in line with work along these lines on earlier years of EEC data (Ehrenberg, 1971a; Nussbaum and Wise, 1977) and for Canada (Laudadio and Percy, 1973) as well as with other studies (see Hamermesh, 1993 for a comprehensive review).

[9] See Devereux (2001), who makes this point in a different context.

derived from a pure demand model with given wages. They are open to the criticism that if the underlying demand model is too restrictive then it may be pointless to modify estimates that were not appropriate to begin with. Building and estimating a labour market model that permits demand and supply influences on the wage resulting from a change in the premium might be expected to give different estimates from estimating a pure demand model and then subsequently overlaying possible supply effects.

Hamermesh and Trejo (2000) provide somewhat stronger support for the work sharing effects of overtime legislation. They concentrate attention on California where up to 1980 a requirement that overtime be paid at time and a half for hours over 8 per day applied to (most) women, but not to men. Thereafter, it applied to both genders. Male and female data from the CPSs on daily and weekly hours – together with other labour force and demographic controls – are collected for a year preceding the male changes and a year after the full change transition. Using a 'difference-in-difference' estimator (Card and Sullivan, 1988), the authors compare male outcomes in the pre- and post-policy periods in California with equivalent outcomes in non-Western states that did not experience these overtime legislative changes. Their results are strongly in line with the predictions from labour demand analysis. Both overtime hours and the incidence of days in which overtime was worked declined substantially among Californian men relative to men in other states. Nor did there appear to be a discernible substitution towards more days worked per week to compensate for the loss of premium hours.

In order to judge maximum possible impacts of US FLSA legislation, it is especially useful to examine the period from 1938 when the Act was first introduced. In a short period of time, many firms and workers experienced large mandatory increases in the premium *and* mandatory reductions in the maximum lengths of weekly standard hours. In October 1938, the Act mandated a time and a half overtime premium for weekly hours in excess of 44 and then, in October 1939 the premium applied after 42 hours, and then in 1940 after 40 hours. At the same time, the Act instituted a concomitant minimum hourly wage in 1938, a rate that grew significantly in real terms over the following decade. The Act covered workers in firms engaged in goods and services involved in inter-state commerce. Initially, it did not apply uniformly across industrial sectors. Two such sectors were wholesale and retail trade. Workers in the former were covered from 1938 while the latter were not covered until 1961. Based on this policy-on/policy-off split, Costa (2000) applies the 'difference-in-difference' estimator – with firms/workers in retail trade acting as the control group – to find out if the Act reduced weekly hours in wholesale trade between 1938 and 1950.[10] We know from the standard labour demand theory of pp. 53–5 that this would be predicted if substitution effects outweighed scale effects.[11] There are two main findings. First, hours worked in the wholesale trade fell significantly relative to retail trade following the 1938 legislation. For example, for those working between 35 and 50 hours in wholesale trade, the 5 per cent reduction in standard hours in 1940 compared to the preceding year associated with a

[10] Costa (2000) incorporates two data sets for the tests: (1) monthly time series from 1935 to 1941 based on firms covered in surveys by the BLS, (2) individual-level data taken from the 1940 and 1950 Censuses.
[11] As noted by Costa, weekly hours in wholesale and retail trade where well above 40 at this time, in contrast to manufacturing that averaged less than 40. Thus, if hours' reactions were to be observed at all, they would be expected to be particularly strong in these two sectors.

weekly hours reduction of 0.4 hours for men and 0.2 hours for women. It also associated with an 18 per cent decline in men and women working more than 40 hours per week. Second, these declines were significantly larger in the South than the North, an observation consistent with the fact that the minimum wage acted more as a binding constraint in the former area than in the latter. In other words, firms in the South had less scope for effecting standard wage offsets. Costa concludes that the estimates of hours reductions in this early period are larger than later US estimates by Trejo (1991, 2003) but less than the European estimates of Hart and Wilson (1988) and Hunt (1999).

Overtime pay regulation also features in the Canadian study of Friesen (2002). Advantage is taken of the fact that both lengths of maximum standard working hours and coverage rules vary across the 10 Canadian provinces. A hazard function approach is adopted that allows estimates of the effects of differences in standard hours on the hours distribution over a given range of weekly hours, *ceteris paribus*. Model estimation is undertaken for the range of 40–50 weekly hours in respect of jobs that require at least 40 hours. A 'double difference' estimator is employed which allows estimation of the effects of coverage by overtime pay regulation. Estimation is undertaken with respect to almost 20,000 individuals.

Simulations based on Friesen's estimates reveal three main features. First, cuts in standard hours had only modest impacts. Costa's wholesale estimates revealed that a 5 per cent reduction in standard hours reduced the proportion working more than 40 weekly hours by 18 per cent. By contrast, Friesen finds that a 20 per cent reduction in standard hours (from 48 to 40) produced only a 27 per cent reduction in the proportion working more than 40 hours. Second, coverage by overtime pay regulations is found to be positively associated with standard wage rates. Third, the constraints imposed by such regulation induced moonlighting among affected workers. This latter reaction tends to extend the total number of jobs held by existing workers and detracts from new job creation. In general, Friesen's findings provide only weak support for the employment creation potential of overtime regulations.

Using data from the 1974, 1976 and 1978 May CPSs, Trejo (1991) sets out to test the relative strength of the overtime predictions from the compensating differentials (or 'fixed-job') model (see section 3.7) versus the workers-hours demand model. He concludes that neither model offers a complete explanation of reactions to FLSA overtime regulations. For example, it is found that workers on minimum wages have significantly lower overtime pay compliance. This lends support to the fixed-job model since, by definition, such workers are not in a position to adjust standard wages to offset the overtime regulation. On the other hand, the 1974 and 1976 data show that workers covered by the FLSA legislation are more likely to work for the maximum 40 weekly hours than uncovered workers. This is supportive of the demand model. This predicts a tendency for firms – that might have had recourse to offer some overtime in the absence of premium pay legislation – to cluster at the kink of the standard-time/overtime isocost functions.[12] It would appear that both models offer

---

[12] Refer to figure 3A.1 (p. 79). It is shown that an increase in the overtime premium, k, serves to steepen the slope of the isocost in the overtime region (i.e. to the right of point e). This accentuates the kink point. (The change in k has no effect on the isocost to the left of point e because there is no overtime in this region.) In turn, in the neighbourhood of the kink point, this increases the likelihood of isoquant/isocost equilibrium tangency point occurring at the kink itself.

some contribution to final outcomes. In fact, from earnings regressions, Trejo concludes that standard wages 'appear to adjust in the direction implied by the fixed-job model, but by less than half as much as would be necessary to offset overtime pay completely' (Trejo, 1991, p. 738).

As far as changes in the mandated premium are concerned, the foregoing studies by no means completely reject the standard labour demand model as offering an explanation of hours effects. Two further studies are much less supportive of this model. Using annual data on eleven US industry groups between 1970 and 1989, Trejo (2003) examines the effects of FLSA coverage by industry on weekly work schedules. After controlling for industrial long-term workweek trends, Trejo finds no evidence that increased coverage is associated with reductions in either overtime incidence or overtime hours. Some caution is expressed about these results, however. At this aggregate level, inter-temporal changes in coverage are not substantial and may, in any case, be significantly reflective of long-term trend influences on work schedules. The work of Johnson (2003) concentrates on a major change in FLSA coverage among state and local government workers. It provides an econometric and case study investigation of the US Supreme Court ruling in 1985 that state and local workers were eligible for overtime coverage. Before the ruling, about 400,000 such workers were eligible for overtime coverage. After it, almost 8 million were covered. The econometric work detects no reductions in either overtime hours or percentage of employees working overtime in this public sector after 1985. In fact, unionised workers experienced increases. Detailed case study evidence for public sector union contracts in Illinois show that 95 per cent of workers enjoyed an explicit agreement concerning overtime and, for many of these, the provisions were not significantly different from those provided by the FLSA.

Much of the latest work concerning government interventions on overtime pay and conditions has addressed the issue of the comparative strength of the two core models that were discussed in chapter 1 and developed at later stages. On the one hand, the labour demand model predicts employment and hours substitution effects of changes in mandatory rules while, on the other, the compensating differential model predicts no effects on average hourly wages, hours and jobs. In earlier work, and especially European-based studies, the labour demand model provided most of the theoretical and empirical action. The United States provides a particularly important test-bed for these comparative approaches because intervention under the FLSA makes for relatively more straightforward testing than several other economies, such as Britain, where a more *laissez faire* approach to overtime working has been followed. Without doubt, the studies reviewed here underscore the view that the labour demand model alone offers only a partial explanation of reactions to changes in legislation. But, in general, they do not dismiss the demand model; a number of US studies find hours and coverage evidence that is consistent with its predictions.

This raises the critical question as to why standard hourly wages do not appear to adjust fully so as to offset exogenous rises in the premium or cuts in the length of the standard workweek. There are several plausible reasons (see also Owen, 1989, pp. 46, 47). In the first place, legislation itself may seek to curb flexibility in standard hourly wages. As we have reported in respect of the study by Costa (2000), minimum wage legislation offers one important constraint in this respect. Second, the strength of the argument that the wage acts as a compensating differential for jobs of different length appears to be most forceful if the job lengths of all comparable employees in a firm are equal. As emphasised in section 2.2, however, only a fraction of employees in many companies work overtime. For most workers, overtime is a voluntary activity. From an industrial relations perspective, it may well be deemed impractical to pay differential standard hourly rates as between non-overtime and overtime workers in the same occupation (see section 4.4). But this is what would be required under the compensating differential model if mandated increases in the premium or reductions in standard hours were to occur for that proportion of the workforce engaged in overtime. The alternative would be to offset the increased costs by reducing the standard wage for all employees but this may lead to justifiable feelings of inequity among those who have chosen not to work overtime. Third, and related, if overtime is a voluntary activity and the recruitment policy of firms is to obtain the best job matches for their vacancies then they will want to offer competitive standard hourly rates because, *a priori*, they will not know if a new potential employee will work overtime. But this objective will be difficult to realise if the level of the standard wage, in part, reflects externally imposed overtime payments.

It might be added that most of the foregoing discussion either explicitly or implicitly concerns overtime regulation in relation to the overtime decision within a single firm. King (1997) attempts to evaluate the effects of mandatory rules at industry level, allowing for firm interactions. The introduction of, or changes in, overtime rules within an oligopoly model is considered. Firms' reactions to increased overtime payments include the familiar employment-hours substitution effect, the substitution of other production factors for labour and a negative scale impact on firms' output. It may prove profitable to firms to support such schemes since, if the scale effect predominates, industry output may fall and firms' revenue increase. This may translate into higher profits[13] or better pay and employment, or both. The interesting feature of this work is that these results hold either under the standard labour demand (fixed wage) or the wage-hours compensating differential (fixed-job) model. It is claimed, therefore, that this broader approach may help to explain the mixed results of Trejo (1991) with respect to testing for the relative strengths of these two approaches.

7.2 Taxes, subsidies, profits and job creation

In most OECD countries there is generally less possibility than in the United States to use the overtime premium as a work sharing policy instrument. While a number of European governments have sought to reduce the length of the standard workweek to achieve similar employment goals, this strategy has been increasingly rejected as a fruitful line to pursue. There is a range of alternative instruments, however. Here, we consider possible interventions concerning payroll taxes, general and marginal employment subsidies and profit sharing compensation systems. As with section 7.1, an underlying labour demand framework is retained.

---

[13] In other words, the scale effect reduces output and raises product prices with revenue increasing more than the increase in marginal labour costs.

Employment taxes and subsidies

Adopting a slightly modified function (3.2), let labour services be given by $L = Ng(h)$. Then, with fixed capital, output (Q) is expressed

$$Q = F[Ng(h)] \qquad (7.2)$$

with $g'(h) > 0$ and $g''(h) < 0$. For present purposes, there is no need to be more specific about the form of the $g(h)$ function. Again, we use a simple homothetic function that we know leads to scale invariance in hours within the broader profit maximising problem.

Labour costs are given by an extended version of (3.4), or

$$C = cN = \{t_1 w[h_s + k(h - h_s)] + t_2 + z\} N \qquad (7.3)$$

where $t_1 \geq 1$ is a payroll tax that varies directly with wage payments and t_2 is an hours-independent payroll tax.[14]

Treating wages, taxes and fixed costs as exogenous, the firm's maximisation problem is

$$\max_{N,h} \pi = F[Ng(h)] - cN. \qquad (7.4)$$

Respective first-order conditions for $\pi_N = \pi_h = 0$ are

$$F_L g(h) = c \qquad (7.5)$$

and

$$F_L N g'(h) = t_1 wkN \qquad (7.6)$$

which combine to give

$$\frac{wk}{w[h_s + k(h - h_s)] + \phi} = \frac{g'(h)}{g(h)} \qquad (7.7)$$

where

$$\phi = \frac{t_2 + z}{t_1}.$$

For simple illustrative purposes, suppose that the government increases the worker-related payroll tax, t_2. This increases the value of ϕ and thus reduces the left-hand side of (7.7). A compensating fall in the right-hand side expression is brought about through an hours-worker substitution. But the rise in t_2 implies an increase in F_L in (7.5) (given $g''(h) < 0$) and so $L = Ng(h)$ declines. This latter effect necessitates a reduction in N since $g(h)$ increases. These results are simply the equivalent of a reduction in h_s explored on p. 54. Both substitution and scale effects act against employment.

By inference, payroll tax policies designed to encourage work sharing should be aimed at effecting reductions in the value of ϕ in (7.7). Three broad types of policy approach are available.

---

[14] For an exhaustive discussion of variable and hours independent payroll taxes, see Hart (1984).

The first approach involves changes in *either* t_1 *or* t_2. This is potentially unattractive to governments, firms and existing workers. Given the foregoing example, an increase in t_1 (the wage-related payroll tax) would have beneficial work sharing implications via workers–hours substitution but these would be offset by a negative scale impact if firms are required to fund all or part of the tax increase. If workers were required to fund the increase then the government would have to take into consideration adverse supply-side reactions. It would appear to be unwise for a government to base variable payroll tax increases – which for most workers are tantamount to rises in income tax – on ambiguous work sharing outcomes.

A second, more attractive, approach involves attempting to eliminate both negative scale outcomes and adverse budgetary impacts. For example, suppose that t_2 were to be reduced and t_1 simultaneously increased in (7.7) such that, with respect to a 'typical' firm, the loss of government revenue derived from the former was offset by the increase stemming from the latter. Then, the value of ϕ would be reduced, substitution would favour employment at the expense of hours, and scale effects would be neutralised. Unfortunately, this strategy is somewhat academic since payroll taxes in most economies are overwhelmingly hours- rather than purely worker-related. For most firms it is simply not feasible to produce reductions in t_1 of comparable magnitudes to increases in t_2.[15]

An alternative strategy would be to structure the payroll tax system so as to mimic the shape of the typical overtime schedule. This would impose a two-tier payroll tax with respect to standard and overtime hours. Let t_s be the tax rate applying to standard hours and t_o the rate attached to overtime, then the cost function becomes

$$C = cN = [t_s w h_s + t_o w k(h - h_s) + t_2 + z]N. \tag{7.8}$$

Entering the costs in (7.8) into the maximisation problem in (7.4) gives the optimising condition, equivalent to (7.7),

$$\frac{wk}{wk(h - h_s) + \psi} = \frac{g'(h)}{g(h)} \tag{7.9}$$

where

$$\psi = \frac{t_s w h_s + t_2 + z}{t_o}.$$

Suppose, initially, that $t_s = t_o$ so that cost functions (7.8) and (7.3) are equivalent. Then, for a 'typical' overtime firm, the government could set $t_s < t_o$ such that the total weekly payroll contribution remained the same. But, clearly, there is now an incentive for the firm to substitute workers for hours with ψ reducing in (7.9) and worker-hours substitution, given diminishing returns in hours, restoring equilibrium. If overtime firms were encouraged to alter their employment mix towards more workers working fewer overtime hours, the cost

---

[15] One example of t_2 arises when payroll taxes levied on firms have an upper-ceiling cut-off limit. Where employees earn above this limit then the payroll tax is effectively hours-independent (see Hart, 1984). In recent times, most major OECD countries have either set very high ceilings in relation to average earnings or, effectively, removed the upper ceiling altogether, and so this tax example is no longer important.

to the government exchequer may be a loss of exchequer tax receipts. This may well be regarded as a relatively modest price for creating new jobs.[16]

This use of a graduated payroll tax structure has some appeal. In fact, it might be thought of as a special variant of established payroll tax schemes that vary tax rates directly with wage earnings levels.[17] Inevitably, it raises several problems. First, the tax incidence would be uneven, with long-overtime firms faring worst. These would experience negative scale impacts that might serve to lessen employment responses. On *a priori* grounds there seems to be no reason to target long-hours firms in this way. In fact, work on the relative returns to workers and hours has been based on the conjecture that firms with long hours tend to be more efficient (see section 5.3). Second, the uneven tax incidence may serve to penalise relatively less well-off employees. There is British evidence (see section 4.2) of a relatively high incidence of long overtime hours among low-paid workers.

As we have seen, a problem with the simplest form of payroll tax intervention – i.e. changes in the single hours-related rate, t_1 – is that it is not possible to achieve favourable work sharing outcomes through *both* scale and substitution effects. What type of related intervention could achieve this dual objective? One device – the so-called 'marginal employment subsidy' (MES) (see Layard and Nickell, 1980) – is to subsidise employment expansions by firms beyond current 'equilibrium' employment levels.

Suppose that in equilibrium the firm employs N^* workers. Suppose that a marginal employment subsidy, σ, is paid with respect to the variable labour costs of each worker employed in addition to N^*. Total subsidy is given by

$$S = \max \left\{ 0, \sigma t_1 w[h_s + k(h - h_s)](N - N^*) \right\} \quad 0 \le \sigma < 1 \tag{7.10}$$

and the revised cost expression is

$$\widetilde{C} = \widetilde{c}N = \{ t_1 w[h_s + k(h - h_s)] + t_2 + z\} N - S. \tag{7.11}$$

Hart (1989) has analysed the implications of introducing this kind of subsidy into the worker-hours demand model. Unsurprisingly it serves to encourage the firm to increase employment and reduce average hours. This is also the case if the subsidy applies to hours-independent costs.

There are three particularly strong objections to introducing MES schemes. First, the cost of identifying employment growth relative to some 'equilibrium' base line may be prohibitively high. Second, there is a clear dead-weight loss problem that is both hard to quantify and to control. Third, MES schemes are not revenue neutral and inevitably introduce the difficult task of assessing the opportunity costs of this type of labour market policy intervention.

---

[16] The tax loss would occur because overtime hours incur higher tax rates. Of course, the loss is offset by the increased tax-take arising from the net addition to the workforce. Osuna and Ríos-Rull (2003) attempt to evaluate overtime taxation within a far more complete model incorporating various economic agents (households, the firm, intermediate insurance companies, etc.). They estimate that a tax rate of 12 per cent on overtime wages is needed to reduce weekly standard hours from 40 to 35.

[17] For example, up to 1998, the UK government imposed a stepped tax schedule that imposed progressively higher rates on higher-earning employees.

Profit and related pay

So far, the discussion has centred on policies designed directly to encourage work sharing through their influence on the relative prices of workers and hours. But these relative price effects are important to understand within the context of policy initiatives that are not ostensibly connected to working time goals. An interesting illustration of this point is contained within the broad subject area of profit-related pay.

There are well-known economic benefits and costs linked to policies to encourage more employees to receive a part of their compensation in the form of either cash-based or share-based profit sharing.[18] However, an aspect of this debate has received relatively little attention. Profit sharing schemes in their various guises generally involve the payment of a fixed, or basic, wage within total compensation. The profit sharing element of pay is designed to reflect, in one way or another, company performance. One of the critical concerns within the broader profit sharing debate is the level of the basic hourly wage in relation to the hourly wage that would have pertained in the absence of a scheme. Under the assumption of positive expected profits, it might reasonably be supposed that switching from a pure wage to a profit sharing compensation structure would involve a reduction in the hourly wage. Then, effectively, the marginal cost of employment would be reduced and, *ceteris paribus*, employment would be stimulated. Extending input factors to include capital would not be expected to harm favourable employment outcomes. Indeed, labour-capital substitution might be encouraged through relative factor price effects. Those outcomes lie at the core of Weitzman's advocacy of a stronger sharing economy (Weitzman, 1984, 1985).

If, however, employment change can occur on the firm's extensive *and intensive* margins, then the employment consequences of profit sharing are more complicated. Would a reduction in the marginal cost of employment result in a rise in the size of the workforce or a rise in the average hours of existing workers, or both? Where firms can alter worker utilisation through changing hours then almost certainly the employment consequences of switching to profit sharing schemes are marred. The intuition follows immediately from the simple cost minimising/profit maximising models of pp. 51–5. Consider that overtime is worked in equilibrium and that there are fixed employment costs. If the hourly wage rate reduces after a switch from a pure wage to a profit sharing compensation structure then this constitutes a fall in variable relative to fixed employment costs. This would lead to an hours-worker substitution effect. The implied reduction in employment would be offset, however, by a positive scale impact of reduced marginal wages. Technical details are provided in Hart (1990) and Hart and Moutos (1995). In companies where significant overtime working is practised, the introduction of profit sharing schemes is likely to have ambiguous net employment impacts.

7.3 Absenteeism

We have already noted a potential link between absenteeism and a supply-side overtime decision in relation to figure 4.1 (see also section 5.3). This involves the demarcation

---

[18] For a useful European discussion of the broader debate in this area, see Commission of the European Communities (1991).

between an exogenously imposed standard work week and overtime hours. If a firm or the government set a standard workday consisting of standard hours that are in excess of a worker's unconstrained hours' preferences then the latter may seek to eliminate some of the 'surplus' hours by taking regular spells of absenteeism. However, there is perhaps a more obvious connection between overtime and absenteeism that relates to workplace hours' setting. It seems reasonable to suppose that overtime is seen in the workplace as a consequence of absenteeism rather than part of a causal mechanism for it. Thus, an apparently strong rationale for overtime working is that it is used to cover for absenteeism among existing employees.

We can imagine that, to some extent, firms can predict rates of absenteeism. Seasonal illnesses, young children in workers' households, knowledge of attitudes to work and the age distribution of the workforce are among key factors that may help firms to anticipate absenteeism rates and to make arrangements to provide adequate cover. As a result, the firm may be able to employ a workforce that contains sufficient slack, or underutilisation, to cover for anticipated rates. In these circumstances, it would appear to be more costly a solution to meet employment shortfalls by recourse to permanent overtime scheduling. But, inevitably, an element of absenteeism is stochastic. A flu epidemic may be abnormally severe and widespread or the implementation of new work practices may provoke unexpected levels of stress in the workplace. Where unanticipated absenteeism combines with binding output constraints then it would seem natural to rely on 'surviving' workers to provide cover by engaging in longer per-period hours. This would especially be the case where high fixed employment costs or labour supply shortages made it prohibitively expensive to hire temporary replacement staff.

The apparent logic stemming from the foregoing arguments is as follows. Where absenteeism is largely erratic and unpredictable then it would be expected to correlate strongly with observed changes in overtime working. Where it is largely anticipated, then it seems reasonable to suppose that the firm would pre-plan for potential employment shortfalls by employing an appropriately-sized stand-by labour force that could fill the absenteeism gaps.[19] In other words, with known absenteeism we might suppose that, *ceteris paribus*, the use of overtime would be lower and the level of employment higher than if high degrees of uncertainty prevailed. Ehrenberg (1970, 1971a) develops strong arguments that suggest that this line of reasoning may well be false.

Adopting the cost minimisation framework of p. 51, we re-express the labour services function in (3.1) to accommodate non-stochastic absenteeism. Thus,

$$L = F(aN, h) \equiv F(\widetilde{N}, h) \tag{7.12}$$

where a is the fraction of the workforce in attendance. Thus, N now describes the potential labour force and $\widetilde{N}$ is the actual labour force.

It is reasonable to suppose that fixed, or hours-independent, costs are incurred in respect of each worker independently of her/his attendance record. The firm would normally be

---

[19] This argument of course abstracts from cases where workforce indivisibilities, union rules and supply-side constraints preclude the employment of workers on a stand-by basis.

required to meet costs related to turnover (hiring, redundancy payments, training costs), as well as private fringe benefits and payroll taxes which contain fixed cost elements, irrespective of the employee's absentee rate. As for variable costs, and in particular standard and overtime pay, these would normally be conditional on work attendance. Assume, as before, that overtime is worked in initial equilibrium. The firm's total labour costs – modified from (3.4) – may be written

$$\tilde{c}\tilde{N} = zN + wh_s\tilde{N} + wk(h - h_s)\tilde{N}$$
$$= \{z/a + w[h_s + k(h - h_s)]\}\tilde{N}, \tag{7.13}$$

using (7.12).

The new cost minimisation problem, equivalent to (3.5) is expressed

$$\min_{h,N} \tilde{C} = \tilde{c}\tilde{N} \tag{7.14}$$

subject to $F(\tilde{N}, h) = \overline{L}$.

The structure of the problem in (7.14) is identical to that explored earlier in (3.5). The fraction of the workforce in attendance, a, serves to modify fixed cost in (7.13) and the number of production workers in (7.12). A fall in a increases the fixed cost per worker in attendance. For given hours, absenteeism requires the firm to employ more labour to meet its production constraint. But per-period fixed costs must be covered whether labour is in attendance or not. Therefore, marginal costs on the extensive margin rise relative to the intensive margin. Again, it should be emphasised that we are assuming that starting equilibrium takes place on the overtime margin. From the results derived on p. 53, it follows that a rise in the rate of absenteeism, $(1 - a)$, will produce an hours-worker (in attendance) substitution, or

$$\frac{\partial h^*}{\partial(1 - a)} > 0, \quad \frac{\partial \tilde{N}^*}{\partial(1 - a)} < 0. \tag{7.15}$$

But what about the effect of the absentee rate on the actual workforce size, as opposed to workers in attendance? Given $\tilde{N} = aN$, we have

$$\frac{\partial N^*}{\partial(1 - a)} = \frac{1}{a}\frac{\partial \tilde{N}}{\partial(1 - a)} + \frac{N}{a}. \tag{7.16}$$

We know from the substitution effect in (7.15) that the first part of (7.16) is negative and so, overall, the expression cannot be signed. The substitution effect is offset by a scale effect.

Therefore, contrary to intuition, a certainty absentee rate is associated with *more* overtime while the effects on the size of the workforce are ambiguous. A rise in the absentee rate is equivalent to a rise in the fixed cost per unit of labour available for work and encourages the firm to utilise its workforce more intensively. Ehrenberg (1971a) proceeds to generalise these findings. He shows that the foregoing results will hold even if absentee workers incur lower fixed costs than do workers in attendance or if they receive sick leave payments.[20]

---

[20] For example, fixed costs may include travel-to-work expenditures and absentees would not normally incur these.

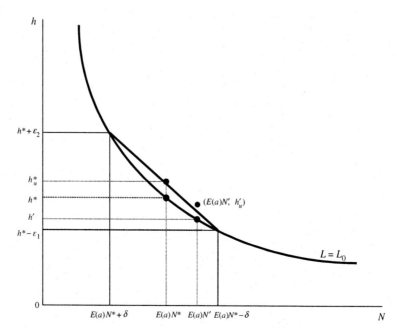

Figure 7.1   Stochastic absenteeism
Source: Ehrenberg (1970).

The results stand as long as absentees are not paid for scheduled overtime and as long as some fixed costs are incurred irrespective of attendance records.

Ehrenberg compares the above outcomes when the attendance rate is treated as a random variable. He assumes a probability density $\psi(a)$ distributed symmetrically around an expected value, $E(a)$. The problem is treated by the cost minimising firm as a two-step decision procedure. First, it chooses N before the actual attendance rate is known. Once the rate is revealed, hours are chosen such that the given production requirement is met. Following Ehrenberg, we discuss outcomes via the graphical illustration in figure 7.1.

Let $L = L_0$ represent the hours-worker trade offs that provide L_0 amount of labour service. It displays a diminishing marginal rate of substitution between the two inputs. (see appendix 3.1, p. 78, for its derivation.) Assume that in the case of a certain absentee rate, equilibrium is given by the $E(a)N^*$, h^* combination. A stochastic absentee rate allows for symmetric fluctuations of $\pm \delta$ around $E(a)N^*$. Given the shape of $L = L_0$, the rate at which hours are substituted for employment rises as employment falls. Consequently, $\varepsilon_2 > \varepsilon_1$ in figure 7.1. Given this property, and assuming a symmetric distribution of attendance around $E(a)N^*$ in the stochastic case, associated average hours, h_u^*, are higher than the certainty-equivalent average hours, h^*. Compared to the certainty outcome, a larger number of hours is required for a given number of workers, or costs on the intensive margin have risen relative to the extensive margin. The cost minimising combination $E(a)N^*$, h^* for the certainty case cannot hold for the stochastic case. At $E(a)N^*$ the firm faces $h_u^* > h^*$ and so cost minimising behaviour will require that this higher intensive margin cost be offset by employing more workers. Let this new employment level be N' with an associated optimal expected level of average hours h'_u. Again, due to the assumption of a diminishing marginal rate of substitution combined with symmetric fluctuations in attendance rates, we know that h'_u associated with N' would lie *above* its non-stochastic equivalent, h'. The new expected workers-hours combination, $E(a)N'$, h'_u, is shown in figure 7.1.

Are expected overtime hours per worker higher or lower in the stochastic compared to the non-stochastic case: i.e. is h'_u greater or smaller than h^*? There is insufficient detail in the present analysis to determine this relative outcome. It appears that generalisations are ruled out and that specific functional forms are needed in order to arrive at unambiguous outcomes. Ehrenberg (1970) shows that if a Cobb–Douglas labour services function is used, equilibrium overtime hours in the stochastic case are *less* than in the non-stochastic case.

Of course, the foregoing models stop well short of complete explanations of relationships between overtime and absenteeism. Perhaps their greatest shortcoming is that absenteeism is regarded as exogenous to the cost minimising problem. Overtime may directly *cause* absenteeism through its effects on workers' health. While we have concentrated attention on equilibrium hours occurring in the region of diminishing marginal productivity, this stops short of accommodating the possibility that overtime hours beyond a certain point may render those workers who wish to be 'in attendance' actually to be absent from work due to detrimental effects. Yanif (1995) modifies Ehrenberg's modelling framework to allow for so-called 'burnout induced absences' due to overtime working. The foregoing results are quite radically altered since potential burnout can lead to marginal cost increases on the intensive margin that are greater than those on the extensive margin.

Using three-digit establishment-level Bureau of Labor Statistics (BLS) data for 1966, classified into two-digit industries, Ehrenberg (1971a) provides estimates of male overtime equations in which absenteeism is included as an explanatory variable.[21] Two-digit industry estimates are provided for manufacturing and for non-manufacturing industries. In both manufacturing and non-manufacturing sectors, results for individual industries are not satisfactory. Coefficients are overwhelmingly negative, although relatively few significantly negative. This outcome is opposite to that predicted in (7.5) for the certainty absentee model. Ehrenberg argues that the weaknesses may result from the fact that it is not possible to separate certainty and stochastic overtime effects.

Ehrenberg's work on absenteeism and overtime has been very influential in both the relatively narrow area of studying the causes of absenteeism and, far more importantly, in the general area of modelling labour utilisation. But caution should be emphasised. The work is demand-driven, ignoring completely individual-based responses in absentee behaviour to the offer of overtime by the firm. In his certainty model, Ehrenberg has the insight that an increase in the absentee rate is equivalent to a rise in fixed labour costs of available workers and cost minimising demand for labour dictates a response by the firm of more utilisation of the active workforce. Overtime and absenteeism are accordingly positively related. But what

---

[21] Two definitions of overtime are used: (a) annual overtime per worker and (b) annual overtime payments at premium rates divided by the overtime premium (time and a half) times the number of employees. Absenteeism is measured as the ratio of paid sick-leave hours to total hours.

if the firm regards high fixed cost not in terms of demand-side labour allocation but in terms of supply preferences? We have considered this possibility in section 4.3. The firm might try to curb higher fixed costs associated with absenteeism by attempting to alter an individual's work/leisure preferences through the mechanism of regular and guaranteed overtime. In other words, the firm's principal strategy may be to influence supply-side tendencies to be absent rather than to concentrate on demand-side reactions to absence. If this were the case, then we would expect to observe a *negative* association between overtime working and absenteeism. Leslie (1982) presents circumstantial British evidence that shows a negative correlation between overtime and rates of absence. At the very least, the supply oriented theoretical approaches provide strong leads as to why demand-based empirics have been largely inconclusive.

More generally, empirical links between overtime working and absenteeism stem from a broad range of studies in the social sciences. It seems fair to report that it is difficult to detect distinct and significant patterns of association between the two variables at this stage of research.[22]

---

[22] Based on a standard neoclassical labour supply model with time series Australian data, Kenyon and Dawkins (1989) investigate the effect of the availability of overtime on labour absence. Their favoured proxy for the former, the percentage of workers working overtime, proved to be weak and, of their other measures of overtime, only average hours of those working overtime entered with a significant negative sign. It is not obvious how this overtime variable matches their theory, however. Chaudhury and Ng (1992) postulate that since overtime might be expected to associate with less flexible work environments and long workdays then it should be found to influence absenteeism positively. However, based on Canadian firm-level data, they obtain only weak support.

8   Is overtime working here to stay?

Throughout OECD countries there are two types of dominant working time arrangements. The first, and most important, is the standard hours contract. This stipulates precise weekly or monthly hours of work and, predominantly, it involves hours that are confined to weekdays. The second is the standard hours contract plus paid overtime. Usually depending on type of work activity, paid-for overtime hours are either mandatory within the terms of an employment contract or voluntarily undertaken by self-selected individual workers. The importance of these standard contracts is illustrated in the case of Britain in figure 8.1 for males and females over the period 1994–2001. Together they account for over 80 per cent of male and 70 per cent of female workers over the period. It should be added that Britain has one of the highest national incidences of paid overtime (see, for example, figure 2.1, p. 13) but the data in figure 8.1 are reasonably indicative of the general picture. As can also be seen in figure 8.1, other main working time contracts account for relatively low percentages of employees, although flexitime arrangements cover 10 per cent of male and about 12 per cent of female workers. In fact, several of these alternatives – the $4\frac{1}{2}$-day week and the 9-day fortnight – are close derivatives of the standard contract. At least in a British context, there has been little recent indication of a movement away from the standard contracts, both with and without overtime.

We also know from broad international trends in average hours that the relative importance of overtime working has not significantly declined in the last three decades (see, for example, figures 2.1 and 2.2, pp. 13 and 14). Why has the use of paid overtime retained this important position? There are two broad answers. First, albeit with some notable exceptions in some industries/sectors/ occupations, overtime hours provide a cost effective means of achieving labour market flexibility in the face of unanticipated economic events. Second, overtime pay and hours arise from firms and workers expressing preferences over work schedules involving indivisible per-period hours. Overtime working arises where relatively long hours are preferred and where the firm faces exogenous standard time/overtime regulations applied either through government legislation or wider union/employers association agreements or custom and practice.

Undoubtedly, many firms view overtime as a useful means of dealing with unanticipated economic events. These include fluctuations in product demand and in rates of absenteeism as well as breakdowns in production/organisational work flow. We know from empirical

Males

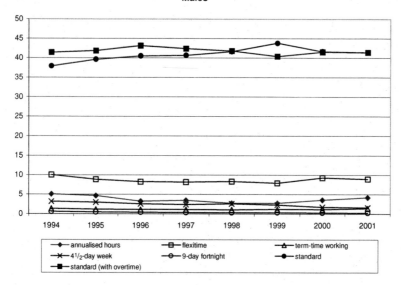

Females

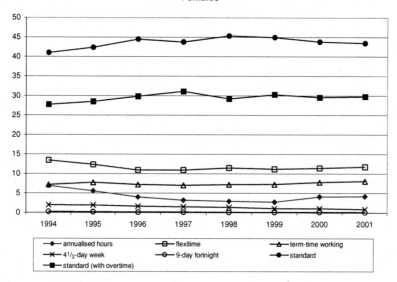

Figure 8.1   Main British working time agreements, 1994–2001
Source: Bell and Hart (2003c).

evidence that overtime offers a speedy short-term response mechanism that is readily reversible. These properties are especially useful to companies that experience high transaction costs of adjusting stocks of employment and capital. They also offer a hedge against uncertainty over the duration of, for example, a product demand rise. The breathing space provided reduces the risk of wasteful investments in human and physical capital. Of course, the effectiveness of using overtime in these ways is predicated on cost advantages compared to other short-term buffers. These include deviations from planned inventory levels as well as changes in the degree to which production and services are subcontracted.

Overtime working designed to accommodate unforeseen, usually short-term, events is likely to remain a permanent feature of the labour market scene. But it is unlikely that it accounts for the major part of overtime activity. As suggested by the national-level data shown in figures 2.1 and 2.2, while overtime activity is highly procyclical it is also an important part of total hours provision during the troughs of the most severe recessionary periods. In fact, when we account econometrically for job-match effects in overtime working, we know that there are important fixed components in individuals' overtime behaviour (see section 5.3).

The leading idea behind the notion of a permanent element of overtime working derives from the Lewis view that the per-period length of working hours defines a *job attribute*. This notion comprises one of the major themes running through this book. If employers and employees reach long-term contractual agreements over job lengths and associated wage earnings then they are unlikely to be overly concerned about the permanency of overtime schedules, whether stemming from government mandate or established custom and practice. Any threatened exogenous change in overtime rules can simply be neutralised by recourse to standard wage manipulation. This is a powerful way of thinking of the persistence of overtime. However, the US evidence to date suggests that it is only a partial explanation, while European labour market researchers have only recently started to evaluate its potency.

In effect, government work sharing policies designed to eliminate, or severely reduce, the practice of overtime working are rendered virtually meaningless if it is established that firms and workers are operating under long-term wage-hours contracts involving agreed daily indivisible hours. But even if such contracts do not represent the dominant experience, the alternative demand-dominated analysis of overtime holds little prospects for the demise of overtime due to government manipulation of factor prices. Research in the United States on increasing the overtime premium in order to reduce hours/increase employment has not, in general, established the likelihood of significant employment impacts. As for reductions in standard hours – an active labour market strategy among major European governments and unions since the 1970s – there is virtually no theoretical or empirical support for significant work sharing repercussions. Crépon and Kramarz (2002) provide a recent evaluation.

While job matching that represents workers and firms agreeing on job length/wage earnings combinations is probably the most appealing argument for the expected longevity of overtime working, it would be wrong to overemphasise this aspect of the employment relationship. The ability to agree over fixed work schedules is almost certainly confined to selected types of work activity. In manufacturing, for example, we would expect it to be far more prevalent in make-to-stock than in make-to-order companies (see pp. 60–1).

Service sector experience will also be mixed in this respect. For example, work scheduling is likely to be important in retailing where regular business-trading hours is the norm. It is less likely in financial and IT services that employ high proportions of skilled professional workers. For instance, we know that many workers from higher occupational/educational groups work significant numbers of unscheduled and unpaid overtime hours.

Undoubtedly, some companies regard overtime working as a financial and organisational burden that requires elimination or severe curtailment. To this end, they seek alternative working time arrangements. Two such examples, linked with recent initiatives on the European scene, are annualised hours contracts and working time accounts.

Under annualised hours contracts, workers and managers agree to the number and scheduling of working hours over a 12-month period. Economic arguments for such contracts from both viewpoints of workers and managers, together with background analysis, are presented by Bell and Hart (2003c). One of the reported motivations behind the introduction of annual hours is to overcome the overtime culture (Incomes Data Services, 1999, 2002). In many annualised hours' contracts, managers and workers agree to a basic number of annual (or *rostered*) hours as well as an annual number of *reserve* hours. These latter hours can be called on by management to meet unforeseen events such as abnormal sales increases or above-normal absenteeism. They can also be used to cover planned events, such as training courses and planning meetings. There are three potential advantages compared to traditional overtime practices. First, reserve hours remove the voluntary nature of hours' extensions that is common in the case of paid overtime. Therefore, adequate cover is ensured. Second, and relatedly, it helps firms to establish robust contingency plans to deal with the labour needs resulting from particularly volatile and unpredictable output fluctuations, Third, it reduces unforeseen severe fluctuations in labour costs due to overtime premium payments.

However, as indicated in figure 8.1, annualised hours contracts account for less than 5 per cent of the working population in Britain and there were no signs in the 1990s of significantly growth in this form of work scheduling. One particularly important offsetting cost consideration is that, *ceteris paribus*, annualised hours contracts involve higher standard hourly wage payments than in equivalent standard contracts with overtime. Several explanations account for this. First, a higher wage may well represent a compensating differential for the fact that annual hours in many firms tend to be arranged in unconventional clusters within complex organisational working timetables. Second, firms may need to pay more for the right of a 'call option' on reserve hours. As analysed by Bell and Hart (2003c), these contracts are particularly suited to large unionised public and private sector companies that require complex work scheduling, such as so-called 'continental shift systems' (3-shift systems that rotate rapidly – e.g. 3 mornings then 2 afternoons then 2 nights).

The use of reserve hours with the annualised hours' structure gives the firm the ability to respond to unforeseen events and to ensure that it can call on adequate cover. If all or part of reserve hours were not called on during a given year then, in any event, workers are typically remunerated for these hours. This raises a general problem over scheduling hours of work in general and overtime hours in particular. Where there is a degree of permanency in the hours structure, it is not always feasible to match hours requirements to work flow.

Even where firms and workers reach contractual agreements over fixed lengths of daily hours and daily earnings subsequent problems of uneven utilisation of scheduled time may have to be faced.

An alternative way of overcoming this sort of problem was especially associated with the German economy in the late 1990s. This involves so-called 'working time accounts'. Such accounts are designed to allow fluctuations in actual hours around standard, or collectively agreed, hours. Over a given period of time an employee is allowed to exceed or fall short of standard hours collecting, respectively, working time credits or debits. These are later 'paid-off' in the form of either additional free time or additional work. The advantages to the firm are, at least, twofold. First, labour input can be better matched to production requirements, thereby smoothing out productive performance. Second, this system gets round a problem of systematic and unproductive provision of overtime. The advantages to workers are not so obvious which perhaps accounts for employers' associations attempting to provide greater worker sovereignty over working time scheduling by offering 'generous deposit limits and/or extended periods for balancing individual working hours accounts' (Pannenberg and Wagner, 2001).

These newer kinds of working time contracts – together with a myriad of flexitime agreements – offer companies and workers real alternatives to traditional overtime working. They have stimulated much media interest in recent years, especially in relation to the goal of achieving more flexible labour markets. There are as yet few compelling signs, however, that they are about to make significant inroads into established practice.

References

Abowd, J.M. and D. Card, 1989. On the covariance structure of earnings and hours changes, *Econometrica* 57: 411–445

Abraham, K.G. and J.C. Haltiwanger, 1995. Real wages and the business cycle, *Journal of Economic Literature* 33: 1215–1264

Akerlof, G.A., 1982. Labor contracts as a partial gift exchange, *Quarterly Journal of Economics* 97: 543–569

Alchian, A. and H. Demsetz, 1972. Production, information costs, and economic organization, *American Economic Review* 62: 777–795

Andrews, M.J., T. Schank and R. Simmons, 2002. Does worksharing work? Some empirical evidence from the IAB Panel, Department of Economics, University of Manchester, mimeo

Andrews, M.J. and R. Simmons, 2001. Friday may never be the same again: some results on work sharing from union-firm bargaining models, *Scottish Journal of Political Economy*, 48: 488–516

Anxo, D. and A. Bingsten, 1989. Working hours and productivity in Swedish manufacturing, *Scandinavian Journal of Economics* 91: 613–619

Arellano, M. and S. Bond, 1991. Some tests of specification for panel data: Monte Carlo evidence and an application to employment equations, *Review of Economic Studies* 58: 277–297

Arellano, M. and O. Bover, 1995. Another look at the instrumental-variables estimation of error component models, *Journal of Econometrics* 68: 29–52

Arnott, R.J., A.J. Hosios and J.E. Stiglitz, 1988. Implicit contracts, labor mobility and unemployment, *American Economic Review* 78: 1046–1066

Ashworth, J., J. McGlone and D. Ulph, 1977. Uncertainty, overtime and the demand for labour, *Zeitschrift für Nationalökonomie* 37: 323–336

Barzel, Y., 1973. The determination of daily hours and wages, *Quarterly Journal of Economics* 87: 220–238

Bauer, T. and K.F. Zimmermann, 1999. Overtime work and overtime compensation in Germany, *Scottish Journal of Political Economy* 46: 419–436

Bell, D.N.F., 1988. Comment on 'Implications of the non-homogeneity of standard and overtime hours on the structure and cyclical adjustment of labor input', in Hart (1988)

Bell, D.N.F. and R.A. Hart, 1991. Effort, worker quality, wage rates and firm-specific human capital, University of Stirling, mimeo

1998. Working time in Great Britain, 1975–1998: evidence from the New Earnings Survey panel, *Journal of the Royal Statistical Society (Series A)* 161: 327–348

1999. Unpaid work, *Economica* 66: 271–290

2000. Overtime working in an unregulated labour market, Department of Economics, University of Stirling, mimeo

2003a. Wages, hours, and overtime premia: evidence from the British labor market, *Industrial and Labor Relations Review* 56: 470–480

2003b. Job match effects in overtime working, Department of Economics, University of Stirling, mimeo

2003c. Annualised hours' contracts: the way forward in labour market flexibility?, *National Institute Economic Review* 185: 64–77

Bell, D.N.F., A. Gaj, R.A. Hart, O. Hübler and W. Schwerdt, 2000. *Unpaid Work in the Workplace: A Comparison of Germany and the UK*, London: Anglo-German Foundation for the Study of Industrial Society

Bellmann, L. and U. Blien, 2001. Wage curve analyses of establishment data from Western Germany, *Industrial and Labor Relations Review* 54, 851–863

Bhattacharya, J., T. DeLeire and T. MaCurdy, 2001. The California experiment: labor demand and the impact of overtime legislation on hours of work, University of Chicago, mimeo

Bils, M., 1985. Real wages over the business cycle: evidence from panel data, *Journal of Political Economy* 93: 666–689

1987. The cyclical behavior of marginal cost and price, *American Economic Review* 77: 838–855

Black, A.J., P.G. Chapman and M. Chatterji, 1993. Earnings, overtime and regional labour markets, *Regional Studies* 27: 637–650

Black, A.J. and F.R. FitzRoy, 2000. Earnings curves and wage curves, *Scottish Journal of Political Economy* 47: 471–486

Blanchard, O. and L.F. Katz, 1997. What we know and do not know about the natural rate of unemployment?, *Journal of Economic Perspectives* 11: 51–72

Blanchflower, D.G. and A.J. Oswald, 1994a. *The Wage Curve*, Cambridge, MA: MIT Press

1994b. Estimating the wage curve for Britain, *Economic Journal* 104: 1025–1043

Böckerman, P., 2002. Overtime in Finland, *Finnish Economic Papers* 15: 36–54

Booth, A. and F. Schiantarelli, 1987. The employment effect of a shorter working week, *Economica* 54: 237–248

1988. Reductions in hours and employment: what do union models tell us?, in Hart (1988)

Borjas, G.J., 2000. *Labor Economics*, Singapore: McGraw-Hill

Brechling, F., 1965. The relationship between output and employment in British manufacturing industries, *Review of Economic Studies* 32: 187–216

Brown, C.V., E. Levin, J. Rosa, R.J. Ruffell and D.T. Ulph, 1986. Payment systems, demand constraints and their implications for research into labour supply, in R. Blundell and I. Walker (eds.), *Unemployment, Search and Labour Supply*, Cambridge: Cambridge University Press

Brown, S., 1999. Worker absenteeism and overtime bans, *Applied Economics* 31: 165–174

Brown, S. and J.G. Sessions, 1996. The economics of absence: theory and evidence, *Journal of Economic Surveys* 10: 23–53

Calmfors, L. and M. Hoel, 1988. Work sharing and overtime, *Scandinavian Journal of Economics* 90: 45–62

1989. Work sharing, employment and shift work, *Oxford Economic Papers* 41, 758–773

Card, D., 1995. The wage curve: a review, *Journal of Economic Literature* 33: 785–799

Card, D. and D. Hyslop, 1996. *Does Inflation 'Grease the Wheels of the Labor Market'?*, NBER Working Paper 5538

Card, D. and D. Sullivan, 1988. Measuring the effect of subsidized training programs on movements in and out of employment, *Econometrica* 56: 497–530

Chaudhury, M. and I. Ng, 1992. Absenteeism predictors: least squares, rank regression, and model selection results, *Canadian Journal of Economics* 25: 615–634

Commission of the European Communities, 1991. *Social Europe*, Supplement 91/3, Brussels: Directorate-General for Social Affairs

Contensou, F. and R. Vranceanu, 2000. *Working Time: Theory and Policy Implications*, Cheltenham: Edward Elgar

Costa, D.L., 2000. Hours of work and the Fair Labor Standard Act: a study of retail and wholesale trade, 1938–1950, *Industrial and Labor Relations Review* 53: 648–664

Crépon, B. and F. Kramarz, 2002. Employed 40 hours or not employed 39: lessons from the 1982 mandatory reduction of the workweek, *Journal of Political Economy* 110: 1355–1389

Dalton, D.R. and D.J. Mesch, 1992. The impact of employee-initiated transfer on absenteeism: a four-year cohort assessment, *Human Relations* 45: 291–304

Deaton, A., 1997. *The Analysis of Household Surveys*. Baltimore: Johns Hopkins University Press

DeBeaumont, R. and L.D. Singell, 1999. The returns to hours and workers in US manufacturing: evidence on aggregation bias, *Southern Journal of Economics* 66: 336–352

Dellaert, N.P. and M.T. Melo, 1998. Make-to-order policies for a stochastic lot-sizing problem using overtime, *International Journal of Production Economics* 56–57: 79–97

Devereux, P.J., 2001. The cyclicality of real wages within employer-employee matches, *Industrial and Labor Relations Review* 54: 835–850

DiNardo, J.E. and J.S. Pischke, 1997. The returns to computer use revisited: have pencils changed the wage structure too?, *Quarterly Journal of Economics* 112: 291–303

Eaple, J.S. and J.H. Pencavel, 1990. Hours of work and trade unionism, *Journal of Labor Economics*, 8 (1, Supplement 2): S150–174

Ehrenberg, R.G., 1970. Absenteeism and the overtime decision, *American Economic Review* 60: 352–357

1971a. *Fringe Benefits and Overtime Behavior*, Lexington, MA: D.C. Heath

1971b. The impact of the overtime premium on employment and hours in US industry, *Western Economic Journal* 9: 199–207

Ehrenberg, R.G. and P.L. Schumann, 1982a. *Longer Hours or More Jobs?*, Cornell Studies in Industrial and Labor Relations 22, Ithaca, NY: Cornell University

1982b. Compliance with the overtime pay provisions of the Fair Labor Standards Act, *Journal of Law and Economics* 25: 159–181

1984. Compensating wage differentials for mandatory overtime?, *Economic Inquiry* 22: 460–477

Fair, R.C., 1969. *The Short-Run Demand for Workers and Hours*, Amsterdam: North-Holland

1985. Excess labor and the business cycle, *American Economic Review* 75: 239–245

Feldstein, M.S., 1967. Specification of the labour input in the aggregate production function, *Review of Economic and Statistics* 34: 375–386

1975. The importance of temporary layoffs: an empirical analysis, *Brookings Papers on Economic Activity* 3: 725–745

1976. Temporary layoffs in the theory of unemployment, *Journal of Political Economy* 84: 937–957

Filer, R.K., D.S. Hamermesh and A. Rees, 1996. *The Economics of Work and Pay*, New York: HarperCollins

FitzRoy, F.R. and R.A. Hart, 1985. Hours, layoffs and unemployment insurance funding: theory and practice in an international perspective, *Economic Journal* 95: 700–713

1986. Part-time and full-time employment: the demand for workers and hours, International Institute of Management, Wissenschaftszentrum Berlin

Frederiksen, A., E.K. Graversen and N. Smith, 2001. Overtime work, dual job holding and taxation, IZA DP 323, Bonn

Friesen, J., 2002. Overtime pay regulation and weekly hours of work in Canada, *Labour Economics* 8: 691–720

Giannelli, G.C. and C. Braschi, 2002. Reducing hours of work: does overtime act as a break upon employment growth?, IZA DP 557, Bonn

Gordon, R.J., 1982. Why US wage and employment behaviour differs from that in Britain and Japan, *Economic Journal* 92: 13–43

Gowler, D., 1969. Determinants of the supply of labour to the firm, *Journal of Management Studies* 68: 73–95

Hall, G.J., 1996. Overtime, effort, and the propagation of business cycle shocks, *Journal of Monetary Economics* 38: 139–160

Hall, R.E. and D.L. Lilien, 1979. Efficient wage bargains under uncertain supply and demand, *American Economic Review* 69: 868–879

Hamermesh, D.S., 1976. Econometric studies of labor demand and their application to policy analysis, *Journal of Human Resources* 11: 507–525

1993. *Labor Demand*, Princeton, NJ: Princeton University Press

Hamermesh, D.S. and S.J. Trejo, 2000. The demand for hours of labor: direct evidence from California, *Review of Economics and Statistics* 82: 38–47

Hansen, G. and T. Sargent, 1988. Straight time and overtime in equilibrium, *Journal of Monetary Economics* 21: 281–308

Hansen, L.P., 1982. Large sample properties of Generalised Method of Moments estimators, *Econometrica* 50: 1029–1054

Hart, R.A., 1984. *The Economics of Non-Wage Labour Costs*, London: Allen & Unwin

1987. *Working Time and Employment*, London: Allen & Unwin

(ed.) 1988. *Employment, Unemployment and Labor Utilization*, London: Unwin Hyman

1989. The employment and hours effects of a marginal employment subsidy *Scottish Journal of Political Economy* 36: 385–395

1990. Profit sharing and work sharing, *Economics Letters* 34: 11–14

2001. Hours and wages in the Depression: British engineering, 1926–1938, *Explorations in Economic History*, 38: 478–502

2003a. Overtime working, the Phillips curve and the wage curve: British engineering, 1926–66, *Manchester School* 71: 97–112

2003b. Worker-job matches, job mobility, and real wage cyclicality, Department of Economics, University of Stirling, mimeo

Hart, R.A. and Y. Ma, 2003. The overtime premium, overtime hours, and leisure preferences, Department of Economics, University of Stirling, mimeo

Hart, R.A. and J.R. Malley, 2000. Marginal cost and price over the business cycle: comparative evidence from Japan and the United States, *European Journal of Political Economy* 16: 547–569

Hart, R.A., J.R. Malley and R.J. Ruffell, 1996. What shapes are overtime premium schedules? Some evidence from Japan, the UK, and the US, *Economics Letters* 53, 97–102

Hart, R.A., J.R. Malley and U. Woitek, 2003. Manufacturing earnings and cycles: new evidence, Department of Economics, University of Glasgow, Discussion Paper in Economics 02-16

Hart, R.A. and P. McGregor, 1988. The returns to labour services in West German manufacturing industry, *European Economic Review* 32: 947–963

Hart, R.A. and T. Moutos, 1995. *Human Capital, Employment and Bargaining*, Cambridge: Cambridge University Press

Hart, R.A. and R.J. Ruffell, 1993. The cost of overtime hours in British production industries, *Economica* 60: 183–201

2000. The effects of straight-time hours reductions on average weekly hours when firms work overtime, Department of Economics, University of Stirling, mimeo

Hart R.A. and N. Wilson, 1988. The demand for workers and hours: micro evidence from the UK metal working industry, in Hart (1988)

Hetrick, R.L., 2000. Analyzing the recent upward surge in overtime hours, *Monthly Labor Review* 123: 30–33

Hoel, M. and P. Vale, 1986. Effects on unemployment of reduced working time in an economy where firms set wages, *European Economic Review* 30: 1097–1104

Hübler, O., 1989. Individual overtime functions with double correction for selectivity bias, *Economics Letters* 29: 87–90

2002. Unpaid overtime, the use of personal computers and wage differentials, *Jahrbuch für Wirtschaftswissenschaften* 53: 88–106

Hunt, J., 1998. Hours reductions as work-sharing, *Brookings Papers in Economic Activity* 1: 349–381

1999. Has work-sharing worked in Germany?, *Quarterly Journal of Economics* 114: 117–148

Idson, T.L. and P.K. Robins, 1991. Determinants of voluntary overtime decisions, *Economic Inquiry* 29: 79–91

Ilmakunnas, P., 1994. Working time and labour demand in Finnish manufacturing: short-run and long-run effects, *Applied Economics* 27: 995–1002

Incomes Data Services, 1997. *Overtime*, Study 617, London: Income Data Services Ltd

1999. *Annual Hours*, Study 674, London: Income Data Services Ltd

2002. *Annual Hours*, Study 721, London: Income Data Services Ltd

Johnson, J.H., 2003. The impact of Federal overtime legislation on public sector labor markets, *Journal of Labor Economics* 21: 43–69

Kahn, S. and K. Lang, 1995. The causes of hours constraints: evidence from Canada, *Canadian Journal of Economics* 28: 914–928

1996. Hours constraints and the wage/hours locus, *Canadian Journal of Economics* 29: S71–S75

Kalwij, A.S. and M. Gregory, 2000. Overtime hours in Great Britain over the period 1975–1999: a panel data analysis, IZA DP 153, Bonn

Kenyon, P. and P. Dawkins, 1989. A time series analysis of labour market absence in Australia, *Review of Economics and Statistics* 71: 232–239

Killingsworth, M.R., 1983. *Labor Supply*, Cambridge: Cambridge University Press

King, S.P., 1997. Oligopoly and overtime, *Labour Economics* 4: 149–165

Kingsman, B., L. Hendry, A. Mercer and A. de Souza, 1996. Responding to customer enquiries in make-to-order companies. Problems and solutions, *International Journal of Production Economics* 46–47: 219–231

Kinoshita, T., 1987. Working hours and hedonic wages in the market equilibrium, *Journal of Political Economy* 95: 1262–1277

Kohler, H. and E. Spitznagel, 1996. Überstunden in Deutschland: eine empirische analyse, Werkstattbericht 4, Institut für Arbeitsmarkt und Berufsforschung (IAB), Nürnberg

Krueger, A.B., 1993. How computers have changed the wage structure: evidence from microdata, 1984–1989, *Quarterly Journal of Economics* 108: 33–60

Laudadio, L. and M. Percy, 1973. Some evidence on the impact of non-wage labour cost on overtime and the environment, *Relations Industrielles* 28: 397–403

Layard, R. and S. Nickell, 1980. The case for subsidising extra jobs, *Economic Journal* 90: 51–73

Lazear, E.P., 1979. Why is there mandatory retirement?, *Journal of Political Economy*, 87: 1261–1284

Leontief, W., 1946. The pure theory of the guaranteed annual wage contract, *Journal of Political Economy* 56: 76–79

Leslie, D., 1982. Absenteeism in the UK labour market, in M. Artis, C.J. Green, D. Leslie and G.W. Smith (eds.) *Demand Management, Supply Constraints and Inflation*, Manchester: Manchester University Press

    1991. Modelling hours of work in a labour services function, *Scottish Journal of Political Economy* 38: 19–31

Leslie, D. and J. Wise, 1980. The productivity of working hours in UK manufacturing and production industries, *Economic Journal* 90: 74–84

Lewis, H.G., 1969a. Employer interests in employee hours of work, University of Chicago, mimeo
    1969b. Notes on the economics of hours of work, University of Chicago, mimeo

Lilien, D., 1980. The cyclical importance of temporary layoffs, *Review of Economics and Statistics* 62: 24–31

Lin, C.C. and C.C. Lai, 1997. The Solow condition in an efficiency wage model with overtime work, *Australian Economic Papers* 36: 342–350

Martin, J., 1971. Some aspects of absence in a light engineering factory, *Occupational Psychology* 45: 77–89

McDonald, I.M. and R.M. Solow, 1981. Wage bargaining and employment, *American Economic Review* 71, 896–908

McDonald, J.F. and R.A. Moffitt, 1980. The uses of Tobit analysis, *Review of Economics and Statistics* 62: 318–321

Mincer, J., 1974. *Schooling, Experience, and Earnings*, New York: National Bureau of Economic Research

Moses, L.N., 1962. Income, leisure, and wage pressure, *Economic Journal* 72: 320–44

Moulton, B.R., 1986. Random group effects and the precision of regression estimates, *Journal of Econometrics* 32: 385–397

Nadiri, M.I. and S. Rosen, 1969. Interrelated factor demand functions, *American Economic Review* 59: 457–471
    1973. *A Disequilibrium Model of the Demand for Factors of Production*, New York: National Bureau of Economic Research

Nakamura, S., 1993. An adjustment cost model of long-term employment in Japan, *Journal of Applied Econometrics* 8: 175–194

Nickell, S.J. and M. Andrews, 1983. Unions, real wages and employment in Britain, 1951–79, *Oxford Economic Papers* 35, Supplement: 183–206

Nussbaum, J. and D. Wise, 1977. The employment impact of overtime provisions of the FLSA. Final report, US Department of Labor Contract J-9-E-6-0105

OECD Employment Outlook, 1998. Working hours: latest trends and policy initiatives, chapter 5, Paris: OECD

Osuna, V. and J.-V. Ríos-Rull, 2003. Implementing the 35 hour workweek by means of overtime taxation, *Review of Economic Dynamics* 6:179–206

Owen, J.D., 1989. *Reduced Working Hours: Cure for Unemployment or Economic Burden?*, Baltimore: Johns Hopkins University Press

Özdamar, L. and T. Yazgaç, 1997. Capacity driven due date settings in make-to-order production systems, *International Journal of Production Economics* 49: 29–44

Pannenberg, M., 2002. Long-term effects of unpaid overtime: evidence for West Germany, IZA DP 614, Bonn

Pannenberg, M. and G.G. Wagner, 2001. Overtime work, overtime compensation and the distribution of economic well-being, IZA DP 318, Bonn

Pencavel, J.H., 1991. *Labor Markets under Trade Unionism*, Oxford: Blackwell

de Regt, E.R., 1984. Shorter working time in a model of the firm – theory and estimation, Institute for Economic Research, Erasmus University, Rotterdam, mimeo

Rosen, S., 1968. Short-run employment variations on Class-1 railroads in the US, 1947–1963, *Econometrica* 36: 511–529

1974. Hedonic prices and implicit markets: product differentiation in pure competition, *Journal of Political Economy* 82: 34–55

Salop, S.C. 1979. A model of the natural rate of unemployment, *American Economic Review* 69: 117–125

Santamäki, T., 1983. The overtime pay premium, hours of work, and employment, Helsinki School of Economics, Working Paper F-75

1984. Employment and hours decisions, and the willingness to work overtime hours, Helsinki School of Economics, Working Paper F-86

1988. Implications of the non-homogeneity of standard and overtime hours on the structure and cyclical adjustment of labor input, in Hart (1988)

Schank, T., 2001. *Estimating Worksharing and Related Issues: Evidence from a German Establishment Panel Data*, PhD thesis, Department of Economics, University of Manchester

2003, *The Impact of Working Time on Employment, Wages and Productivity*, Nürnberg: Bundesanstait für Arbeit, BeitrAB 269

Schlicht, E., 1978. Labour turnover, wage structure and natural unemployment, *Zeitschrift für die gesamte Staatswissenschaft* 134: 337–346

Schmidt-Sørensen, J.B., 1991. An efficiency-wage-hours model and shorter working hours, *Scottish Journal of Political Economy* 38: 113–131

Shapiro, M.D., 1986. The dynamic demand for capital and labor, *Quarterly Journal of Economics* 101: 513–542

Solon, G.R., Barsky and J.A. Parker, 1994. Measuring the cyclicality of real wages: how important is composition bias?, *Quarterly Journal of Economics*, 109: 1–25

Tachibanaki, T., 1987. Labour market flexibility in Japan in comparison with Europe and the US *European Economic Review* 31: 647–684

Topel, R.H., 1982. Inventories, layoffs, and the short-run demand for labor, *American Economic Review* 72: 769–787

Trejo, S.J., 1991. The effects of overtime pay regulation on worker compensation, *American Economic Review* 81: 719–740

1993. Overtime pay, overtime hours, and labor unions, *Journal of Labor Economics* 11, 253–278

2003. Does the statutory overtime premium discourage long workweeks?, *Industrial and Labor Relations Review* 56: 530–551

Ulph, A. and D. Ulph, 1990. Union bargaining: a survey of recent work, in D. Sapsford and Z. Tzannatos (eds.), *Current Issues in Labour Economics*, London: Macmillan

Weitzman, M.L., 1984. *The Share Economy*, Cambridge, MA: Harvard University Press

    1985. The simple macroeconomics of profits sharing, *American Economic Review* 75: 937–953

Wright, M. and P. Edwards, 1998. Does teamworking work, and if so, why? A case study in the aluminium industry, *Economic and Industrial Democracy* 19: 59–90

Yanif, G., 1995. Burnout, absenteeism, and the overtime decision, *Journal of Economic Psychology* 16: 297–309

Yura, K., 1994. Production scheduling to satisfy workers' preferences for days off and overtime under due-date constraints, *International Journal of Production Economics* 33: 265–270

Index of names

Index of subjects

absenteeism 2–3, 47, 96–7, 145–8, 150
adjustment speed *see* overtime – adjustment
  speed
annualised hours *see* hours – annualised
approximately efficient contracts 84–6
Australia 12, 19, 21

bargaining models 44, 67–70
  Nash 69
Britain *see* United Kingdom
business cycle
  marginal cost 126–8
  overtime 7, 12–17
  wages 8

Canada 12, 139, 150
capital stock 59
compensating differentials
  job length 3, 4
  number of hours 49
  overtime pay 49, 119–20
Cost minimisation 51–3, 60, 61–2, 64, 65, 78–9,
  135–6, 147
Custom and practice *see* overtime premium – custom
  and practice

demand *see* labour demand
  and supply *see* hours – demand and supply
  workers–hours *see* workers-hours demand
discriminating monopsonist 47

earnings
  by hours of overtime 28, 29
  cyclical *see* business cycle – wages
  distributions 39–2
  longitudinal micro studies *see* micro studies
  metal working 130
  paid-for and effective 41, 129–31
  versus wage rates 37, 118–20
earnings decomposition 35–6, 37,
  118–19
  frequency domain 128–9
effort 60, 65–6
employment subsidies 142–4

employment taxes 142–4
engineering 81, 123–4, 125
Europe 98, 134
European Working Time Directive 30

Fair Labor Standards Act (FLSA) 9, 30, 36, 48, 73,
  83, 123, 138–40
Finland 19, 21, 101, 107
Fixed job model *see* hours – indivisibility

Germany 12, 17–19, 24–5, 27, 39–42, 100–1, 102,
  105–6, 108, 109, 111–12, 113–15, 131, 135, 136,
  155

heterogeneous preferences *see* preferences –
  heterogeneous
hours 100–16
  actual and desired 111–13
  annualised 154–5
  demand and supply 67
  job attribute 44, 153
  shift working 59–60
  standard/overtime and production 57–9
  standard/total 26
  stock of capital *see* capital stock
  yearly 27
hours curves 132–3
hours indivisibility 3, 4, 70–3, 90, 153
  and earnings 119

industrial relations *see* overtime premium – industrial
  relations
institutional compensation rules *see* overtime
  premium – legislation
interrelated factor demand 6
inventories 128

Japan 2, 12, 34, 35, 127–8

labour demand 2, 44, 50–65, 134–5, 140
  for workers and hours *see* workers-hours demand
labour supply 2–3, 5, 43–4, 45–9
labour service 50–1
legislation 1, 29–30, 31, 70–3